Evidence Management for the Paralegal

WEST LEGAL STUDIES

Options.

Over 300 products in every area of the law: textbooks, CD-ROMs, reference books, test banks, online companions, and more—helping you succeed in the classroom and on the job.

Support.

We offer unparalleled, practical support: robust instructor and student supplements to ensure the best learning experience, custom publishing to meet your unique needs, and other benefits such as West's Student Achievement Award. And our sales representatives are always ready to provide you with dependable service.

Feedback.

As always, we want to hear from you! Your feedback is our best resource for improving the quality of our products. Contact your sales representative or write us at the address below if you have any comments about our materials or if you have a product proposal.

Accounting and Financials for the Law Office • Administrative Law • Alternative Dispute Resolution • Bankruptcy • Business Organizations/Corporations • Careers and Employment Civil Litigation and Procedure • CLA Exam Preparation • Computer Applications in the Law Office • Contract Law • Court Reporting • Criminal Law and Procedure • Document Preparation • Elder Law • Employment Law • Environmental Law • Ethics • Evidence Law • Family Law • Intellectual Property • Interviewing and Investigation • Introduction to Law Introduction to Paralegalism • Law Office Management Law Office Procedures Legal Nurse Consulting • Legal Research, Writing, and Analysis • Legal Terminology • Paralegal Internship • Product Liability • Real Estate Law • Reference Materials • Social Security Sports Law • Torts and Personal Injury Law • Wills, Trusts, and Estate Administration

---

West Legal Studies
5 Maxwell Drive
Clifton Park, New York 12065-2919

For additional information, find us online at:
www.westlegalstudies.com

THOMSON
✳
DELMAR LEARNING

Evidence Management for the Paralegal

STACEY HUNT
ELLEN SHEFFER

THOMSON

DELMAR LEARNING

Australia Canada Mexico Singapore Spain United Kingdom United States

THOMSON
DELMAR LEARNING

WEST LEGAL STUDIES

EVIDENCE MANAGEMENT for the PARALEGAL
Stacey Hunt and Ellen Sheffer

Career Education Strategic Business Unit:

Vice President:
Dawn Gerrain

Director of Learning Solutions:
John Fedor

Acquisitions Editor:
Shelley Esposito

Managing Editor:
Robert L. Serenka, Jr.

Editorial Assistant:
Melissa Zaza

Director of Production:
Wendy A. Troeger

Senior Content Production Manager:
Betty L. Dickson

Art Director:
Joy Kocsis

Technology Project Manager:
Sandy Charette

Director of Marketing:
Wendy Mapstone

Marketing Manager:
Gerard McAvey

Marketing Coordinator:
Jonathan Sheehan

Cover Design:
DC design

Library of Congress Cataloging-in-Publication Data

Hunt, Stacey.
  Evidence management for the paralegal / Stacey Hunt, Ellen Sheffer.
      p. cm. -- (West legal studies)
  Includes index.
  ISBN 978-0-7668-5963-0 (0-7668-5963-0) 1. Evidence (Law)--United States-- Outlines, syllabi, etc. I. Sheffer, Ellen. II. Title.
  KF8539.Z9H86 2007
  347.73'6--dc22
2007018256

NOTICE TO THE READER

Contents

CHAPTER 4 Depositions 68

CHAPTER 5 Reports, Tests, and Expert Witnesses 92

CHAPTER 6 Video and Audio Recordings 114

CHAPTER 7 Electronic Evidence 126

Preface

INTRODUCTION

High-quality paralegal education programs provide the foundation necessary for paralegals to confidently enter the marketplace. Workplace mentoring, training, and experience then build upon academic knowledge, contributing to a satisfying and rewarding career. Continuing education and professional development can help the paralegal maintain and sharpen skills and knowledge about changes in laws, technology, specific areas of the law, and career opportunities. Local, state, and national associations present opportunities for professional interaction with fellow paralegals.

At the heart of legal matters is identifying, gathering, and analyzing evidence to support or dispute facts. These tasks often appear overwhelming and the amount of information gathered may be staggering, especially in our age of advanced technology with its oceans of paperwork and data. Well-educated and trained paralegals have the skills required to methodically and thoroughly sort through hard documents, electronic data, and objects in order to help the attorney determine the relevancy and best use of evidence.

This book is not intended for use solely by paralegals working in civil litigation and criminal matters, although that is, of course, the emphasis. Thoroughness, organization, and attention to detail are important in all paralegal work. For example, probate and estate planning require that a paralegal be skilled at examining documents concerning assets and finances. Paralegals working in corporate law will spend a great deal of time examining financial documents and records. Paralegals must be aware that any document may at some time become evidence.

WHY WE WROTE THIS BOOK

The American Bar Association defines "paralegal" as follows:

> A legal assistant or paralegal is a person, qualified by education, training or work experience who is employed or retained by a lawyer, law office, corporation, governmental agency or other entity and who performs specifically delegated substantive legal work for which a lawyer is responsible.

A primary opportunity for paralegals to be of service to attorneys is to follow a case, client, or matter from the initial retention to resolution. A competent paralegal may be the primary contact with the client and work closely with the development of the case. A well-trained paralegal is crucial to the gathering and interpretation of evidence to support issues involved in a lawsuit in a cost-effective manner.

We found that there is a dearth of educational materials available to assist the paralegal educator and student in gathering and analyzing evidence. The scarcity is particularly glaring because this knowledge is especially suited to a paralegal's unique skill set and is one area where a paralegal can be most helpful to an attorney. As paralegals entering the field today often have specialized education, that is, two- or four-year degrees in addition to paralegal education, they are often well prepared to assist in matters involving a wide variety of technical issues.

Educators, students, and working paralegals can use this book as a resource in gathering and analyzing evidence. The information provided will assist the paralegal in working with the attorney to carefully determine the evidence needed to support or dispute the facts presented, locate and gather that evidence, and preserve and maintain it for use in settlement, alternative dispute resolution, and trial.

HOW THE BOOK IS ORGANIZED

The Chapter Objectives set out the goals of the chapter. The Introduction to each chapter briefly summarizes what is to follow. In an effort to include practical applications, we have included four different scenarios with fact patterns as examples of real-life issues the paralegal may encounter. The fact patterns cover various areas of the law including intellectual property, medical malpractice, criminal law, and product liability. The scenarios allow the student to observe methods of gathering and analyzing specific kinds of evidence and apply the methods to actual cases. Because the nature of paralegal work is hands-on and practical, the case scenarios throughout the book let the paralegal student practice the skills being taught.

Topics covered include the following:

Chapter 1 – The Use of Evidence in a Lawsuit

What evidence is and how it is used in a case
The different types of evidence
Real evidence and demonstrative evidence

Chain of custody
The paralegal's role in gathering evidence
The rules of admissibility of evidence

Chapter 2 – Documentary Evidence

The investigation stage of a case
What documents consist of in the legal context
The discovery phase of a case
Interrogatories and requests for production of documents
The purpose and use of a discovery plan

Chapter 3 – Using the Formal Discovery Process to Obtain Documents

The Federal Rules of Civil Procedure governing the formal discovery process
The primary methods of obtaining evidence using the formal discovery process
Propounding and responding to discovery

Chapter 4 – Depositions

Taking the deposition of a party, witness, or expert witness
Preparing a witness for a deposition
Summarizing deposition testimony

Chapter 5 – Reports, Tests, and Expert Witnesses

Pre-litigation and post-litigation reports
Where to look for relevant pre-litigation reports
How expert witnesses are used in a case
Finding an expert witness for your case
The paralegal's role in working with a retained expert

Chapter 6 – Video and Audio Recordings

The Federal Rules of Evidence relating to recordings
The various types of videotaped and audiotaped evidence

Chapter 7 – Electronic Evidence

Examples of electronic evidence
The Federal Rules of Evidence governing electronic evidence
Discovery tools used to gather electronic evidence

Chapter 8 - Physical Evidence

The Federal Rules of Civil Procedure that relate to physical evidence
How to preserve physical evidence
Preparing a request for inspection of physical evidence
Conducting an inspection

Chapter 9 - Demonstrative Evidence

The Federal Rules of Evidence relating to demonstrative evidence
The different types of demonstrative evidence and their uses
Steps for planning the use of demonstrative evidence
The difference between real and demonstrative evidence

Chapter 10 - The Use of Evidence at Settlement and Trial

The various methods of resolving a lawsuit
Preparing evidence for trial
The use of trial subpoenas
Assisting the attorney at trial

Chapter 11 - Evidence After Case Resolution and Additional Resources

Post-trial procedures
Maintaining evidence after alternative dispute resolution and final
resolution
Ethics and the paralegal
Professional development and continuing education

The Key Terms and glossary assist in the introduction of terminology. Including the Federal Rules of Evidence and pertinent Federal Rules of Civil Procedure and Federal Rules of Criminal Procedure as appendixes gives the student access to important materials within one book. Examples of actual forms required by the courts (for example, subpoenas) are used throughout the book. Examples from a variety of federal and state courts demonstrate to the student that care must be taken to select forms appropriate to the venue and jurisdiction.

Applicable Web sites have been included wherever possible. The Internet is a frequently used resource for forms, rules, and statutes, and we have made every attempt to include Web site references for this purpose in the text.

As experienced paralegals and educators, we examined how we have previously needed to supplement the well-written textbooks and course materials we have used. Therefore, we have included Tips that provide helpful hints, interesting trivia, and cautions about common pitfalls. In addition, the Career Options suggest various traditional and nontraditional careers for persons with paralegal skills.

At the end of each chapter there are opportunities to review and apply the knowledge gained in the chapter. Applying What You Have Learned requires the student to answer questions from the material presented in the chapter. In addition, pertinent portions of an actual published opinion are set out at the end of each chapter and the student is asked to answer questions relating to the chapter topics that are addressed in the particular decision. In this way, the student is testing his or her understanding of the chapter against an actual case decision.

We have attempted to apply gender-neutral language throughout the text by referring to both males and females as paralegals and as examples in our case scenarios.

Ethics is an important component of all professional endeavors. We have woven ethical considerations throughout the book and have included in Appendix D the Code of Ethics and Professional Responsibility developed by the National Association of Legal Assistants as well as in Appendix E the Code of Ethics developed by the National Federation of Paralegal Associations.

INSTRUCTOR'S MANUAL

The Instructor's Manual contains a suggested syllabus for teaching the material contained in the book. Additional Web resources can be used to direct the student to specific topics covered in each chapter. The entire text of each decision in the book is included for the instructor's reference as well as for additional assignments for students. The test bank includes a variety of questions including essay, true-false, multiple-choice, and short answer. We have suggested additional assignments for students to undertake both individually and in groups in order to further solidify their understanding of the material.

Acknowledgments

No work product is achieved in a vacuum. The authors are fortunate indeed to have experienced fine support from teachers, co-workers, friends, and family. Their knowledge, willingness to mentor, kindnesses, and encouragement have contributed to this undertaking.

Stacey Hunt would like to thank Tom Saville, Cathy Crum, Chuck Plemons, and Leslie Parkinson for sharing their talent and artwork with me for use in this book; Jill Harvey, typist extraordinaire, who recreates difficult forms; Steve Appleby of Appleby & Co. for explaining how sub-rosa investigations work; criminal defense paralegals Connie Scorza and Amy Brumfeld and attorney Matthew E. Guerrero, who enlightened me about their line of work; Walter J. Millar and Michael R. Jencks, two wonderful attorneys who helped me with aspects of this book and who patiently waited for their work to get done when I put it aside to write; Barbara Price, our very patient and knowledgeable editor, who made great suggestions and answered every question; and Rhonda Gregory, who taught me what it means to be a professional.

Ellen Sheffer wishes to thank Deputy District Attorney Kirk Wilson for his help in creating the criminal case scenario; Ronald Goldfarb for his encouragement; Patricia-Ann Stoneman for her support of my work as director of the paralegal studies program at California State Polytechnic University; Craig R. Oliver Esq. for believing in the paralegal profession and those who work in it; our editor, Barbara Price, for her flexibility and ability to guide me down this new and exciting path; Chere Estrin for providing the opportunity to combine my passions for education and the paralegal profession; Stacey Hunt for her knowledge and expertise and the joy of working with her; and Linda Murphy. Finally, thank you to Michael, Jane, and Robin: you bring out the best in me.

CHAPTER 1

The Use of Evidence in a Lawsuit

■ OBJECTIVES

After studying this chaper, you will be able to:

❑ understand what evidence is and how it is used in a case.

❑ describe the different types of evidence.

❑ explain the difference between real evidence and demonstrative evidence.

❑ know what chain of custody is and why it is important.

❑ understand the paralegal's role in gathering evidence.

❑ have a working knowledge of the rules of admissibility of evidence.

INTRODUCTION

When confronted with a crime on one of those old television shows, the accused would often challenge the authorities by saying, "Oh yeah? Prove it!" How do lawyers and paralegals go about "proving it"? Convincing a judge or jury that the lawyer's clients should prevail is done through the use of evidence. In fact, the value of a case rests largely on the quality and quantity of the evidence that supports it. For

■ **TRIER OF FACT**

The jury, or the judge if there is no jury.

example, no **trier of fact** is going to accept your client's word alone that she was the subject of workplace harassment. The client must have witnesses or documents that will support her allegations.

Perhaps your firm represents a pest control company that is being sued in a wrongful death case. The complaint alleges that chemicals used by your client caused the death of an employee. What sort of evidence can be used to show that the pest control company properly stored its chemicals and posted all necessary warnings? It is the job of the attorney and paralegal to gather sufficient evidence to prove this.

All the evidence in the world, however, won't help you if it is not admissible in court. We have all heard lawyers in movies and on television object to a particular line of questioning or to the introduction of a piece of evidence. We have heard newscasters report on high-profile celebrity trials where a particular piece of key evidence was not allowed by the judge.

This chapter will discuss the various types of evidence, why each is important, and how each is used during the course of a lawsuit and at trial. There will also be a brief discussion about the rules of evidence and an overview of the paralegal's role in the process.

Case Scenario

The first case scenario you will be working with throughout this book is a fictional intellectual property case entitled *Cellutronics, Inc. v. Microcell Manufacturing*.

Your firm's client is a consumer electronics company called Cellutronics, Inc. In December 2000, Cellutronics applied to the U.S. Patent Office for a design patent for a new type of cellular telephone that also contains a digital camera and personal digital assistant. In March 2002, Cellutronics was awarded its patent. Cellutronics began manufacturing the new phone/camera/PDA under the product name Omniphone, and it hit the shelves in major electronics stores in January 2003.

In March 2003, a key employee of Cellutronics, Jacob Richmond, quit the firm following a salary dispute. Jacob was the manager of the group that developed the Omniphone. A month after Jacob left the company, Cellutronics heard a rumor that he was working for its chief competitor, Microcell Manufacturing. Jacob's girlfriend, Sonya, allegedly told her girlfriend, Trina Campbell, that Jacob had gone to work for Microcell. Trina just happened to be part of the management team at Cellutronics, and she immediately reported the conversation to her superiors.

In December 2003, Microcell began selling the Pictophone, a product that is suspiciously similar to the Omniphone. Cellutronics asks your firm to bring a lawsuit against Microcell Manufacturing for patent infringement and against Jacob Richmond for disclosing company secrets.

WHAT IS EVIDENCE?

Oran's *Dictionary of the Law* defines **evidence** as "any information that might be used for a future trial." The gathering of evidence is a painstaking procedure that comprises the majority of time spent by a firm during a lawsuit, beginning on the day the client walks through the door. The phase of a case during which the bulk of the evidence is obtained is commonly known as **discovery**. (See Exhibit 1-1, which shows the various stages of civil and criminal actions.) First, the attorney and paralegal identify and isolate each fact that needs to be proven in a case. Then they search for the right combination of information that will cause the judge or jury to believe their client's version of the facts and not the opposing party's. For example, the chart in Exhibit 1-2 breaks down some facts in our Case Scenario No. 1, and the types of evidence that might be used to prove them.

■ **EVIDENCE**

Any information that might be used for a future trial.

■ **DISCOVERY**

The formal and informal exchange of information between sides in a lawsuit.

EXHIBIT 1-1   THE LIFE OF AN ACTION

CIVIL	CRIMINAL
Investigation	Investigation
Pleading	Arrest
Discovery	Indictment (or Information)
Settlement Conference/ADR	Arraignment
	Discovery
Trial	Plea Bargaining
	Trial

EXHIBIT 1-2   FACTS FOR CASE SCENARIO NO. 1

CELLUTRONICS, INC. V. MICROCELL MANUFACTURING AND JACOB RICHMOND

FACT	EVIDENCE
1. Cellutronics applied to the U.S. Patent Office in December 2000 for a design patent for a new type of cellular telephone that also contains a digital camera and personal digital assistant.	Patent application.
2. Cellutronics was awarded a patent from the Patent Office in March 2002.	Patent.

(continues)

EXHIBIT 1-2   FACTS FOR CASE SCENARIO NO. 1 *(continued)*

3. Cellutronics began manufacturing the Omniphone and it hit the shelves in major electronics stores in January 2003.	Cellular phone/camera/PDA product.
4. In March 2003, one of the key employees who developed the new product, Jacob Richmond, quit Cellutronics following a dispute over salary.	Resignation letter.
5. A few months later, Jacob turned up working for a competing technology company, Microcell Manufacturing.	Jacob's girlfriend, Sonya Davis, told her friend, Trina Campbell, who happens to be a member of Cellutronics' management team.
6. In December 2003, Microcell began selling its competing product, the Pictophone.	Sample of the Pictophone purchased at a store.
7. The Pictophone was disassembled and analyzed and found to be almost identical to the Omniphone.	Reports of engineers who performed the testing and analysis.
8. Jacob Richmond assisted Microcell Manufacturing in building the infringing product by using knowledge he obtained while working for Cellutronics.	Tape recording of a telephone conversation between Jacob and Sonya, during which he admitted this.

■ **DOCUMENTARY EVIDENCE**

Evidence supplied by writings and all other documents.

■ **TANGIBLE EVIDENCE**

Evidence that can be touched; real. Also known as physical evidence.

■ **TESTIMONY**

Evidence given by a witness under oath.

Let's take a look at some of the kinds of evidence that has been gathered in this case. The patent application (item 1), patent (item 2) and resignation letter (item 4) are all examples of **documentary evidence**. Documentary evidence is all of the paperwork that will support a party's claims, such as contracts, correspondence, memos, budgets, checkbooks, and grant deeds. Documents will normally compose the bulk of the evidence gathered in a case, and paralegals have an extremely vital role in locating and maintaining them. They must take care to make sure that each document is authentic and that someone is available who can identify it as an authentic record. The paralegal's role in gathering and organizing documentary evidence is discussed in detail in Chapter 2.

Your client's patented phone/camera/PDA (item 3) and the competing product (item 6) are illustrations of what is known as **physical** or **tangible evidence**, that is, evidence that has physical substance. The most common example of tangible evidence is the proverbial smoking gun, the murder weapon that is still warm from use. In fact, that term is now often used to mean any critical piece of evidence in a case.

Another type of evidence is witness **testimony**, that is, words spoken by a person who has firsthand knowledge of a particular fact. Item 5, the girlfriend's mention to a Cellutronics manager that her boyfriend, Jacob Richmond, had gone to work for the competing company, is an example of witness testimony. The credibility or admissibility of witness testimony often comes into question and will be discussed later in this chapter and in Chapter 4.

Attorneys often rely on the work of **expert witnesses** to assist the judge and jury in understanding more complicated evidence. An expert witness is someone who, through education, training, or experience, is qualified to give **opinion evidence** about a subject that is beyond the knowledge of the average person. In the patent infringement case outlined in Exhibit 1-2, the client would probably need to employ engineers such as the ones who tested and analyzed the competing product (see item 7) to explain to the jury how the two competing cellular phones were similar and why an inference could be drawn that the second version was pirated from the first.

In today's modern cases, technology often plays an important role as evidence in a lawsuit. Audio recordings are used, for example, to capture witness statements or as part of the official record of different government proceedings, such as city council meetings or planning commission hearings. Video recordings are used to show traffic levels at a busy intersection where an accident happened, or during **sub-rosa investigations**, where investigators follow and catch on camera a supposedly severely injured plaintiff who is playing volleyball or helping a friend move furniture. Paralegals are sometimes called upon to either perform the audio and videotaping themselves or, more traditionally, arrange to have it done.

Many other types of evidence will be discussed in this book, including photographs, test results, drawings, depositions, charts, blowups, medical records, and models. The most creative paralegals will have a large arsenal of possible evidence to draw from and have open minds on the best way to combine evidence types to tell a story that the jury will relate to and sympathize with.

THE EFFECTIVE USE OF EVIDENCE

Psychologists have told us that the most effective way to reach a person is by stimulation of multiple senses. Following this school of thought, successful advocacy will draw upon as many senses as possible in order to prevail in a lawsuit. In the examples above, we have discussed only evidence that would stimulate a juror's sense of sight or hearing. While it is true that these are the most common pieces of evidence, depending on the issues in your lawsuit other choices may be even more persuasive.

Let's suppose a city has built a sewage treatment plant right in the middle of the community, over the protests of angry citizens. Residents of homes closest to the plant claim they are now practically uninhabitable because of the odors emanating from the plant operations. The owners of those homes have now sued the city for inverse condemnation, the taking of private property by the authorities without just compensation. As part of the evidence to present in convincing a jury to make an award in favor of the property owners, the trial team might make arrangements to have the jury transported from the courthouse to the neighborhood in question. One whiff downwind from a sewer is infinitely more powerful evidence than hours and hours of impassioned testimony on the witness stand.

How can a clever trial team use the sense of touch? Suppose your firm represents a client whose two-year-old child choked to death on a small part of a toy. It would have an undeniable effect on a jury to pass around the offending part so they could

---

■ EXPERT WITNESS

A person possessing special knowledge or experience who is allowed to testify at trial not only about facts (like an ordinary witness) but also about the professional conclusions he or she draws from these facts.

■ OPINION EVIDENCE

Evidence of what a witness thinks, believes, or concludes about facts, rather than what the witness saw, heard, etc. Opinion evidence is usually accepted only from an expert witness.

■ SUB-ROSA INVESTIGATION

A confidential, secret, private or covert investigation.

! TIP

When the ancient Romans congregated for a secret meeting, a rose was tacked up on the doorway to indicate that what was said "under the rose" (Latin – *sub rosa*) was to be kept secret. This is the origin of the word sub-rosa, which is now used to mean a "secret surveillance."

not only see but feel it and imagine it lodged in the child's throat. The jury's sense of touch will subliminally underscore the knowledge that a part that small should never have been used on a toy meant for a toddler.

A creative way to combine different types of evidence for a more powerful effect is through the use of **multimedia** presentations. Multimedia can be used to juxtapose contradictory statements made by an opposing party in order to call the party's credibility into question. For example, let's suppose your firm represents a software company that is suing a competing company for copyright infringement on a computer application program. Your firm has taken the videotaped deposition of the CEO of the defendant software company, who testifies under oath that he had never heard of your client's program. During your review of the documents produced during the case, you stumble upon a memorandum written by this same CEO to his research and development department. The memo instructs the employees to write a program that will compete directly with your client's program. Those two pieces of evidence could be introduced separately from each other during the course of the trial. However, using modern technology, it is possible to create a split-screen image on a television monitor, with the videotaped denial of the CEO running next to the image of the memorandum that makes him a liar, thereby creating a much more powerful effect.

DEMONSTRATIVE EVIDENCE

The types of evidence we have been discussing so far are known as **real evidence**. This is evidence that is an actual part of the transactions or events that are the subject of the litigation. Real evidence is what the attorneys and paralegals gather during the investigation and discovery phase of the lawsuit.

There is another type of evidence that paralegals should be familiar with called **demonstrative evidence**. Demonstrative evidence is evidence created for the trial of the matter that is used for illustrative purposes only. Its primary purpose is to clarify a particular point or issue for the trier of fact or to re-create or demonstrate an event. Examples of demonstrative evidence are computer animations that re-create how an accident happened, scientific experiments that are videotaped elsewhere and shown in the courtroom, a skeleton used by an expert witness to show where on the human body a particular injury occurred, or an aerial photograph of a blind intersection.

Demonstrative evidence will be discussed in greater detail in Chapter 9. It is important for paralegals to know the difference between real and demonstrative evidence and the role each plays in the courtroom. Relevant and authentic real evidence will almost always be admitted by the judge, and the jury will be allowed to consider it when making a verdict. On the other hand, the admission of demonstrative evidence is at the discretion of the trial judge. Remember, demonstrative evidence is not actually a part of the actual events of the lawsuit; rather it was created to act as a visual aid to the jury in understanding the facts of the case and the testimony of the

Sidebar

■ **MULTIMEDIA**
Software programs used to integrate documents, graphics, and video clips to produce presentations that can be made to the jury during a trial.

■ **REAL EVIDENCE**
Objects seen by the jury; for example, wounds, fingerprints, weapons used in a crime, etc.

■ **DEMONSTRATIVE EVIDENCE**
Visual aids that have been created specifically to illustrate or demonstrate a key point or issue during a trial, such as charts or graphs.

CAREER TIP

There are many companies across the nation that specialize in designing and creating demonstrative evidence for law firms. These companies often hire paralegals, whose knowledge of the law and what attorneys need is invaluable.

witnesses. The jury may or may not be allowed to take the demonstrative evidence back into the deliberating room.

Conceiving ideas for demonstrative evidence is among the most enjoyable and creative tasks in trial preparation for paralegals. However, it is not a substitute for relevant, admissible real evidence for properly proving a case.

RULES OF EVIDENCE

Evidence law came about to promote the search for truth in adversarial proceedings. A system of rules was created to ensure fairness and to prevent the jury from being exposed to prejudicial, unreliable, confusing, or irrelevant evidence. It is the trial judge who acts as the gatekeeper for the admission of evidence and will make rulings from the bench as to what is allowed in and what is excluded.

Paralegals should familiarize themselves with the Federal Rules of Evidence (see Appendix A) and the rules of evidence for the state in which they live. Having a basic understanding of what evidence the court will consider **relevant** (i.e., tending to prove or disprove a fact in issue) or **admissible** (i.e., able to be considered by the jury in reaching a verdict) will help you in making decisions about which evidence will ultimately be used in the trial of your case.

Hearsay

Rules of evidence normally forbid the use of **hearsay** testimony, although there are some exceptions. Hearsay is basically secondhand knowledge, a statement that was made outside the courtroom but offered inside the courtroom as evidence to prove that what was said was true. The statement was usually made by someone other than the witness who is testifying in court. For example, in item 5 of Exhibit 1-2, Trina Campbell doesn't know from her own experience that Jacob Richmond has gone to work for Microcell Manufacturing. She only knows what she has been told by Sonya Davis. This type of secondhand knowledge, that is, hearsay, is not normally admissible in court. If your firm attempted to call Trina as a witness to testify about her conversation with Sonya in order to prove that Jacob was working for Microcell, Microcell's attorneys would certainly object and this evidence would not be admitted. Another method of proving this fact will need to be found. For example, you could ask Jacob himself on the witness stand; however, he might not be truthful about this information. Another way around the problem would be to **subpoena** Sonya Davis herself. Another possibility would be to subpoena the employee records of Microcell Manufacturing during the discovery phase and obtain documentary evidence of when Jacob began working there.

Rules 803 and 804 of the Federal Rules of Evidence (see Appendix A) list many exceptions to the hearsay rule. Keep in mind that there is no guarantee that the

RELEVANT
Tending to prove or disprove a fact that is important to a claim, charge, or defense in a court case.

ADMISSIBLE
Proper to be used in reaching a decision; describes evidence that should be "let in" or introduced in court, or evidence that the jury may use.

HEARSAY
A statement about what someone else said (or wrote or otherwise communicated).

SUBPOENA
A court's order to a person that he or she appear in court to testify in a case.

questionable statement will be admitted, but if it falls under one of the exceptions, you are past the first hurdle.

As another example of admissibility, look at item 8 in Exhibit 1-2. Trina Campbell put a bugging device on Sonya's telephone during one of her visits. This was done without Sonya's knowledge. The device picked up a conversation between Sonya and Jacob, during which he bragged to Sonya that he got even with Cellutronics by using his knowledge of the Omniphone technology to help Microcell build the Pictophone. This is very damning evidence, to be sure, but is it admissible? Federal law prohibits the interception and disclosure of wire, oral, or electronic communications (18 U.S.C. § 2511) without a warrant, so although well intentioned, what Trina did was probably not legal and the tape would be precluded from being admitted into evidence.

How else could this information be introduced? Perhaps Sonya could be subpoenaed to appear and testify. But since this is information she received secondhand from Jacob, it may be objectionable hearsay. Jacob would almost certainly not admit to this in open court. Perhaps corroborating evidence will come from subpoenaed records from Microcell Manufacturing. Or perhaps during depositions taken during the discovery phase of the case, Microcell employees will testify that Jacob was instrumental in developing the Pictophone. Paralegals need to keep in mind that there often is more than one solution to evidentiary problems and that as they gain experience, their bag of tricks will continue to grow.

Authentication of Records

Paralegals should also become familiar with the evidentiary rules relating to authentication of records (Rules 901–1008; see Appendix A). Federal rules require the presence of the original document in court. However, if the original is unavailable, a duplicate of the document is admissible to the same extent as the original unless (1) the authenticity of the duplicate is called into question or (2) it would be unfair to admit the duplicate into evidence. For example, refer to item 4 in Exhibit 1-2. Cellutronics wants to introduce into evidence the resignation letter of Jacob Richmond. Suppose the original letter was misplaced and only a copy is available. Now let's also suppose that Jacob denies that he resigned, but insists that he was fired by Cellutronics. He has now called into question the authenticity of the resignation letter and the judge will have to make a decision about whether or not the copy will be admitted.

Documents that have been issued by, submitted to, or filed with a public agency are considered **public documents**. These include such documents as birth and death certificates, deeds, passport applications, and business licenses. There are special rules pertaining to the admissibility of these types of records. It would be impractical for parties to have to subpoena the county clerk, for example, to testify about the authenticity of a public record. Business at the clerk's office would come to a standstill if the clerk was always on the stand in court. The Rules of Evidence allow for the self-authentication of public records, either under seal or by certified copies (see

■ PUBLIC DOCUMENTS

Documents that have been submitted to, filed with, or prepared by a public agency.

Rule 902). Therefore, looking at item 2 in Exhibit 1-2, all the paralegal needs to do to have Cellutronics' patent for the Omniphone admitted into court is to purchase from the U.S. Patent Office a certified copy. It takes time to gather these types of records from public agencies and it is wise to begin this process very early in the case.

Privilege

An important concept of admissibility for paralegals to understand is that of **privilege**. Privilege is a rule of law that allows a witness to refuse to give testimony on a particular subject and to prevent others from so testifying. The Fifth Amendment sets forth the only privilege based in the U.S. Constitution, the privilege against self-incrimination. That is why witnesses who are asked questions on the stand that may incriminate them will "take the fifth," which means they are invoking the protections set forth in the Fifth Amendment. The other privileges in evidence law have their roots in the common law and are known as **confidential relations**. The law protects these confidential relationships and the communications made therein even over and above the need to search for the truth.

The confidential communications privilege most familiar to paralegals is the attorney-client privilege. The historical purpose of this privilege was to encourage clients to make the fullest possible disclosures to their attorneys to enable the attorney to properly advise the client. The clients must be confident that the attorney could never be forced to disclose what was said between them. Unless the client waives the privilege, the attorney may never reveal the conversation. (As always, there are exceptions, and one exception to the attorney-client privilege occurs when the client sues the attorney for malpractice.) Fortunately, the attorney-client privilege rules also extend to paralegals. Therefore, no court of law can require you to divulge a client's confidence unless the client waives that privilege.

Other types of privileges include the marital privilege, doctor-patient privilege, clergy-penitent privilege, and journalist-source privilege. If testimony is needed to prove a point, and that testimony will be inadmissible if a claim of privilege is raised, then the trial team will have to find another way to get that evidence in.

CHAIN OF CUSTODY

One of the important requirements of evidence is that it be **authentic**. Rule 901(a) of the Federal Rules of Civil Procedure states: "The requirement of authentication or identification as a condition precedent to admissibility is satisfied by evidence sufficient to support a finding that the matter in question is what its proponent claims." In other words, if a defendant is arrested on a charge of driving under the influence, and his blood is drawn for testing, the laboratory had better not mix the defendant's blood sample up with someone else's and send back the wrong results.

■ **PRIVILEGE**
The right to prevent disclosure, or the duty to refrain from disclosing, information communicated within a specially recognized confidential relationship; for example attorney-client privilege, clergy's privilege, doctor-patient privilege, executive privilege, journalists' privilege, and marital communications privilege.

■ **CONFIDENTIAL RELATION**
Any relationship where one person has a right to expect a higher than usual level of care and faithfulness from another person.

■ **AUTHENTIC**
Evidence that is proven to be what it seems to be.

■ CHAIN OF CUSTODY

The chronological list of those in continuous possession of a specific physical object. A person who presents physical evidence at a trial (such as a gun used in a crime) must account for its possession from the time of receipt to the time of trial in order for the evidence to be "admitted" by the judge. It must thus be shown that the chain of custody was unbroken.

The burden on the party offering the evidence is to show to the satisfaction of the court that it is reasonably certain that there has been no alteration, intentional or unintentional, of the evidence. How can the legal team meet this burden? By establishing a **chain of custody,** the attorney and paralegal can ensure that unnecessary doubts concerning the identity and authenticity of evidence are removed.

Chain of custody issues most often arise with physical evidence in the context of criminal matters. While it is equally important that evidence be properly maintained and accounted for in civil matters, the issue of authenticity comes up much less frequently.

In their commentary on Rule 901 in the United States Code Service, Lawyers Edition (Federal Rules of Evidence, 1998), Stephen A. Saltzburg, Daniel J. Capra, and Michael M. Martin provide the following information:

In criminal cases, a question of authenticity arises where something is seized from the defendant and then introduced at trial, and then the defendant disputes that it is his or argues that the thing has been altered in some way. . . .

The strictness with which a chain of custody requirement is applied should depend on the importance of the evidence and the extent to which its probative value depends on its unchanged condition. . . .So, for example, in the usual drug case, the most important chain of custody is the one from the original seizure of the evidence to the analysis of the substance. Given the fungibility of drugs, it is essential to make a connection between the substance seized from the defendant and the substance actually tested. Any substantial gap in this chain of custody or any indication of alteration should be treated as fatal, since otherwise there is an unacceptable risk that the test does not reflect the contents of the substance seized.

One of the major problems in the prosecution's presentation of the infamous O. J. Simpson case was that the chain of custody on some of the key blood evidence was broken; thereby creating the possibility that it had been tampered with. Suspect evidence will be either inadmissible in court or unpersuasive to a jury.

Law enforcement personnel and U.S. and district attorneys' offices will have procedures in place to ensure that the chain of custody is not broken. Usually chain of custody is established by police officers who can testify that they took possession of a particular item of evidence, such as the seized drugs in the above example, and took it to police headquarters. From there, detectives or other personnel should be able to testify that they delivered the drugs to a laboratory for testing. Lab personnel must be able to confirm that they received the drugs, tested them, and came up with specific results.

Paralegals who work for prosecutors will be trained to follow these procedures. Paralegals who work on the other side of the fence, for public defenders or private attorneys who do criminal defense work, will be on the lookout for the weakest links in the chain of custody. By establishing that a vital link in the chain of custody is unaccounted for, and that the evidence analyzed was not the evidence originally received or was tainted somehow, the trial team may be in a position to ask the court to exclude key evidence. On the other hand, if there is only speculation that an item was tampered with, it is more likely the court will allow the evidence to be introduced and let the jury decide how much weight the evidence will be given.

Saltzburg, Capra, and Martin go on to state that the degree of proof necessary to support a chain of custody will also depend on the nature of the evidence proffered. "If the evidence is unique and resistant to change (e.g., an ancient pearl-handled scimitar), then the chain of custody is relatively unimportant. On the other hand, 'if the evidence is open to alteration or tampering, or is not readily identifiable, the trial court requires a more elaborate chain of custody to establish that the evidence has not been tampered with or altered.'" (Citing from *United States v. Clonts*, 966 F.2d 1366 (10th Cir. 1992)).

This explains why chain of custody issues do not often arise in civil matters. Physical evidence in a civil case is usually unique and easily identifiable, for example, a vehicle owned by a party that was involved in an accident. The most common sort of evidence tampering in civil matters is the alteration of documents. But documents and photocopies of those documents are difficult to keep control of, and usually no chain of custody can be established. Admissibility of documents is discussed in more detail in Chapter 2.

THE PARALEGAL'S ROLE

The paralegal's specific role in the procurement of and management of evidence may vary depending on the size of the employing law firm and the type of law practice. For example, in large law firms where lead trial counsel may have several associates assigned to the case, paralegals may have less of a role in formulating a discovery plan or interviewing witnesses. In smaller firms or for sole practitioners, the paralegal may truly be the right hand of the attorney, taking part in minor and major decisions involving the case. Large law firms may have in-house graphics departments or computer technology departments that will create blowups and charts, electronic presentations, or other demonstrative or high-tech wizardry, whereas that task may fall on the paralegal in the smaller firm.

The paralegal's responsibilities will also vary depending on the size of the case. A complex case with thousands of documents will require a more complex system of organization than one with only a few boxes of records. In some cases, less than a dozen depositions are taken during the course of discovery; in others, a dozen are taken every week for months. The paralegal must learn different strategies for dealing with both types of cases. Large-firm paralegals in charge of massive document productions may have teams of assistants working for them, coding documents into large databases for future retrieval. In small firms with little or no support staff, the paralegal will personally handle literally every piece of paper in the case.

CONCLUSION

Discovery is a major part of any lawsuit, and a paralegal's organizational skills are ideal for dealing with the sometimes massive volumes of information that will come pouring in. Paralegals, therefore, have a major role in gathering evidence, reviewing and organizing it, and preserving it for trial. The following chapters of this book will cover different types of evidence and strategies for the paralegal to use in dealing with them. Finally, there will be a section on trial preparation, in which the evidence that will best prove the client's case is chosen and turned into trial exhibits and demonstrative evidence.

■ KEY TERMS

admissible	evidence	real evidence
authentic	expert witness	relevant
chain of custody	hearsay	subpoena
confidential relation	multimedia	sub-rosa investigation
demonstrative evidence	opinion evidence	tangible evidence
discovery	privilege	testimony
documentary evidence	public documents	trier of fact

■ REVIEW QUESTIONS

1. In what phase of a lawsuit is the majority of the evidence obtained?
2. What is the difference between real evidence and demonstrative evidence?
3. What type of witness is qualified to give opinion evidence?
4. Why does technology play such an important role in modern trials?
5. Explain the difference between relevancy and admissibility.
6. Explain why establishing a chain of custody is so important for certain types of physical evidence.
7. Which is the only privilege provided in the U.S. Constitution?
8. List three types of confidential communications privileges.

■ APPLYING WHAT YOU HAVE LEARNED

1. In the case of *Cellutronics v. Microcell*, Sonya Davis testifies during her deposition that her boyfriend, Jacob Richmond, told her that Microcell wanted to hire him on the condition that he turn over as much information as possible about the Omniphone. At the time of the trial, Sonya is in Europe on business and cannot be served with a subpoena. Can her deposition be used under a hearsay exception?
2. Review the Federal Rules of Evidence on relevancy (Rules 401–403). Does your state have similar rules? If there are differences, discuss them.

3. Statements made by parties to a civil action during settlement negotiations are normally not admissible if the settlement attempts are unsuccessful and the case proceeds to trial. Find the rule of evidence for your state that prohibits the admission of such statements.

4. Your attorney asks you what other witnesses you think should be deposed or interviewed or what documents you would like to obtain (from either party) in the *Cellutronics v. Microcell* case. Provide a list and explain why the people/documents you have chosen are important to prove your case against Microcell and Richmond.

ILLUSTRATIVE CASE

Read the following case, excerpted from the U.S. Supreme Court's opinion, and answer the following questions:

1. How did the Special Prosecutor meet his burden of showing that the missing tapes were relevant to the criminal charges?

2. How does the court dispose of hearsay objections made to admissibility of the tapes?

EXCERPT FROM UNITED STATES V. NIXON, PRESIDENT OF THE UNITED STATES, ET AL., 414 U.S. 683 (1974)

CERTIORARI TO THE UNITED STATES COURT OF APPEALS FOR THE DISTRICT OF COLUMBIA CIRCUIT, CASE NO. 73-1766

Burger, C.J., delivered the opinion of the Court, in which all Members joined except Rehnquist, J., who took no part in the consideration or decision of the case.

This litigation presents for review the denial of a motion filed in the District Court on behalf of the President of the United States, to quash a third-party subpoena duces tecum issued by the United States District Court for the District of Columbia, pursuant to Fed. Rule Crim. Proc. 17(c). The subpoena directed the President to produce certain tape recordings and documents relating to his conversations with aids and advisors. The court rejected the President's claim of absolute executive privilege, of lack of jurisdiction, and of failure to satisfy the requirements of Rule 17(c).

On March 1, 1974, a grand jury of the United States District Court for the District of Columbia returned an indictment charging seven named individuals (Mitchell, Haldeman, Ehrlichman, Colson, Mardian, Parkinson and Strachan) with various offenses, including conspiracy to defraud the United States and to obstruct justice. Although he was not designated as such in the indictment, the grand jury named the President, among others, as an unindicted co-conspirator. On April 18, 1974, upon motion of the Special Prosecutor, a subpoena duces tecum was issued pursuant to Rule 17(c) to the President by the United States District Court and made returnable on May 2, 1974. This subpoena required the production, in advance of the September 9 trial date, of certain tapes, memoranda, papers, transcripts, or other writings relating to certain precisely identified meetings between the President and others. The Special Prosecutor was able to fix the time, place and persons present at these discussions because the White House daily logs and appointment records had been delivered to him. On April 30, the President publicly released edited transcripts of 43 conversations; portions of

(continues)

ILLUSTRATIVE CASE *(continued)*

20 conversations subject to subpoena in the present case were included. On May 1, 1974, the President's counsel filed a "special appearance" and a motion to quash the subpoena under Rule 17(c). This motion was accompanied by a formal claim of privilege. At a subsequent hearing, further motions to expunge the grand jury's action naming the President as an unindicted co-conspirator and for protective orders against the disclosure of that information were filed or raised orally by counsel for the President . . . . The District Court held that the judiciary, not the President, was the final arbiter of a claim of executive privilege. The court concluded that, under the circumstances of this case, the presumptive privilege was overcome by the Special Prosecutor's prima facie "demonstration of need sufficiently compelling to warrant judicial examination in chambers . . ." The court held, finally, that the Special Prosecutor had satisfied the requirements of Rule 17(c) . . . .

Rule 17(c) provides:

"A subpoena may also command the persons to whom it is directed to produce the books, papers, documents or other objects designated therein. The court on motion made promptly may quash or modify the subpoena if compliance would be unreasonable or oppressive. The court may direct that books, papers, documents or objects designated in the subpoena be produced before the court at a time prior to the trial or prior to the time when they are to be offered in evidence and may upon their production permit the books, papers, documents or objects or portions thereof to be inspected by the parties and their attorneys."

A subpoena for documents may be quashed if their production would be "unreasonable or oppressive," but not otherwise. The leading case in this Court interpreting this standard is *Bowman Dairy Co. v. United States,* 341 U.S. 214 (1951). This case recognized certain fundamental characteristics of the subpoena duces tecum in criminal cases: (1) it was not intended to provide a means of discovery for criminal cases, id., at 220; (2) its chief innovation was to expedite the trial by providing a time and place before the trial for the inspection of subpoenaed materials. As both parties agree, cases decided in the wake of *Bowman* have generally followed Judge Weinfeld's formulation in *United States v. Iozia,* 12 F.R.D. 335, 338 (SDNY 1952), as to the required showing. Under this test, in order to require production prior to trial, the moving party must show: (1) that the documents are evidentiary and relevant; (2) that they are not otherwise procurable reasonably in advance of trial by exercise of due diligence; (3) that the party cannot properly prepare for trial without such production and inspection in advance of trial and that the failure to obtain such inspection may tend unreasonably to delay the trial.

Against this background, the Special Prosecutor, in order to carry his burden, must clear three hurdles: (1) relevancy; (2) admissibility; (3) specificity. Our own review of the record necessaril l3y affords a less comprehensive view of the total situation than was available to the trial judge and we are unwilling to conclude that the District Court erred in the evaluation of the Special Prosecutor's showing under Rule 17(c). Our conclusion is based on the record before us, much of which is under seal. Of course, the contents of the subpoenaed tapes could not at that stage be described fully by the Special Prosecutor, but there was a sufficient likelihood that each of the tapes contains conversations relevant to the offenses charged in the indictment. With respect to many of the tapes, the Special Prosecutor offered the sworn testimony or statements of one or more of the participants in the conversations as to what was said at the time. As for the remainder of the tapes, the identity of the participants at the time and place of the conversations, taken in their total context, permit a rational inference that at least part of the conversations relate to the offenses charged in the indictment.

(continues)

ILLUSTRATIVE CASE *(continued)*

We also conclude there was a sufficient preliminary showing in each of the subpoenaed tapes containing evidence admissible with respect to the offenses charged in the indictment. The most cogent objection to the admissibility of the taped conversations here at issue is that they are a collection of out-of-court statements by declarants who will not be subject to cross-examination and that the statements are therefore inadmissible hearsay. Here however, most of the tapes apparently contain conversations to which one or more of the defendants named in the indictment were a party. The hearsay rule does not automatically bar all out-of-court statements by a defendant in a criminal case. Declarations by one defendant may also be admissible against other defendants upon a sufficient showing, by independent evidence of a conspiracy among one or more other defendants and the declarant and if the declarations at issue were in furtherance of that conspiracy. The same is true of declarations of co-conspirators who are not defendants in the case on trial. Recorded conversations may also be admissible for the limited purpose of impeaching the credibility of any defendant who testifies or any other co-conspirator who testifies. Generally the need for evidence to impeach witnesses is insufficient to require its production in advance of trial . . . .

From our examination of the materials submitted by the Special Prosecutor to the District Court in support of his motion for the subpoena, we are persuaded that the District Court's denial of the President's motion to quash the subpoena was consistent with Rule 17(c). We also conclude that the Special Prosecutor has made a sufficient showing to justify a subpoena for production before trial. The subpoenaed materials are not available from any other source, and their examination and processing should not await trial in the circumstances shown.

For additional resources, visit our Web site at www.westlegalstudies.com

2

Documentary Evidence

■ OBJECTIVES

After studying this chapter, you will be able to:

❏ understand and describe the investigation stage of a case.

❏ understand what documents are, as that term is used in a case.

❏ understand and describe the discovery phase of a case.

❏ draft basic interrogatories and requests for production of documents.

❏ prepare a discovery plan.

INTRODUCTION

In this chapter, we will discuss what documents are, how to gather documents in the investigation stage and the discovery stage of a lawsuit, and how to manage them. The use of documents during trial is covered in Chapter 10.

Many everyday words take on new meaning when you understand their legal definitions. A legal dictionary is an important resource for every paralegal and you should refer to it often. It is unwise to assume that the meanings of words remain the same when they appear in statutes, codes, or cases. Even a relatively innocent-seeming word such as *document* has specific definitions when used in a legal context. It is not uncommon for statutes, codes, and rules to furnish definitions for particular words.

Besides definitions used in legal dictionaries, laws themselves frequently offer their own definitions of terms. For example, Article X, Federal Rules of Civil Procedure, Rule 1001, defines "documents" as follows:

Rule 1001. Definitions

For purposes of this article the following definitions are applicable:

(1) Writings and recordings.—"Writings" and "recordings" consist of letters, words, or numbers, or their equivalent, set down by handwriting, typewriting, printing, photostating, photographing, magnetic impulse, mechanical or electronic recording, or other form of data compilation.

(2) Photographs.—"Photographs" include still photographs, x-ray films, video tapes, and motion pictures.

(3) Original.—An "original" of a writing or recording is the writing or recording itself or any counterpart intended to have the same effect by a person executing or issuing it. An "original" of a photograph includes the negative or any print there from. If data are stored in a computer or similar device, any printout or other output readable by sight, shown to reflect the data accurately, is an "original".

(4) Duplicate.—A "duplicate" is a counterpart produced by the same impression of the original, or from the same matrix, or by means of photography, including enlargements and miniatures, or by mechanical or electronic re-recording, or by chemical reproduction, or by other equivalent techniques which accurately reproduces the original.

Thus, it is important to consider word definitions when drafting documents of any sort.

The progression of a lawsuit follows a rather formal and logical path. There may be starts and stops, twists and turns, the occasional dead end or detour, but the way is governed by rules and laws that give structure to the journey. At this point, we are at the beginning of the road.

CASE SCENARIO

In this chapter we will introduce our next fact pattern, *Olde v. Convalescent Care, Inc.* We will continue to use this case throughout the book so you will need to refer to it at times.

Your firm is representing Mrs. Mary Olde, an 82-year-old widow who lives alone and independently. Her daughter, Joan Young, checks in with her mother frequently, either in person or by telephone. On February 2, 2001, Mrs. Olde fell in her home, fracturing her hip. She had surgery on February 3, 2001, and remained in the hospital for six days post-surgery. On February 9, 2001, Mrs. Olde was transported from the hospital directly to Convalescent Care, Inc. (CCI), to complete her recovery and receive physical therapy. Mrs. Olde's primary care physician had told Mrs. Olde that she would remain in CCI for approximately three weeks, or until she was completely ambulatory and could care for herself at home once again.

On March 29, 2001, Mrs. Olde lost consciousness at CCI and was transported by ambulance to the emergency room. The emergency room doctor found Mrs. Olde to be severely dehydrated and malnourished. Mrs. Olde remained in the hospital, where she received treatment for these conditions, until April 12, 2001.

She was then released to the care of her daughter, Joan Young. Mrs. Olde refused to return to CCI or any other convalescent facility, stating that meals were often late or missing altogether and that CCI staff often failed to check on her or respond to her requests for help. Mrs. Olde continued to receive physical therapy and nursing care at her daughter's home.

In an effort to understand the treatment Mrs. Olde received at CCI, her daughter obtained a complete copy of her mother's medical records from CCI.

Mrs. Olde and her daughter have come to your firm seeking advice regarding any legal remedies that might be available to Mrs. Olde as a result of her mistreatment at the hands of CCI. Your firm has determined that Mrs. Olde may sue CCI for medical malpractice, negligence, and perhaps other torts.

During the discovery phase of the development of the case, you requested copies of all of Mrs. Olde's records directly from CCI. You had previously reviewed the records provided by your client's daughter. Upon receipt of the records obtained through discovery, you found that they had been altered so as to falsely indicate that Mrs. Olde received much more frequent care than was reported on the records received by Mrs. Olde's daughter.

A fact summary of our case is found in Exhibit 2-1.

EXHIBIT 2-1 FACTS FOR CASE SCENARIO NO. 2	
OLDE V. CONVALESCENT CARE, INC.	
FACT	**EVIDENCE**
1. Your client entered Convalescent Care, Inc. (CCI) on February 9, 2001.	Ambulance records. CCI admission records.
2. Your client received care from CCI from February 9 through March 29, 2001.	CCI medical records (including lab results, tests, X-rays, nurse's notes, prescriptions, etc.). CCI billing records (including, if applicable, bills sent to insurance and records of payments).
3. Your client was transported by ambulance to the hospital on March 29, 2001.	Ambulance records. Hospital admission and treatment records. 911 dispatch records. Statements from neighbors who witnessed the event.
4. Your client was hospitalized until April 12, 2001.	Hospital treatment records. Hospital billing records.
5. Your client's daughter obtained medical records from CCI.	CCI records from Joan Young.

DISCOVERY PLAN

The purpose of a discovery plan is to outline how best to acquire information and evidence in an organized, orderly, and cost-efficient manner. Keep in mind that litigation is a stressful and often nearly all-consuming event for your client. Of course, this is to be expected when the client is unfamiliar with the court system and legal proceedings. Lay people often have pre-conceived notions of the legal profession based upon movies, books and newspaper and magazine articles. However, even those experienced in navigating the legal system, such as corporate CEOs, would much rather focus their attention on the day-to-day business of making money for their business than become embroiled in lawsuits. In either case, the bottom line is to proceed efficiently and economically toward the end result.

A discovery plan will address the following areas:

- Clarifying the claims made, including those in the complaint or petition and any cross-complaints or complaints in intervention or counterclaims, aids in the preparation of discovery and in investigation.

- Sources of proof to support or dispute the claims are important in order to determine what witnesses and documents are necessary.

- You may conduct investigation and informal discovery from the very beginning, even before any lawsuit has been filed. Gathering as much information as possible at this early stage assists in determining how to pursue and may help lead to early resolution of the matter.

Formal discovery is conducted in accordance with the governing rules. Methods of discovery and deadlines are imposed by the codes, rules, and statutes of the particular jurisdiction and venue and must be closely monitored.

Trial preparation should always be in the back of your mind as you gather information. You must determine the need for expert witnesses and take depositions of parties and witnesses. Some documents, things, and records may need to be officially certified in order to be allowed at trial.

All the preparation pays off at trial or alternative dispute resolution. Documents and other tangible items will be selected to be used as trial exhibits. You will have formed a complete picture of the facts that support your case and be ready to present it at trial.

Under these broad headings will be subparts setting out in detail what is known, what needs to be known, and the time and money required to complete each item. Carefully thinking about and addressing each item will contribute to the development of a successful strategy.

The nature of the suit, number of parties, cooperation of the client, complexity of the issues, attorney caseload, and office staffing all contribute to the discovery timeline. Any discovery plan must begin with a thorough understanding of the federal and local rules regarding procedure, discovery, and trial preparation. The person creating and implementing the plan (most likely a paralegal) must ensure that these rules are followed at all times.

DOCUMENTARY EVIDENCE

In all litigation, the tangible or physical evidence that you will most commonly work with will be documentary evidence. Documentary evidence is most frequently a writing that is offered into evidence. This evidence may include letters, business records, school records, medical records, e-mail, e-mail attachments, all sorts of printed matter, photographs, charts, drawings, plans, transcriptions of oral records, and so forth. The use of e-mail and other forms of electronic evidence is discussed in detail in Chapter 7. The documents must be both **material** and **relevant** to the case at hand. Use of documentary evidence is governed by the Rules of Evidence, Rules of Civil Procedure, and Rules of Criminal Procedure (see Appendixes A, B, and C).

The purpose for requesting and gathering evidence is to substantiate your party's claims as well as to disprove the opposing party's claims. It is vital that you critically analyze each piece of evidence in light of how it may be used to either support or undermine your case. Many documents may support a claim in part and weaken a claim in part. Carefully consider how each piece of evidence can best be presented to strengthen your client's claims. You should not brush aside weaknesses merely because the strengths appear to outweigh them. Rather, examine each document with an eye toward how it may be used against your client. This can be a difficult task to do while advocating strongly for your client. However, you must occasionally take a step back and try to think like opposing counsel. Ask yourself: How could the other side turn this evidence against us? Where are the holes? How will the jury interpret this document? Finding weaknesses in your case early provides ample time to gather additional documents, perform additional research, clarify issues, and generally bolster any weaknesses or perhaps even turn them into strengths.

Documentary evidence is often used as proof of **allegations**, for example, when medical records are used to corroborate personal injuries cited in a lawsuit for medical malpractice. A document is authenticated by a witness who identifies it or by witnesses who establish a chain of custody for it.

Gathering evidence requires knowledge of basic interviewing and investigative techniques combined with an understanding of the discovery rules found in statutes relating to civil and criminal procedure. When you accumulate evidence you must determine the relevance of each document without a thorough understanding of the legal and factual theories of a case, it is impossible to appropriately evaluate the evidence. The conscientious paralegal will frequently turn to the applicable codes and statutes to make sure the developing facts fit the legal premises and also will consult treatises and hornbooks to ascertain the best procedures for building the case. Of course, the paralegal will be working with a supervising attorney and other members of the legal team to make sure best practices are being followed.

For example, in our fact pattern, employees of CCI appear to have falsified the medical records of Mrs. Olde. To prove her case, Mrs. Olde's attorney will introduce both the falsified records and the real records into evidence at trial. You will have obtained these documents during the discovery process. Most likely, a document expert witness will be retained to testify as to the falsification of the records. Another expert might be retained to testify regarding the standard of care to which CCI should have adhered in its care and treatment of Mrs. Olde. In addition, you will have obtained medical records from all of Mrs. Olde's medical providers for at least 10 years prior to this incident and continuing to the present time. In order to substantiate damages, all documents pertaining to financial loss suffered as a result of the incident will need to be identified and obtained. But long before introducing the exciting "case-making" exhibits, a great deal of information gathering must take place in order to meticulously and thoroughly lay the best possible factual

■ **MATERIAL**
A document or person determined to be useful for or made the object of consideration or study.

■ **RELEVANT**
Tending to prove or disprove a fact that is important to a claim, charge, or defense in a court case. Information must be relevant to be admitted as evidence in a case. All relevant evidence is admissible in a case unless excluded by a specific rule, such as the hearsay rule. Relevant evidence may also be excluded if its value as evidence is outweighed by the possibility of unfair prejudice, the time wasted in presenting it, the possibility of confusing the issues, etc.

■ **ALLEGATION**
A statement in a pleading that sets out a fact that the side filing the pleading expects to prove.

foundation based upon documents that have been catalogued, sorted, analyzed, and summarized. This behind-the-scenes legwork represents the day-in day-out attention to detail and document maintenance procedures that result in a successful outcome for the client. This work requires a well-organized, knowledgeable, and meticulous paralegal.

GENERAL REQUIREMENTS FOR DOCUMENTARY EVIDENCE

The genuineness of every document must be proven. Having its author appear as a witness, calling a witness who was present when it was signed, or calling one who can identify the handwriting may authenticate a writing. In the Olde case, the fact that there is a dispute about the genuineness of CCI records of Mrs. Olde's treatment at that facility raise questions of authentication. Before trial, these uncertainties may be addressed by using the questionable records as exhibits at the depositions of various parties and asking the deponents about who wrote the records, who had access to them, who has custody of them, and how they were maintained and stored. Mrs. Olde and her daughter will most likely be questioned by opposing counsel regarding their allegations that the records have been falsified. A handwriting expert may be retained by one or both of the parties to render an opinion regarding authenticity and alterations of the records.

Authentication

In proving the contents of a writing, the original of the writing is the best evidence of its contents and must, therefore, be introduced (except in certain situations). When an admissible writing has been lost or destroyed or cannot be produced, the contents may be proven by an authenticated copy or by the testimony of a witness who has seen and can remember the writing. Again, in the present fact pattern, an expert witness may be hired to identify which original documents were tampered with. Copies are typically used as the working documents. All originals must be maintained in a secure location.

When documentary evidence is lengthy, the court (to save time) may permit a witness who has studied the papers to attest to their meaning. The opposing party, of course, has the right to examine the documentary evidence and to cross-examine the witness. In our case, treating physicians will attest to the meaning of the various medical records.

Unofficial charts, sketches, diagrams, plans, notes, or drawings representing items that cannot be described clearly and easily by a witness are admissible when proven to be authentic. Proof that such a piece of evidence is a true and accurate representation is sufficient. For example, anatomical drawings may be introduced in order to educate the jury about Mrs. Olde's medical conditions.

The terms of a written document cannot be altered by oral testimony. Oral testimony intended to explain the meaning of a document, however, is admissible. In other words, just because a party testifies that the document means something other than what the words on the document indicate, the document itself is the best evidence of its meaning. However, testimony may be used to clarify the meaning of the document.

Documentary evidence must be introduced by presenting it to the court and identifying it. A document must be offered in full. Even though only those portions pertinent to the testimony of the witness referring to it may be read to the court, the entire document must be received in evidence. A desired document that is not in the possession of the party wishing to introduce it may be produced in court by serving a subpoena on the holder requiring that he or she appear at trial with the document.

The Federal Rules of Evidence describes the requirements regarding documentary evidence in detail. Refer to the Appendixes for additional information.

TIP

Although the entire document must be introduced at trial, the attorney may wish to use only particular portions with the jury. Be sure to have those portions that will be read to the jury available and highlighted so that the attorney may refer to them easily.

Official Records

Properly authenticated copies of government records are admissible in lieu of the originals. Governmental entities do not release original records, but upon request and, usually, the payment of a fee, they will provide an authenticated copy of a record. The authentication may consist of a raised seal or a stamp applied to the document. In the Olde case, such records may consist of licenses granted to CCI by various governmental agencies. In the Omniphone case, the records may include applications made to the U.S. Patent Office.

An official chart is admissible as an official record. There are businesses that specialize in preparing charts for use at trial. Such a business might prepare an intricate chart of an intersection that was the scene of an automobile accident, for example. Such businesses produce professional charts and diagrams based upon impartial materials provided to them, such as police reports. They usually employ or consult with specialists in the areas needed to produce an accurate, fair rendering. In the Olde case, a business specializing in medical drawings might be retained to create an accurate rendition of a healthy hip and a hip that has suffered a fracture similar to Mrs. Olde's. A treating or expert physician could refer to the drawing while testifying about the nature of Mrs. Olde's injury to the jury.

Be aware that these drawings or models are not inexpensive, although they may serve a valuable purpose in educating the judge and jury. They must be prepared by a reputable company and with no appearance of bias. In addition, they often take several days to weeks to prepare. Take the cost and time required into consideration when preparing your discovery plan.

Entries and records of an organization (such as attendance reports, master sheets, and hotel registers) are admissible, provided it is the practice of the organization to keep such records in the regular course of business. It is not appropriate to request that an organization manufacture records it does not normally keep. Many businesses keep records in the ordinary course of business that may be requested and used as evidence. For example, the telephone company keeps records of phone calls as a part of its business. Be aware, however, that many businesses have accepted practices detailing the length of time it is required to keep records. It is important to acquire such records as early as possible. In the Olde case, we may use time cards for various CCI personnel showing when they were on duty and where, as that information relates to our case.

The rules on the admissibility of letters and photographs hold that a letter written, dictated, or signed by a party to the lawsuit may be submitted as evidence. A letter sent to a party to the lawsuit is admissible only if it can be shown that he or she answered or acted upon it. The letters and photographs must be relevant to the issues in the lawsuit. For example, the fact that Mrs. Olde has a letter from her primary physician advising that she undergo a bone density test has no bearing on the fact that she broke her hip.

Photographs and X-rays that are proven to be true pictures are admissible. Proof that photographs are true pictures can be established by the negatives. If the negatives are lost, the owner of the photos may verify their authenticity or the parties may agree to accept them as authentic. The doctor or facility where the X-ray was taken would verify its authenticity.

Originals Versus Duplicates

Rule 1002 of the Federal Rules of Evidence states: "To prove the content of a writing, recording, or photograph, the original writing, recording, or photograph is required, except as otherwise provided in these rules or by Act of Congress." This may seem daunting but, fortunately, the immediately following Rules deal with the admissibility of duplicates: "Rule 1003. Admissibility of Duplicates. A duplicate is admissible to the same extent as an original unless (1) a genuine question is raised as to the authenticity of the original or (2) in the circumstances it would be unfair to admit the duplicate in lieu of the original." In the Olde case, copies of Mrs. Olde's income tax records will be admissible since the original returns are in the possession of the Internal Revenue Service.

Rule 1004 provides that the original of a document is not required and other evidence of the contents of a writing, recording, or photograph is admissible if

(1) Original lost or destroyed.—All originals are lost or have been destroyed, unless the proponent lost or destroyed them in bad faith; or

(2) Original not obtainable.—No original can be obtained by any available judicial process or procedure; or

(3) Original in possession of opponent.—At a time when an original was under the control of the party against whom offered, that party was put

on notice, by the **pleadings** or otherwise, that the contents would be a subject of proof at the hearing, and that party does not produce the original at the hearing; or

(4) Collateral matters.—The writing, recording, or photograph is not closely related to a controlling issue.

When documentary evidence is used as a kind of real evidence (such as CCI's records proving Mrs. Olde's stay at its facility), it is authenticated the same way as any other real evidence. A witness will identify it or, less commonly, witnesses will establish a chain of custody for it. If the evidence was previously introduced and authenticated at a deposition or as a result of discovery, the parties may agree to stipulate to its authenticity. If any party questions the authenticity, the original will need to be produced at trial and authenticated by the author, photographer, or other originator of the evidence.

IDENTIFYING POTENTIAL PROBLEMS

During investigation as well as during the discovery phase, you should scrutinize each document carefully and subject it to a checklist of questions in order to become aware of and deal with problems as early as possible in the litigation process. The questions to ask are the following:

1. Is there a parol evidence problem?
2. Is there a best evidence problem?
3. Is there an authentication problem?
4. Is there a hearsay problem?

Parol Evidence

With regard to question number 1, the **parol evidence rule** bars the admission of extrinsic evidence to vary the terms of a written agreement. This issue is a matter of substantive law, not a rule of evidence. **Substantive law** is law that creates or defines rights, duties, obligations, and causes of action that can be enforced by law. In contrast, **procedural law** provides the procedures and methods for enforcing rights and duties and for obtaining redress. In other words, substantive law deals with the issues of the dispute (e.g., a contract, assault and battery, medical malpractice, or rape). Procedural law deals with the process of navigating the legal system. In the Olde case, substantive law includes the allegations of negligence (medical malpractice) and fraud (alteration of records), among others. Procedural law includes the rules that govern the discovery process.

■ **PLEADING**

The process of making formal, written statements of each side of a civil case.

■ **PAROL EVIDENCE RULE**

The principle that the meaning of a written agreement, in which the parties have expressly stated that it is their complete and final agreement, cannot be contradicted or changed by using prior oral or written statements or agreements as evidence.

■ **SUBSTANTIVE LAW**

The basic law of rights and duties (contract law, criminal law, accident law, etc.) as opposed to procedural law (law of pleading, law of evidence, law of jurisdiction, etc.).

■ **PROCEDURAL LAW**

The rules of carrying on a civil lawsuit or a criminal case (how to enforce rights in court) as opposed to substantive law (the law of the rights and duties themselves).

Best Evidence Rule

The **best evidence rule** provides that, where a writing is offered in evidence, a copy or other secondary evidence of its content will not be received in place of the original document unless an adequate explanation is offered for the absence of the original, as stated above in Rule 1002 of the Federal Rules of Evidence.

The best evidence rule arose during the days when a copy was usually made by a clerk or, worse, a party to the lawsuit. Courts generally assumed that if the original was not produced there was a good chance of either a scrivener's error or fraud. Today, the term "copy" usually means "photocopy." Courts have acknowledged that photocopying a document rarely creates an error, as opposed to the old days when illegibility was a concern. In addition, courts are reluctant to require needless effort and delay where there is no dispute about the fairness and adequacy of a photocopy. Before the computer age, the old laws governing documentary evidence preferred original documents and considered machine-produced documents to be "copies" of originals, clearly an unsuitable position for our computer world.

Rules of evidence today establish that the evidentiary value of a document is determined by knowledge about the way the document was created, used, and maintained. This knowledge is usually obtained by having either the creator of the document or someone directly familiar with it testify about the particular document.

Accordingly, the federal rules allow the use of mechanically produced duplicates unless a party has raised a genuine question about the accuracy of the copy or can show that its use would be unfair, as noted in Rule 1003, cited above. Remember, however, a party can always question the authenticity of a document. Therefore, unless you have a stipulation to the contrary, or your document fits one of the exceptions listed in the statute, you must be ready to produce originals of any documents involved in your case or to produce evidence of why you can't. Always know where the original document is and how to obtain it should the need arise. If you are unable to produce the original you must be ready to defend your reasons.

Compilations

Under the federal rules, compilations or summaries of voluminous records may be received where the originals are available for examination by the other parties, as set out in Rule 1006: "The contents of voluminous writings, recordings, or photographs which cannot conveniently be examined in court may be presented in the form of a chart, summary, or calculations. The originals, or duplicates, shall be made available for examination or copying, or both, by other parties at reasonable time and place. The court may order that they be produced in court."

For example, referring to the Omniphone scenario set out in Chapter 1, the drawings of the competing phone may consist of hundreds of pages of highly intricate and technical drawing from the device's inception through research and development and through the production process. As discussed above, information pertinent to the lawsuit may be synthesized and presented in a chart or a simpler drawing that may be more easily explained to and understood by the jury. The paralegal will participate in determining how best to make such technical information accessible to a jury of laypersons. As stated above, the original drawings must be available to be produced, if necessary.

Authenticity

As noted above, the Rule provides that documents can be authenticated the same way as any other real evidence, but material alterations must be accounted for. The Rules of Evidence also list specifically approved methods of authenticating documents, including the submission to the finder of fact of a known exemplar of a signature for comparison with the signature on a disputed document.

Authenticity is important in the Olde case, since medical records are signed by the care provider and there is a question of falsified records. Rule 901(a) of the Federal Rules of Evidence states that the requirement of authentication or identification as a condition precedent to admissibility is satisfied by evidence sufficient to support a finding that the matter in question is what its proponent claims. This could be a complicated process in the Olde case, since authentication goes to the heart of some of the claims made against the care facility. The jury will determine whether or not the records were altered based upon the testimony of expert witnesses.

In addition, some documents, such as certified copies of public records, official documents, newspapers, periodicals, trade inscriptions, documents to prove acknowledgment, certificates of the custodians of business records, and certain commercial paper and related documents are, to one extent or another, self-authenticating under the federal rules.

Hearsay Exceptions

Rule 801(c) of the Federal Rules of Evidence defines hearsay as follows: "'Hearsay' is a statement, other than one made by the declarant while testifying at the trial or hearing, offered in evidence to prove the truth of the matter asserted."

Hearsay is not admissible. Of course, as in everything else, there are exceptions to this rule. For purposes of our fact pattern, the hearsay exceptions that apply include Federal Rules 803 (3), (4), (5), and (6):

(3) *Then existing mental, emotional, or physical condition.* Mrs. Olde may testify as to her physical abilities before and after she fell in her home. She may also testify regarding her pain and mental status, that is, anxiety, fear, and anger resulting from the lack of adequate care provided by CCI. Her daughter may also testify about her observations of her mother's state of mind and her impressions when she visited her mother. The opposing party may object to the latter statements on the grounds of hearsay since Mrs. Olde will be available to testify on her own behalf. However, if a party has died or is otherwise unavailable to testify on his or her own behalf, the court may consider statements made by others as to that party's frame of mind.

(4) *Statements for purposes of medical diagnosis or treatment.* It is a usual practice for medical providers to include statements as to the patient's level of pain or statements made by the patient regarding his or health. In our case, these statements are certainly pertinent to decisions made about the diagnosis and treatment of Mrs. Olde. The rule provides that statements made for purposes of medical diagnosis or treatment and describing medical history, or past or present symptoms, pain, or sensations, or the inception or general character of the cause or external source thereof insofar as reasonably pertinent to diagnosis or treatment are exceptions to the hearsay rule.

(5) *Recorded recollection.* The rule reads: "A memorandum or record concerning a matter about which a witness once had knowledge but now has insufficient recollection to enable the witness to testify fully and accurately, shown to have been made or adopted by the witness when the matter was fresh in the witness' memory and to reflect that knowledge correctly. If admitted, the memorandum or record may be read into evidence but may not itself be received as an exhibit unless offered by an adverse party."

In our case, it is certainly conceivable that Mrs. Olde would have a difficult time remembering specific medical bills, treatment dates, and so forth. Records could be used to refresh her memory. She could not be expected to recall who provided care for her on specific dates. The records of CCI and the hospital will be used to help her remember.

(6) *Records of regularly conducted activity.* These documents would consist of records, memoranda, reports, or data compilations such as medical records, notes, and lab results that were made in accordance with the custom and practice of the medical providers. The rule requires that the documents describing acts, events, conditions, opinions, or diagnoses be made at or near the time by, or from information transmitted by, a person with knowledge, if kept in the course of a regularly conducted business activity, and if it was the regular practice of that business activity to make them. The records will be authenticated by the testimony of the custodian or other qualified witness, or by certification that complies with Rule 902(11), Rule 902(12), or a statute permitting certification, unless the source of information or the method or circumstances of preparation indicate lack of trustworthiness.

GATHERING DOCUMENTS TO SUPPORT A CLAIM

It is important to remember that documents and other records are the lifeblood of any corporation. Corporations depend on their financial records, payroll records, personnel records, correspondence, advertising documents, and all other records, documents, and various printed matter. While employees come and go and change jobs within an organization, the documents created and left behind by those employees are a historical record of the activities of that particular entity. Documents can merely record this history or they can significantly help or hurt a party, such as a manufacturer involved in product liability litigation.

Corporations do not usually provide easy access to their records. Issues of privacy, confidentiality, privilege and trade secrets must be addressed. Corporations will closely parse the language used in discovery requests in the light most favorable to producing the fewest possible documents. It is important to have a clear understanding of the documents sought in order to craft discovery requests to successfully obtain them.

Client Records

After our discussion of the definitions and rules surrounding documents, it should be clear that the procedures used to gather documents are very important. Long before a lawsuit is filed and the discovery process begins, relevant information concerning any claim must be gathered. Prior to the first meeting with the client, determine, to the extent possible, what documents the client has to support her claim. Instruct her to bring all supporting documentation that may have any bearing whatsoever on the claim, whether or not she feels it is relevant. Often a client may be too distraught to think clearly about which documents may be relevant. You should talk with the potential client to determine, in broad terms, the nature of the complaint. Through gentle questioning and using good communication skills, you can learn from the client what documents she has in her possession and request that she bring those with her. A staff member can make copies of the client's materials during the meeting in order to save the client the bother of doing so.

The nature of the relationship between the client and the law office staff will determine how forthcoming the client will be about sharing documentation and other information. Clients rarely withhold vital information purposely; rather, as a result of their unfamiliarity with the legal system and lack of knowledge about how evidence is used, they may share only what they deem to be important. It must be made clear that the attorney and paralegal need to obtain as much factual information from the client in the form of documents and oral information as the client has. The adage "forewarned is forearmed" is certainly true when gathering information. It is at least embarrassing and at most harmful to be surprised by information your client was aware of but chose not to divulge to you when it is discovered at deposition or trial.

However, there are times when a client may select those documents that he feels most strongly support his case and neglect to bring in those that he feels are not necessary, much to his legal peril. Surprise can be disastrous. For example, in a personal injury case it is important that the client advise her attorney of all prior hospitalizations and injuries, not just those she feels are relevant to the instant matter. Learning from opposing counsel that your client suffered similar injuries several years prior to the injury she is currently complaining of, whether or not the prior injury is determined to be relevant to the current injury, is harmful to all concerned. In order to provide the best possible representation, the paralegal may find herself at times in the role of persuader, confidant, and confessor. A paralegal often is more available to the client than the attorney and is in a better position to gather the background information necessary to have a complete picture of the matter at hand.

For example, in our case we ask Joan Young and Mary Olde to bring all medical records for Mrs. Olde, including any records from before the incident in question arose. The reason for gathering these records is to determine Mrs. Olde's state of health leading up to the fall that resulted in her initial hospitalization. Be aware that, due to Mrs. Olde's advanced age, these records may be voluminous. Also, we want to see medical bills, both for the time leading up to the incident and for ongoing medical care. This information will aid in the determination of her financial damages suffered as a result of this incident. We want to see any available photographs of Mrs. Olde shortly before her fall that precipitated the chain of events leading to the claim. Also, photographs taken during her hospitalization, convalescent care, and since moving into her daughter's house will be very useful. The photographs will be used to show the jury how Mrs. Olde appeared before her fall and then after her injuries. If Mrs. Olde received any brochures or marketing information about CCI, she should bring that in.

In order to properly evaluate Mrs. Olde's financial damages, we need information documenting her income from all sources. Presumably, she receives Social Security. We need to analyze and summarize any additional income of whatever nature, such as stock dividends, trust funds, and so forth. The same is true for information regarding her expenses. Mrs. Olde most likely is in control of these documents. We will provide her with a list and a period of time to gather the documents and records together and present them to us to copy, analyze, and summarize. Copies of the prior five years of tax returns are necessary to complete her financial picture.

What we are trying to do is to get as clear a picture as possible of the entire claim and the events surrounding it. This is done by collecting evidence. Documentary evidence is most commonly used to do this. The case will be developed and built upon the documents that support the other kinds of evidence. All of the evidence is interrelated and works together to create a clear picture of events. Documentary evidence will support witness statements and testimony and be the basis for demonstrative evidence used at trial.

After we have obtained and analyzed the client's documentary evidence, gaps in evidence will become apparent. Some evidence can be gathered only during the discovery process, but much can be found during the investigation phase. Again, using our example, we may need an investigator to photograph or videotape the grounds and buildings of the CCI facility where Mrs. Olde received care. During trial, these photos will aid in providing the jury with a sense of location.

After thoroughly reviewing the entire document, they can be culled and irrelevant and immaterial documents pulled out and stored elsewhere.

FREEDOM OF INFORMATION ACT

Using our fact pattern, it may be necessary to make a request under the **Freedom of Information Act (FOIA)** to obtain federal records regarding complaints made against CCI. The FOIA provides access to all agency records, except those that are specifically exempted. An agency record means printed documents or other information-bearing materials such as photographs, computer tapes, or databases that satisfy the following two conditions:

- The agency record must already exist and have been created or obtained by a federal agency; FOIA does not require an agency to create a record just to satisfy your request.
- The record must be within both the possession and the control of the federal agency at the time you make your FOIA request. An agency does not have to retrieve a requested record it doesn't possess at the time your request is made.

An agency has control over a record if it has the power to dispose of it. You have the right to obtain this information from these agencies even if it can be collected from another source. Many states have laws similar to the federal FOIA and the procedure for obtaining agency records will be similar or identical.

In order to obtain such documents, contact the Department of Justice or the agency from which you want information. In this case, a logical place to start would be the federal Department of Health and Human Services and the Department for Consumer Affairs for the state. Then get the specific mailing address for its FOIA office by referring to the Code of Federal Regulations (CFR), available at any law library and many public libraries, or online at *http://www.gpoaccess.gov/cfr/index.html*. Your request must reasonably describe the records you are seeking. This means the description must be specific enough that a government employee familiar with the agency's files will be able to locate the records within a reasonable amount of time and without an unreasonable amount of effort. Be aware that each agency may have slightly different procedures for requesting and obtaining documents.

You need not explain why you want the information you are seeking. However, this explanation might be necessary if you want the agency to waive its fees or comply more fully with your request. The more precise and accurate your request, the more likely you are to get a prompt and complete response and the lower the search fees will be. You must contact the agency you are requesting records from in order to determine fees. Although it may be difficult, due to the extent government entities now rely upon automated telephone services, it may be worth the effort to contact an agency by phone and speak with a person familiar with the agency's procedures regarding FOIA requests. You may also be able to establish contact using e-mail. It is always useful to have the name and contract information of the individual assisting you with the request. In addition, establishing rapport with the agency may smooth the way for future requests or clarification.

■ **FREEDOM OF INFORMATION ACT** (5 U.S.C. § 552) A 1966 federal law that makes all records held by the federal government, except for certain specific types of records (such as certain military secrets), available to the public. Procedures are set up to get these records and to appeal decisions to withhold them.

DETERMINING THE DOCUMENTS NEEDED TO SUPPORT CLAIMS

At this time in the development of the lawsuit, you should make a checklist to determine documents needed and how to obtain them. Exhibit 2-2 is a sample checklist featuring documents pertaining to the Olde case.

EXHIBIT 2-2   DOCUMENTS CHECKLIST

DOCUMENT	HOW OBTAINED	DATE OBTAINED
Medical Records:		
Prior to Incident:		
Dr. A	Medical Records Release	
Dr. B	Medical Records Release	
Clinic 1	Medical Records Release	
Clinic 2	Medical Records Release	
Pertinent to Incident:		
Ambulance	Medical Records Release	
Hospital	Medical Records Release	
Primary Care MD	Medical Records Release	
From CCI:		
Treatment Records	From Client Medical Records Release Request for Production	
CCI Corporate Info:		
Articles of Incorporation	Request for Production	
Certificate of Good Standing	Secretary of State	
Financial Data	Dow Jones, Hoovers – online	
Reports regarding inspections	Freedom of Information Act	
Background Documents:		
Other lawsuits filed against CCI	Interrogatories, then from applicable court	
Consumer complaints against CCI	Freedom of Information Act	

This checklist is for in-house organizational purposes. It will help you to keep track of documents ordered or requested, when they come in, and what else is needed. Later, we will discuss managing the documents received. All in-house lists like this will be fluid; it is common for the analysis of one document to lead to the need for another. Witnesses may mention documents that were previously unknown. The evolution of the case will determine the necessity of additional documents, records, statements, and so on. It is in the exciting nature of lawsuits that learning some information leads to the need to learn more.

Once you have determined what documents are needed, it is time to begin gathering them. Documents may be obtained in a variety of ways, including by ordering them in writing, demanding them from opposing counsel, or via the Internet. The methods for collecting documents are varied, depending upon the documents and who has possession of them.

In gathering our client's medical records, we must first obtain a signed release from her authorizing us to collect the records on her behalf. Such an authorization will include the following:

- patient's name, address, telephone number, date of birth, and Social Security number
- name and address of provider
- a paragraph stating that the patient is authorizing the provider to release all records pertaining to her medical care, including treatment notes, progress notes, operative notes, laboratory test results, diagnostic tests, and X-rays patient's signature and date of signing

Before ordering the records, call the medical care provider and ask about copy fees and how payment should be made. Many providers charge a flat fee for providing records, others charge by the page, and others may require a medical copying service to make arrangements, provide a subpoena, and do the copying. Making this call will also give you an opportunity to open the door to a positive relationship with the office staff for each provider. Remember, you are ordering records for the client you represent, and having the friendly cooperation of the medical care providers will make your job easier.

Once the authorizations have been completed and signed and dated, you may prepare a cover letter to each provider. The cover letter will reference the patient information (name, date of birth, Social Security number) and include payment for the records. You should prepare a list of all requests for records sent out, to whom they were sent, and date sent. Then the list should reflect receipt of each set of records received in response to the requests. Using such a list enables you to track the requests and follow up on slow responses. Client authorizations can be used to obtain any other personal records as well, such as banking, telephone, employment, or educational records.

SUBPOENAS

The procedure for seeking records about an opposing party or from nonparty witnesses is different. In our case, the attorney for CCI will need to use a **subpoena duces tecum** to acquire Mrs. Olde's medical records. See Exhibit 2-3 for an example of a subpoena duces tecum. The attorney for Mrs. Olde may need to use a subpoena duces tecum in order to acquire financial records from CCI. There are vendors that provide legal support services to law offices (often referred to as attorney services), including the preparation and service of subpoenas duces tecum, based upon information provided by the law firm. The attorney service will also make the necessary arrangements and copy the records requested in the subpoena duces tecum. If the records must be obtained using a copy service and a subpoena duces tecum, the process is different. Absent the use of an attorney service, the paralegal must be familiar with procedures regarding preparation and service of subpoenas.

The subpoena duces tecum is a procedure compelling production of certain specific documents. A form is used to designate a specific person, either by name or by title or capacity, to appear to testify and bring documents, records, papers, or other tangible things to the examination.

Rule 45 of the Federal Rules of Civil Procedure discusses subpoenas. It is very important to be familiar with this rule governing preparation and service of subpoenas. Rule 45 is set out in full in Appendix B.

Criminal Cases

Evidence may be obtained from third-party witnesses via a subpoena duces tecum. As opposed to civil cases, where the subpoenaed records are delivered directly to the parties, evidence obtained via subpoena in a criminal matter is turned over to the court where the case is pending. A judge will then decide whether the requesting party is entitled to see the evidence and, if so, will disseminate it to the parties.

■ **SUBPOENA DUCES TECUM**
A subpoena by which a person is commanded to bring certain documents to court or to an administrative agency.

CAREER TIP

Many attorney services employ paralegals to work with law firm clients regarding subpoenas and obtaining documents.

EXHIBIT 2-3 SUBPOENA DUCES TECUM

AO88 (Rev. 1/94) Subpoena in a Civil Case

Issued by the

UNITED STATES DISTRICT COURT

Seventeenth _____ DISTRICT OF _____ Anystate

MARY OLDE,

V.

CONVALESCENT CARE, INC., et al.

SUBPOENA IN A CIVIL CASE

Case Number:[1] 12 34 567

TO: John Black, Director of Human Resources, Convalescent Care, Inc.

☐ YOU ARE COMMANDED to appear in the United States District court at the place, date, and time specified below to testify in the above case.

PLACE OF TESTIMONY	COURTROOM
	DATE AND TIME

☐ YOU ARE COMMANDED to appear at the place, date, and time specified below to testify at the taking of a deposition in the above case.

PLACE OF DEPOSITION	DATE AND TIME

☑ YOU ARE COMMANDED to produce and permit inspection and copying of the following documents or objects at the place, date, and time specified below (list documents or objects):

Time cards, complete employment records, sign-in records, sign-out records, notes, and any other documents you or your staff possess for and and all employees employed by Convalescent Care, Inc. in any position between the dates of February 9, 2001 and March 29, 2001 and who had or may have had any contact with Mary Olde at any time.

PLACE	DATE AND TIME
Law Offices of Cecilia K. Perkins, 8910 Main Street, Suite 234, Anytown, Anystate 00010	1/8/2003 10:00 am

☐ YOU ARE COMMANDED to permit inspection of the following premises at the date and time specified below.

PREMISES	DATE AND TIME

Any organization not a party to this suit that is subpoenaed for the taking of a deposition shall designate one or more officers, directors, or managing agents, or other persons who consent to testify on its behalf, and may set forth, for each person designated, the matters on which the person will testify. Federal Rules of Civil Procedure, 30(b)(6).

ISSUING OFFICER'S SIGNATURE AND TITLE (INDICATE IF ATTORNEY FOR PLAINTIFF OR DEFENDANT)	DATE
Cynthia K. Perkins	12/10/2002

ISSUING OFFICER'S NAME, ADDRESS AND PHONE NUMBER
Cecilia K. Perkins, 8910 Main Street, Suite 234, Anytown, Anystate 00010
555-555-1111

(See Rule 45, Federal Rules of Civil Procedure, Parts C & D on next page)

[1] If action is pending in district other than district of issuance, state district under case number.

(continues)

EXHIBIT 2-3   SUBPOENA DUCES TECUM *(continued)*

AO88 (Rev. 1/94) Subpoena in a Civil Case

PROOF OF SERVICE

	DATE	PLACE
SERVED		

SERVED ON (PRINT NAME)   MANNER OF SERVICE

SERVED BY (PRINT NAME)   TITLE

DECLARATION OF SERVER

I declare under penalty of perjury under the laws of the United States of America that the foregoing information contained in the Proof of Service is true and correct.

Executed on _____
                    DATE

_____
SIGNATURE OF SERVER

_____
ADDRESS OF SERVER

Rule 45, Federal Rules of Civil Procedure, Parts C & D:

(c) PROTECTION OF PERSONS SUBJECT TO SUBPOENAS.

(1) A party or an attorney responsible for the issuance and service of a subpoena shall take reasonable steps to avoid imposing undue burden or expense on a person subject to that subpoena. The court on behalf of which the subpoena was issued shall enforce this duty and impose upon the party or attorney in breach of this duty an appropriate sanction which may include, but is not limited to, lost earnings and reasonable attorney's fee.

(2) (A) A person commanded to produce and permit inspection and copying of designated books, papers, documents or tangible things, or inspection of premises need not appear in person at the place of production or inspection unless commanded to appear for deposition, hearing or trial.

(B) Subject to paragraph (d) (2) of this rule, a person commanded to produce and permit inspection and copying may, within 14 days after service of subpoena or before the time specified for compliance if such time is less than 14 days after service, serve upon the party or attorney designated in the subpoena written objection to inspection or copying of any or all of the designated materials or of the premises. If objection is made, the party serving the subpoena shall not be entitled to inspect and copy materials or inspect the premises except pursuant to an order of the court by which the subpoena was issued. If objection has been made, the party serving the subpoena may, upon notice to the person commanded to produce, move at any time for an order to compel the production. Such an order to comply production shall protect any person who is not a party or an officer of a party from significant expense resulting from the inspection and copying commanded.

(3) (A) On timely motion, the court by which a subpoena was issued shall quash or modify the subpoena if it

(i) fails to allow reasonable time for compliance,

(ii) requires a person who is not a party or an officer of a party to travel to a place more than 100 miles from the place where that person resides, is employed or regularly transacts business in person, except that, subject to the provisions of clause (c) (3) (B) (iii) of this rule, such a person may in order to attend

trial be commanded to travel from any such place within the state in which the trial is held, or

(iii) requires disclosure of privileged or other protected matter and no exception or waiver applies, or

(iv) subjects a person to undue burden.

(B) If a subpoena

(i) requires disclosure of a trade secret or other confidential research, development, or commercial information, or

(ii) requires disclosure of an unretained expert's opinion or information not describing specific events or occurrences in dispute and resulting from the expert's study made not at the request of any party, or

(iii) requires a person who is not a party or an officer of a party to incur substantial expense to travel more than 100 miles to attend trial, the court may, to protect a person subject to or affected by the subpoena, quash or modify the subpoena, or, if the party in whose behalf the subpoena is issued shows a substantial need for the testimony or material that cannot be otherwise met without undue hardship and assures that the person to whom the subpoena is addressed will be reasonably compensated, the court may order appearance or production only upon specified conditions.

(d) DUTIES IN RESPONDING TO SUBPOENA.

(1) A person responding to a subpoena to produce documents shall produce them as they are kept in the usual course of business or shall organize and label them to correspond with the categories in the demand.

(2) When information subject to a subpoena is withheld on a claim that it is privileged or subject to protection as trial preparation materials, the claim shall be made expressly and shall be supported by a description of the nature of the documents, communications, or things not produced that is sufficient to enable the demanding party to contest the claim.

CONCLUSION

The importance of the paralegal's role in case development and case management cannot be over-emphasized. A well educated, organized, detail oriented paralegal will have the skills to assist in determining the nature of the evidence required to develop the facts, prove the case for the client and disprove, or at least cast doubt on, the opposing side. The ability to communicate clearly with all those who have a vested interest in the outcome of the matter is essential. The paralegal is often the member of the legal team who possesses the time and skill in answering clients' questions and helping them through the legal process.

■ KEY TERMS

allegation

best evidence rule

Freedom of Information Act

material

parol evidence rule

pleadings

procedural law

relevant

subpoena duces tecum

substantive law

■ REVIEW QUESTIONS

1. Give two examples of how documents may be authenticated.
2. Under what circumstances will the court allow a summary of documents?
3. What is the difference between a subpoena and a subpoena duces tecum?
4. What is required in order for a duplicate of a document to be admissible?
5. What is the parol evidence rule?
6. What is the best evidence rule?
7. What is the hearsay rule?
8. What is the difference between substantive and procedural law?
9. How are documents obtained using the Freedom of Information Act?
10. What are interrogatories?
11. What is the purpose of a discovery plan?

■ APPLYING WHAT YOU HAVE LEARNED _____

1. Compare and contrast the local rules for the federal district court where you reside and the rules found in the Federal Rules of Civil Procedure.

2. Develop a discovery plan for the Cellutronics case from Chapter 1.

3. Read the following case and answer these questions:

   a. How did the court determine that accident reports and inspection reports are business records?

   b. How did the court determine that the accident report was properly admitted as evidence?

ILLUSTRATIVE CASE

Read the following case, excerpted from the U.S. Court of Appeals, Second Circuit's opinion, and answer the following questions:

1. What effect does the fact that Talbott completed the personal injury report based on information supplied to him by a third person, Campbell, have on the admissibility of the report? Explain your answer.

2. Explain the judge's reasoning behind allowing that evidence regarding the truthfulness of statements made on the employment application.

Excerpt from *Lewis v. Baker*, 526 F.2d 470 (2nd Cir. 1975)

CLIFFORD J. LEWIS, JR., PLAINTIFF-APPELLANT V.
GEORGE P. BAKER ET AL., DEFENDANTS-APPELLEES

NO. 195, DOCKET 75-7134

UNITED STATES COURT OF APPEALS, SECOND CIRCUIT

ARGUED OCTOBER 7, 1975; DECIDED NOVEMBER 20, 1975; 526 F.2D 470 (2ND CIR. 1975)

APPEAL FROM THE UNITED STATES DISTRICT COURT
FOR THE SOUTHERN DISTRICT OF NEW YORK.

BEFORE WATERMAN, OAKES AND MESKILL, CIRCUIT JUDGES.

WATERMAN, CIRCUIT JUDGE:

Plaintiff, Clifford J. Lewis, Jr., brought this action in the United States District Court for the Southern District of New York pursuant to the Federal Employers' Liability Act, 45 U.S.C. § 51 *et seq.* and the Federal Safety Appliance Act, 45 U.S.C. § 1 *et seq.* alleging he suffered a disabling injury while employed by the Penn Central Railroad. Judgment was entered in favor of defendants after a jury trial. Plaintiff appeals and seeks a new trial on the following grounds: (1) accident reports were improperly admitted into evidence; (2) the trial court erred in charging the jury that they might infer

(continues)

ILLUSTRATIVE CASE *(continued)*

proper functioning of the brake from evidence of the brake's condition before and after the accident; and (3) the trial court erred in charging that the jury might consider plaintiff's response to a question in his employment application on the issue of his credibility. Finding no merit to the above contentions, we affirm.

On the date of his injury, October 26, 1969, plaintiff was employed as a freight brakeman or car dropper in the Penn Central railroad freight yard in Morrisville, Pennsylvania. His work called for him to move freight cars in a railroad yard by riding them down a slope while applying the brake manually. Plaintiff testified that immediately before the incident in question, he climbed onto the lead car of two box-cars, stationed himself on the rear brake platform of that car, applied the brake to test it, and found that the brake held. Upon his signal, another employee of the railroad released the two box-cars from the rest of the train at the top of a hill, at which time they started to roll down the slope. Plaintiff then started to turn the vertical brake wheel so that the car would slow down as it descended the slope and would ease into the train with which it was to couple on a track beyond the bottom of the slope. He claims that the brake did not hold, that the car continued to gather momentum, and that he then decided to leap off the car to avoid injury. As a result of the fall, he claims to have sustained substantial knee injury and the aggravation of a preexisting psychiatric condition which has precluded his returning to his job. There were no witnesses to the accident other than the plaintiff.

At the trial, defendants sought to rebut plaintiff's allegations of a faulty brake with evidence that the brake had functioned properly immediately prior to the accident when the plaintiff tested it, and immediately after the accident when it was checked in connection with the preparation of an accident report. It was the defendants' contention that plaintiff improperly set, or forgot to set, a necessary brake handle, panicked, and then leapt from the car.

In support of their interpretation of the events, defendants offered into evidence a "personal injury report" and an "inspection report." Frank Talbott, a trainmaster, testified that the personal injury report was signed by him and prepared under his supervision. The information had been provided to him by William F. Campbell, the night trainmaster. Talbott confirmed the authenticity of the record and testified that he was required to make out such reports of injuries as part of the regular course of business. At the trial David W. Halderman, an assistant general foreman for the defendants, identified the inspection report which had been prepared by Campbell and by Alfred Zuchero, a gang foreman. This report was based upon an inspection of the car Campbell and Zuchero had conducted less than four hours after the accident. Halderman testified that Zuchero was dead and that Campbell was employed by a railroad in Virginia. The latter was thus beyond the reach of subpoena. Halderman also confirmed that following every accident involving injury to an employee his office was required to complete inspection reports, and that such reports were regularly kept in the course of business. Over objection, the court admitted both reports into evidence.

Determination of the admissibility of these reports under the Federal Business Records Act[1] involves two problems: whether the reports are business records within that statute, and whether the fact that the accident report was prepared by an employee who had neither firsthand knowledge of the accident nor had inspected the purportedly defective car and brake affects admissibility into evidence.

As a preliminary matter, there is little doubt that these reports are each a "writing or record, whether in the form of an entry in a book or otherwise, made as a memorandum or record of any act, transaction, occurrence, or event. . ." 28 U.S.C. § 1732 (1966). Furthermore, it is beyond dispute that these reports were made pursuant to a regular

(continues)

ILLUSTRATIVE CASE *(continued)*

procedure at the railroad yard, and that Talbott, Campbell and Zuchero made the reports within a reasonable time after the accident. Appellant argues, however, that notwithstanding the presence of those factors which would indicate a full compliance with 28 U.S.C. § 1732, the Supreme Court's decision in *Palmer v. Hoffman,* 318 U.S. 109, 63 S.Ct. 477, 87 L.Ed. 645 (1943), precludes their admission into evidence. There the Court upheld the inadmissibility of an accident report offered by the defendant railroad that had been prepared by one of its locomotive engineers. The Court stated that since the report was not prepared "for the systematic conduct of the business as a business," it was not "made 'in the regular course' of the business" of the railroad. 318 U.S. at 113, 63 S.Ct. at 481. We find significant differences between the report and the circumstances of its making in that case and the facts here, and we uphold the district court's admission of the records below.

In *Palmer v. Hoffman,* the engineer preparing the report had been personally involved in the accident, and, as Circuit Judge Frank stated in his opinion for the Court of Appeals, the engineer knew "at the time of making it that he [was] very likely, in a probable law suit relating to that accident, to be charged with wrongdoing as a participant in the accident, so that he [was] almost certain, when making the memorandum or report, to be sharply affected by a desire to exculpate himself and to relieve himself or his employer of liability." 129 F.2d 976, 991 (2d Cir. 1942) (italics omitted). Here there could have been no similar motivation on the part of Talbott, Campbell or Zuchero, for not one of them was involved in the accident, or could have possibly been the target of a lawsuit by Lewis. In *United States v. New York Foreign Trade Zone Operators,* 304 F.2d 792 (2d Cir. 1962), we sustained the admissibility of a similar report by the co-employee of the injured party which had been prepared as part of the regular business of the defendant pier-owner and operator. As we explained there, the mere fact that a record might ultimately be of some value in the event of litigation does not *per se* mandate its exclusion. In *Palmer v. Hoffman,* "[o]bviously the Supreme Court was concerned about a likely untrustworthiness of materials prepared specifically by a prospective litigant for courtroom use." 304 F.2d at 797. The fact that a report embodies an employee's version of the accident, or happens to work in favor of the entrant's employer does not, without more, indicate untrustworthiness. In the absence of a motive to fabricate, a motive so clearly spelled out in *Palmer v. Hoffman,* the holding in that case is not controlling to emasculate the Business Records Act. Therefore the trial court must look to those earmarks of reliability which otherwise establish the trustworthiness of the record. (Citations omitted.)

Here the ICC requires the employer to prepare and file monthly reports of all accidents involving railroad employees. Assistant general foreman Halderman testified that following every injury he was required to inspect the equipment involved and to report the results of the inspection on a regular printed form.[2] As we stated in *Taylor v. Baltimore & Ohio R. R. Co., supra,* "[i]t would ill become a court to say that the regular making of reports required by law is not in the regular course of business." In addition to their use by the railroad in making reports to the ICC, the reports here were undoubtedly of utility to the employer in ascertaining whether the equipment involved was defective so that future accidents might be prevented. These factors, we think, are sufficient indicia of trustworthiness to establish the admissibility of the reports into evidence under the Federal Business Records Act.[3]

The fact that the trainmaster Talbott completed the personal injury report based on information supplied to him by a third person, Campbell, does not render the report inadmissible. 28 U.S.C. § 1732 explicitly states that "lack of personal knowledge by the entrant or maker" shall not affect the admissibility of the record, and may only affect its

(continues)

ILLUSTRATIVE CASE *(continued)*

weight. Nor does the fact that the entrant does not testify preclude the admission of the record. All that is required is that someone who is sufficiently familiar with business practices be able to testify that the record was made regularly as part of those business practices and that the record is a truly authentic one. Witnesses Talbott and Halderman met those requirements.

Appellant next contends that the district court erred in charging the jury that if the brake operated properly before the accident, that the jury might "presume that the functioning would have continued . . . at the time of plaintiff's accident," and that if the brake was found to be functioning normally and properly when it was later inspected by the trainmaster and gang foreman, that they might "infer or conclude . . . it would have operated normally and properly at the time of the accident, and, therefore, was not defective." During the trial, the plaintiff testified that the brake had in fact operated properly when he tested it prior to the release of the car. The information contained in the inspection report showed that Campbell and Zuchero had found nothing wrong with the brake in question when they inspected it after the accident.

When the state of an object at a particular time is in issue, we have repeatedly upheld the relevancy of evidence of that object's condition before and after the time in question. While the weight to be given evidence of prior and subsequent condition differs in each case and is of course a question for the trier of fact, it was proper for the trial judge to tell the jury that they might conclude or presume from that evidence a proper functioning during the interim. He additionally instructed that: If you find there was failure of the hand brake owing to unexplained reasons as distinguished from a known or explainable condition, then it is not material that the hand brake performed properly at another time.

Thus, it was made clear to the jury that if they believed defendants' evidence, they might infer continuance forward and back; but if they believed plaintiff's testimony, then the prior and subsequent condition of the brake was not material. That was a correct statement of the applicable law.

Appellant's final contention pertains to the trial judge's charge to the jury that it might consider on the issue of his credibility an employment application containing an admittedly untruthful statement regarding his psychiatric disorder. At the time of his application for employment with the defendant, Lewis was asked to complete a form which contained questions regarding his medical history and confinement in a hospital or sanitarium. He certified his negative answers to those questions to be true answers at the time he completed the form, but he admitted at trial that the negative answers were not truthful in view of his confinement to a psychiatric hospital and treatment less than five years prior to his employment with Penn Central. He now claims that it was improper for Judge Levet to charge the jury that those untruthful statements were relevant to any issue relating to his credibility.

It is well-settled that the trial judge is accorded great discretion in his assessment of the matters which should properly be raised on cross-examination as bearing on the credibility of a party or witness. The relevancy of testimony which aids in the jury's determination of a party's credibility and veracity has been repeatedly affirmed. Although an opponent is not permitted to adduce extrinsic evidence that a party lied on a previous occasion, he may nonetheless ask questions to that end.

The employment application involved here was a form completed by Lewis as a prerequisite to his obtaining the job of car dropper for Penn Central. His failure truthfully to inform his future employer of a psychiatric condition which defendants argue could have affected his judgment on the evening in question was thus not without probative value on

(continues)

ILLUSTRATIVE CASE *(continued)*

the issue of his veracity. Particularly, as the jury's ultimate task was to decide whether they would believe plaintiff's or defendants' account of the events on October 29, such evidence bearing directly on a party's capacity for truth-telling was relevant. Thus the testimony regarding prior falsification of the application was properly elicited from Lewis, and we uphold the propriety of the trial judge's charge that that evidence might be considered by the jury on the issue of plaintiff's credibility.

    Affirmed.

---

[1] 28 U.S.C. § 1732 provides, insofar as is applicable:
    Record made in regular course of business:
    (a) In any court of the United States and in any court established by Act of Congress, any writing or record, whether in the form of an entry in a book or otherwise, made as a memorandum or record of any act, transaction, occurrence, or event, shall be admissible as evidence of such act, transaction, occurrence, or event, if made in regular course of any business, and if it was the regular course of such business to make such memorandum or record at the time of such act, transaction, occurrence, or event or within a reasonable time thereafter.
    All other circumstances of the making of such writing or record, including lack of personal knowledge by the entrant or maker, may be shown to affect its weight, but such circumstances shall not affect its admissibility.
    The term "business," as used in this section, includes business, profession, occupation, and calling of every kind.

[2] 45 U.S.C. § 38 provides in relevant part:
    It shall be the duty of the general manager, superintendent, or other proper officer of every common carrier engaged in interstate or foreign commerce by railroad to make to the Secretary of Transportation a monthly report, under oath, of all . . . accidents resulting in death or injury to any person. . . .
    Although 45 U.S.C. § 41 provides that neither the report required by section 38 nor any part thereof "shall be admitted as evidence . . . in any suit or action for damages growing out of any matter mentioned in said report or investigation," we think it clear that the reports prepared by Talbott and by Campbell and Zuchero were not themselves monthly reports under section 41, and there is no indication that any part of the information contained in those reports will ever become part of the monthly report. Rather, it would appear that the forms completed by those employees were supplied by the employer, and that wholly different forms are utilized in complying with the federal reporting regulations, as prescribed by 49 C.F.R. § 225.1 *et seq.* Only the latter are barred by section 41 from admission in accident-related litigation.

[3] The reports would also be admissible under the New York statute relative to business records, CPLR § 4518(a). *Toll v. State of New York*, 32 A.D.2d 47, 299 N.Y.S.2d 589 (1969); *Bishin v. New York Central R. R.*, 20 A.D.2d 921, 249 N.Y.S.2d 778 (1964).

For additional resources, visit our Web site at www.westlegalstudies.com

CHAPTER 3

Using the Formal Discovery Process to Obtain Evidence

■ OBJECTIVES

After studying this chaper, you will be able to:

❏ generally describe the Federal Rules of Civil Procedure governing the formal discovery process.

❏ understand the primary methods of obtaining evidence using the formal discovery process.

❏ understand the differences between propounding discovery and responding to discovery.

INTRODUCTION

Formal discovery is the process of obtaining documents and other evidence using the methods set out in and governed by the Federal Rules of Evidence. Rule 102 describes the purpose and objectives of the formal discovery process: "These rules shall be construed to secure fairness in administration, elimination of unjustifiable expense and delay, and promotion of growth and development of the law of evidence to the end that the truth may be ascertained and proceedings justly determined."

When involved in a lawsuit, each party has a variety of tools and methods available to discover facts and obtain documents from all other parties and from nonparties. Nonparties include lay witnesses and

■ CONTENTION

A point or assertion put forward as part of an argument.

> ! **TIP**
>
> Formal discovery may be conducted only with the named parties to the lawsuit.

expert witnesses. By use of the formal discovery process, a party can also discover a great deal about the opponent's **contentions**, allegations, defenses, and the factual bases, documents, and potential witnesses relevant to them. When used to its fullest extent, discovery creates a framework that limits each party to a specified position or positions.

Each discovery tool serves a unique function and carries with it particular limitations. The discovery process is the only reliable means of obtaining information in a form that is admissible as evidence at trial. Factual information obtained by private investigation into the facts involved in the matter may be stipulated to by the parties; however, it is not uncommon for factual information discovered informally to have to be repeated within the confines and limitations of the formal discovery process. For example, in the Omniphone case, the paralegal may be requested to obtain patent records from the client. Certified copies of the documents may have to be requested from the U.S. Patent Office in order to be used at trial. Obviously, the discovery process may be costly, but it is necessary in order to obtain evidence that can be introduced at trial. In the Olde case, medical records obtained from Joan Young on behalf of her mother may have to be requested from the medical providers. Even though the client may have copies of particular records or documents, copies to be used at trial will be ordered using a subpoena duces tecum. The records obtained in this manner may be introduced into evidence through the person who produced them by order of the subpoena.

A great deal of information may be obtained via the Internet in an information search. One school of thought holds that to minimize costs, as much discovery as possible should be conducted informally. This is valid so long as opposing parties stipulate to the evidence so gathered. Then formal discovery is used to obtain those documents not attainable otherwise and to acquire information in admissible form. In a document heavy case, it may be more cost efficient to learn about documents before using the formal discovery process to obtain the documents themselves. For example, the paralegal may be able to learn quite a bit about the business practices of Omniphone by perusing its Web site and looking for articles reported in the media. This information will provide valuable background information that may be useful when preparing witnesses for depositions or considering categories of documents to request from the opposing party.

THE PURPOSE OF DISCOVERY

The main purposes of discovery are to find evidence, avoid surprises, narrow the issues, and perpetuate testimony. This process will facilitate trial preparation and preparation for **dispositive** motions. Discovery will further develop strengths in your own case and reveal weaknesses in the opponent's case, which may facilitate settlement. At this fairly early stage you can address any weaknesses in your case that appear as a result of discovery. Keeping the discovery goals for each case in mind will lead to the wise use of discovery options, avoiding unnecessary and expensive work.

■ DISPOSITIVE

Clearly settling a legal issue or dispute.

The most obvious purpose of discovery is to acquire evidence of any nature. Your opponent or a nonparty commonly has documents or other evidence necessary to establish, explain, clarify, or bolster your party's claims or defenses. It is crucial to know the evidence the opposition is relying upon in order to be in a position to appropriately respond to it. As you review your evidence, you should determine if it is useful to your client or if it may be useful to the opposition. If it is useful to your client, consider how the opposition may refute it. If it is useful to the opposition (and the opposition is aware of it or will obtain it) think about what evidence you have to counter it.

Narrowing Issues

Initial pleadings are often vague, and the issues raised may be so general that it is unclear what facts are at issue. The claims raised in the complaint may be unspecific regarding details of the allegations. Often a general **denial** filed in answer to the complaint is also unclear. The goal of discovery is to provide the structure to the issues raised and to learn exactly and in detail what the facts are and what the opponent is relying on to prove the facts. You will meet these goals and obtain useful responses only by wisely framing **interrogatories** or requests. The ability to successfully request and obtain discovery utilizes the paralegal's skills of analyzing the known facts, locating and gathering the evidence available from the client and other informational sources, and then identifying evidence that must be obtained using the formal discovery process.

Perpetuating Evidence

It is an uncomfortable fact of life and business that evidence can disappear. Witnesses die, forget, or move out of the **jurisdiction**, or simply do not want to be involved. Documents may be misplaced or disposed of during the normal course of business. In some cases, the cost to obtain evidence may simply be prohibitive. Physical evidence may be lost or altered so as to be useless.

A witness's testimony may be perpetuated by taking his or her **deposition**, either orally or upon written questions. If the witness later disappears, leaves the state, forgets, or becomes otherwise unavailable, the record of his or her answers, if properly authenticated, will be admissible. This is an exception to the hearsay rule, and is available only where all the parties to the action have had a fair opportunity to question the witness. Mere declarations or other forms of recorded statement do not fall under this exception, so a noticed deposition must be taken in order to use the statements at trial in the event that the witness becomes unavailable.

A request to inspect documents or other items can also preserve your evidence. For example, in a **product liability** lawsuit, the exact product that caused or was involved in the injury may be requested in order to prevent it from being disposed of

DENIAL
A refusal or rejection; for example, a denial of welfare benefits to a family that makes too much money to qualify.

INTERROGATORIES
Written questions sent from one side in a lawsuit to another, attempting to get written answers to factual questions or seeking an explanation of the other side's legal contentions.

JURISDICTION
The geographical area within which a court or a public official has the right and power to operate.

DEPOSITION
The process of taking a witness's sworn out-of-court testimony. The questioning is usually done by a lawyer, with the lawyer from the other side given a chance to attend and participate.

PRODUCT LIABILITY
The responsibility of manufacturers (and sometimes sellers) of goods to pay for harm to purchasers (and sometimes other users or even bystanders) caused by a defective product.

or altered and to preserve it in its present state. In a case that is relying upon a claim that a product malfunctioned, resulting in injuries to the operator of the product, preserving the product just as it was at the time it allegedly caused the injury is crucial. If the product is repaired or otherwise altered, the opposition may claim that it is no longer possible to determine the exact condition of the product at the time the injury occurred. Once you make such a request, the disposition of the evidence you have requested may result in sanctions ordering the termination of the issue or preclusion of that evidence. For example, the particular evidence acquired may be so strong that the attorney may wish to immediately initiate settlement discussions or perhaps file a motion for summary judgment.

Early requests are important to make of nonparties, especially businesses such as telephone companies, police departments, and brokerage firms. These entities may keep records for only a very short time, so if you are not prompt with your subpoena, your evidence may be lost forever. Early inspection of real evidence allows for the opportunity to memorialize its condition or perform tests before it is too late. It is crucial to examine such evidence before it has been altered (i.e., repaired) in any way. A business entity may be put on notice early on in the development of a case that its records must not be destroyed due to an ongoing investigation. The purpose of the notice is to prevent the entity from destroying or tampering with records in any manner until notified either that it must produce records or that the matter has been resolved and it may destroy records in the ordinary course of business.

Financial Considerations

It may be difficult to know when enough discovery has been obtained. Cost will be a factor, as well as the client's wishes and the attorney's experience regarding elimination of all possible risk. It is certainly not necessary to depose each and every witness. The benefits of informal discovery are more obvious in cases with many witnesses. Thorough interviews can be conducted by either a private investigator or a paralegal to determine who possesses enough information to be deposed or subpoenaed to appear at trial. Factual research performed early on by the legal team may result in many documents or leads on documents. Decisions may then be made as to which leads to pursue in informal or formal discovery.

The parties may stipulate to certain noncontroversial records or documents in order to avoid the expense of obtaining additional copies. Gathering evidence is a seductive process: one piece of evidence leads to another and that leads to another and so on and so on. The skill lies in keeping perspective so that you do not begin gathering evidence for its own sake. There comes a time in every lawsuit when time and financial considerations must prevail.

However, some cases certainly demand extensive discovery. The discovery plan that has been developed in the office, as discussed in Chapter 2, should be discussed with the client in order to explain the expense and necessity of the discovery needed to develop the case satisfactorily. The client must understand the risks involved if he or she does not wish specific discovery to occur because of the expense. It is important to reduce decisions regarding discovery to writing in a confirmation letter to the client.

COMMON DISCOVERY MISTAKES

Propounding and responding to discovery requires care to avoid common pitfalls. It is crucial to remember that if you do not make a written response to discovery in a timely manner, you may waive any objections to the discovery in question, including claims of privilege. For example, while an extension of time to respond includes an extension of time to object, in some jurisdictions an extension of time to answer interrogatories or to produce documents may not, so be careful in your choice of words. It may also be up to the party granting the extension as to whether or not objections are included in the extension.

Another pitfall is failing to provide facts or evidence in your possession in response to a proper request. In this case, the party neglecting to provide or reveal this information or material may be precluded from using it at trial. Therefore, it is important to be sure that all responses reflect all the information that you have or can reasonably obtain. The only way to legally withhold evidence from a requesting party is through an appropriate objection.

It is good practice to request that the opposing party supplement discovery response shortly before the discovery cutoff date with any additional information obtained after the previous responses were filed.

If your client mistakenly makes a damaging answer in response to a question in a deposition, an interrogatory, or **request for admissions**, a motion for **summary judgment** may be based on it. If your attorney opposes the motion with a declaration seeking to explain or correct the mistake, the damaging evidence may be disregarded. Thus, it is possible to recover from damaging evidence but it is best, of course, to know what the evidence is and what the testimony will be in order to respond in a manner that best serves your client. Careful preparation of the witnesses and thorough knowledge of the evidence are key to avoiding costly mistakes.

Additionally, bear in mind that the client probably does not understand either the importance of careful responses to discovery requests or the language that is usually used to make them. Accordingly, it is very dangerous just to send document requests or interrogatories to the client with instructions to send you copies of the responsive documents or his answers without careful oversight. Responding to discovery provides an opportunity for the paralegal and the client to clarify issues, expose weaknesses, discover surprises, and further detail strategies. This is the time to further foster the positive, open, and trusting relationship with the client. The client is crucial to providing all information regarding evidence sought by the opposing party. The attorney will decide whether to produce the evidence after the client has provided all evidence in her possession and to the best of her knowledge. It is much better to have a client who provides more information than is needed than to have a client who withholds information for any reason.

■ **PROPOUND**

To offer, propose, or put forward something. For example, to propound discovery is to put discovery forward.

■ **REQUEST FOR ADMISSIONS**

A discovery request by one side in a lawsuit giving a list of facts to the other and requesting that they be admitted or denied. Those admitted need not be proved at the trial.

■ **SUMMARY JUDGMENT**

A final judgment for one side in a lawsuit, or in one part of a lawsuit, without trial, when the judge finds, based on pleadings, depositions, declarations, etc., that there is no genuine factual issue in the lawsuit, or in one part of the lawsuit.

SEEKING AND OBTAINING DISCOVERY

As with all other evidentiary matters, the formal discovery process is included in the Federal Rules of Civil Procedure and in the Federal Rules of Evidence. The rules state that parties "may seek and obtain discovery regarding any matter not privileged, that is relevant to the claim or defense of any party, including the existence, description, nature, custody, condition, and location of any books, documents, or other tangible things and the identity and location of persons having knowledge of any discoverable matter." Not all evidence obtained through discovery need be admissible at trial. If, at the time it is requested, the discovery appears reasonably calculated to lead to admissible evidence, the information sought will be considered relevant. It would indeed be cumbersome, inefficient, and costly to introduce each and every piece of evidence obtained through discovery into evidence at trial. Also, as the case proceeds, it is not uncommon for the focus to shift and clarify. Documents and other evidence must be analyzed and culled, leaving that which is most meaningful and will have the greatest impact to use at trial.

DISCOVERY TOOLS USED TO OBTAIN DOCUMENTS

The tools used to obtain evidence include the following:

- interrogatories
- requests for production of documents and items
- depositions
- requests for admissions

Each of these tools is discussed in detail below. Since every fact situation is different, choices regarding which discovery tool to use will vary. Sometimes each method for gathering evidence will be employed, other times a combination of a few of them will be used. The first three in the list are by far the most commonly used discovery tools.

Interrogatories

■ **OBJECT**

To claim that an action by your adversary in a lawsuit (such as the use of a particular piece of evidence) is improper, unfair, or illegal, and ask the judge for a ruling on the point.

Interrogatories are written questions prepared and sent to the opposing party for answering. Interrogatories are often the first discovery tool employed because the answers will provide useful background information that may be used to direct further discovery. The recipient usually has 30 days in which to respond or **object** to the interrogatories propounded. Interrogatories provide a fairly inexpensive way to obtain basic information about an individual party such as employment history, medical history, personal data, financial information, witnesses, and involvement in prior lawsuits. In the case of a corporate party, interrogatories will lead to knowledge about the nature of the corporation's business, its corporate status, directors, shareholders, and assets. More detailed interrogatories can address more specific issues and hone in on particular topics.

In federal court, no party may serve more than 25 interrogatories, including sub-parts, without either a stipulation between the parties or leave of court. Leave of court is obtained by filing the appropriate motion and stating the reasons for needing to propound the additional interrogatories. Be sure to look at the applicable state court rules, if pertinent, regarding limits on numbers of interrogatories. The answers must be signed, or **verified**, by the party answering them. Objections to the inter-rogatories are signed by the attorney for the answering party. Rule 33 of the Federal Rules of Civil Procedure covers interrogatories to parties. Refer to this rule in Appendix B.

It is wise to begin, shortly after deciding to file a lawsuit, to prepare interrogato-ries on behalf of your party as well as to consider interrogatories your party will receive. Pondering potential interrogatories will begin the thinking process regarding evidence already known and evidence needed. Since answers must be based upon all the information that your client has or can obtain with reasonable effort, it is impor-tant not to delay in the investigation of the case.

When interrogatories are served by an opposing party, you should first review them in detail to determine which will be answered and which may be objected to, either in part or in whole. Of course, the final decisions will be made by the attor-ney. Then you may wish to either send the interrogatories themselves to the client or a summary of the questions you need the client to answer, or both. The client will be instructed to either prepare answers or perhaps to make an appointment to come into the office to discuss the interrogatories and answers. If enough background work has already been performed, draft answers may be prepared and sent to the client for careful review. In the meantime, you should determine if you already have information to respond. Sometimes it is easier for the law firm to obtain particular information on behalf of the client. For example, if the client has negatives of pho-tos but not the photos, the paralegal can have the negatives developed. Perhaps the client has boxes of documents and is uncertain as to which contain the information responsive to particular interrogatories. The paralegal has the legal, organizational, and analytical skills to sift through many documents to determine those that contain information that may be responsive to the interrogatories and present that informa-tion to the attorney to make the final determination. A draft response would be pre-pared well in advance of the deadline for responding. The paralegal can then thoroughly review the draft and work with the attorney to determine additional information needed. It is customary for interrogatory answers to go through several drafts as responses are clarified, objections are raised, and appropriate wording is decided upon. It is a good practice to ascertain that the client has not overlooked any information or facts that may be relevant to establishing a claim or defense. Whenever you are propounding or responding to discovery, you should see this as an opportunity to again review the file and documents already in your possession. Additional evidence may develop as answers are drafted, and the responses should be updated accordingly.

■ **VERIFY**

To swear in writing to the truth or accuracy of a document.

Interrogatories, like all documents prepared by the attorney and filed with the court, are typed on pleading paper with numbered lines. Each set of interrogatories should have preliminary introductory language containing specific instructions and definitions for the responding party. Exhibit 3-1 is a brief sample of that language for a set of interrogatories.

EXHIBIT 3-1   SAMPLE FORM LANGUAGE FOR INTERROGATORIES

You are hereby notified to answer under oath the interrogatories numbered from _____ to _____, inclusive, as shown below, within 30 days after service of the interrogatories in accordance with Rule 33 of the Federal Rules of Civil Procedure.

[Plaintiff or defendant] requests that the [defendant or plaintiff] answer the following interrogatories in writing and under oath pursuant to Rule 33 of the Federal Rules of Civil Procedure, and that the answers be served on the plaintiff within 30 days after service of these interrogatories.

In answering these interrogatories, you must furnish all information, however obtained, including hearsay, that is available to you and information known by or in possession of yourself, your agents and your attorneys, or appearing in your records.

If you cannot answer the following interrogatories in full after exercising due diligence to secure the full information to do so, state and answer to the extent possible, specifying your inability to answer the remainder, stating whatever information or knowledge you have concerning the unanswered portion, and detailing what you did in attempting to secure the unknown information. If you cannot furnish exact information, such as dates, periods, or amounts, supply estimated information to the extent possible and indicate that the information is estimated.

A question that seeks information contained in or information about or identification of any documents may be answered by providing a copy of such document for inspection and copying or by furnishing a copy of such document without a request for production.

If you object to furnishing any information requested by these interrogatories on the grounds of privilege, work product, or other grounds, your response should state the existence of the information, document, or communication, identify the specific grounds on which your objection is based, and identify the information objected to by furnishing its date, participants (e.g., names of speakers or authors or addressees), and a general description of the nature rather than the substance of the purportedly protected information. If the objected-to information contains relevant nonobjectionable matter, you should disclose it.

These interrogatories shall be deemed to be continuing until and during the course of trial. Information sought by these interrogatories that you obtain after you serve your answers must be disclosed to the plaintiff by supplementary answers. You are obligated

(continues)

EXHIBIT 3-1   SAMPLE FORM LANGUAGE FOR INTERROGATORIES *(continued)*

to supplement your responses to these interrogatories no later than 30 days after the discovery of the new information and in no event later than 15 days before the first day of trial.

DEFINITIONS

The following definitions apply to these interrogatories:

1. Communication. The term "communication" means the transmittal of information (in the form of facts, ideas, inquiries, or otherwise) by any methods, including electronic.

2. Document. The term "document" is defined to be synonymous in meaning and equal in scope with the usage of this term in Rule 34(a) of the Federal Rules of Civil Procedure. A draft or nonidentical copy is a separate document within the meaning of this term.

3. Identify.

   a.   With Respect to Persons. When referring to a person, "to identify" means to give, to the extent known, the person's full name, present or last known address, and when referring to a natural person, additionally, the present or last known place of employment. Once a person has been identified in accordance with this subparagraph, only the name of that person need be listed in response to subsequent discovery requesting the identification of that person.

   b.   With Respect to Documents. When referring to documents, "to identify" means to give, to the extent known, the (i) type of document; (ii) general subject matter; (iii) date of the document; and (iv) author(s), addressee(s), and recipient(s).

4. Parties. The terms "plaintiff" and "defendant" as well as a party's full or abbreviated name or a pronoun referring to a party mean the party and, where applicable, its officers, directors, employees, partners, corporate parent, subsidiaries, or affiliates. This definition is not intended to impose a discovery obligation on any person who is not a party to the litigation.

5. Person. The term "person" is defined as any natural person or any business, legal, or governmental entity, or association.

6. You or Your. The words "you" or "your" mean the [*party*], its present and former members, officers, agents, employees, and all other persons acting or purporting to act on its behalf, including all present or former members, officers, agents, employees, and all other persons exercising or purporting to exercise discretion, making policy, and making decisions.

INTERROGATORY NO. 1

INTERROGATORY NO. 2

INTERROGATORY NO. 3

When you receive interrogatories, you must review them carefully in order to determine the appropriate response. If the interrogatory requests information that is discoverable, then the information must be provided. The Federal Rules state that each interrogatory shall be answered separately and fully in writing under oath, unless it is objected to.

Objecting to Interrogatories

A party that objects to a particular interrogatory shall state the reasons for objection and shall answer to the extent the interrogatory is not objectionable. All grounds for objections must be stated with specificity, stating a particular reason the particular interrogatory is objectionable. Blanket objections are unacceptable. However, if the interrogatory, as phrased, is objectionable, then the answer must contain the bases for the objection. Reasons for objecting to a particular interrogatory include the following:

- The interrogatory is outside the scope of discovery under Rule 26, Federal Rules of Civil Procedure.

- The interrogatory is burdensome. An interrogatory objectionable for this reason may seek information or evidence not directly related to the facts raised in the complaint.

- The interrogatory seeks a response that would constitute the opinion of the responding party rather than fact.

- The interrogatory is overly broad.

- The interrogatory is too vague to formulate an answer.

- The interrogatory requests information that is privileged, is attorney work-product, or has been prepared in anticipation of trial.

Be aware that objections may not be used to avoid answering interrogatories. The responding party must answer interrogatories in good faith and supply the requested information unless there is a solid basis for objection. Remember, if an objection is made, the objecting party has the burden of proof on each and every objection. So, when boilerplate, nuisance objections are inserted, be prepared to supply the facts to sustain each objection or to pay **sanctions** for abuse of the discovery process by frivolous objection. Courts do not look kindly upon frivolous objections, and if a motion for sanctions is filed by the interrogating party, monetary sanctions may well be ordered. Having said that, it is not the purpose of interrogatories to demand onerous or unreasonable answers. If information asked for is not in the custody or control of the answering party, or if the information is in the public domain and equally available to the requesting party, the responding party is not required to provide it. A responding party cannot be forced to compile reports or summaries that are not required by the Federal Rules or that do not already exist if the cost, time, and difficulty would be similar for either party. The answering party must, however, explain its reasons for not providing the requested information and specifying the records that contain the information in order that the propounding party may obtain the information requested.

■ **SANCTION**
A court-ordered payment by the side in a lawsuit that abused the discovery process, made to the side that was hurt by the abuse.

Responses, whether answers or objections, must be signed by the attorney representing the answering party. Answers or objections improperly made are subject to sanctions. Refer to Rule 26 for procedures regarding signing discovery requests, responses, and objections.

It is a good idea to maintain a current interrogatory bank. A binder containing, for example, interrogatories used in prior cases as well as common and unusual objections provides a simple and useful way to cull prior discovery and reuse what has worked before.

Request for Production

Requests for production are covered by Rule 34, Federal Rules of Civil Procedure (refer to Appendix B for the rule). A request for production asks that the responding party gather and turn over certain relevant, requested documents or other tangible things, such as photographs, medical records, financial records, drawings, and charts.

When drafting a request for production, don't ask for too many documents; be specific in what you request, or you may find yourself buried in paper. Word the request carefully in order to avoid objections. Review the facts and any documents in your possession in order to determine where the gaps are and whether or not the opposing party may be in possession of the documents needed to adequately prepare your case.

As in all discovery, when you receive a request for production it is important to first carefully analyze the requests. Then advise the client of the documents requested. It is a good idea to ask the client to send you copies of everything that may be remotely related to the requests or the case itself. The importance of continually asking the client for additional or supplemental or updated information cannot be emphasized too strongly. The client does not always understand that simply providing information to the attorney does not mean it will be made available to the opposition. It is not uncommon for the client to attempt to decide what is really being requested and then to make a decision, often incorrect. Again, a good relationship with the client will help the client trust that only necessary documents will be provided to the opposition. Further, the client will realize that the more information his or her attorney has, the more informed the attorney will be and, therefore, able to provide better representation.

Copies of the documents are produced, together with a log of privileged documents. Privileged documents might include proprietary information, such as specific parts and plans used in the making of the cell phone from the earlier case scenario. They might include financial information from a privately held corporation. Employment records having to do with disciplinary issues may be privileged. If documents are voluminous, the responding party may choose to make them available for inspection and copying by the propounding party. They agree on a mutually convenient time and place to review the documents. The producing party may elect to make copies at the time of inspection or later provide copies of documents identified by the

TIP

When you comb prior discovery to use in a current case, be sure to tailor the discovery to the case at hand in order to avoid incorrect party names, incorrect gender identification, or other embarrassing mistakes.

■ **REQUEST FOR PRODUCTION**

A discovery request served by one party on another party seeking the inspection of specified documents or things or permission to enter on and inspect land and property in the responding party's possession or control.

propounding party. The person making the inspection must keep a careful record of the documents inspected and those documents identified for production.

Analyzing Documents to Be Produced

When you have reviewed and received documents from the client, again analyze them thoroughly in light of the requests for production. Select the documents that are responsive to the particular requests. There will most likely be documents that are important to the case but are not responsive to the requests. Those must be logged and tracked in the office. Confirm that the client has no additional documents that may or may not be entirely responsive to the requests.

You should always analyze documents with an eye towards how they may be used to bolster advocacy for the client as well as how they may be used against the client. Again, all documents must be thoroughly reviewed, analyzed, and categorized. All responsive documents, privileged and unprivileged, should be identified with a serial tracking number. Privileged documents should then be pulled out and maintained in a separate file.

At this point the written response to the document request is drafted. Applicable objections may now be safely made and documents that are not harmful can be completely produced. This is the way to avoid the production of a "smoking gun." Keep careful track of what is produced. It is important to keep an exact copy of any responses to production as you have sent them to opposing counsel, even though all the documents attached appear elsewhere in the file.

As with interrogatories, a request for production of documents will contain fairly standard introductory language. Exhibit 3-2 is a brief example of the opening paragraphs of a request for production of documents.

EXHIBIT 3-2   SAMPLE FORM LANGUAGE FOR REQUEST FOR PRODUCTION OF DOCUMENTS

[Plaintiff/defendant] [*name*] requests [defendant/plaintiff] [*name*] to respond within 30 days to the following requests that:

(1) [Defendant/plaintiff] produce and permit [plaintiff/defendant] to inspect and to copy each of the following documents: [*List the documents either individually or by category and describe each of them.*]

[*Here state the time, place, and manner of making the inspection and performance of any related acts.*]

(2) [Defendant/plaintiff] produce and permit [plaintiff/defendant] to inspect and to copy, test, or sample each of the following objects: [*List the objects either individually or by category and describe each of them.*]

(continues)

EXHIBIT 3-2   SAMPLE FORM LANGUAGE FOR REQUEST FOR PRODUCTION OF DOCUMENTS *(continued)*

[*Here state the time, place, and manner of making the inspection and performance of any related acts.*]

(3) [Defendant/plaintiff] permit [plaintiff/defendant] to enter [*describe property to be entered*] and to inspect and to photograph, test, or sample [*describe the portion of the real property and the objects to be inspected*].

[*Here state the time, place, and manner of making the inspection and performance of any related acts.*]

As with interrogatories, requests for production may be objected to on similar grounds. Again, take care in both answering and objecting to a request for production. Do not produce privileged documents or work product. Identify documents that are responsive to the request but privileged. Maintain a privilege log identifying those documents and what discovery request they are responsive to.

Request for Admissions and Genuineness of Documents

A request for admissions and genuineness of documents or other evidence is a discovery tool that poses a series of written questions requesting the answering party to admit the truth of statements or opinion of fact, the application of the law to the fact, or the genuineness of a document. The purpose of a request for admissions is not to produce documents or other items but, instead, to identify them as being genuine. Doing so reduces the need for formalized proof via witness testimony, resulting in greater efficiency in terms of time and money at trial. Responses to requests for admissions are typically concise, either "admit" or "deny." Requests may be admitted in part and denied in part.

Rule 36 of the Federal Rules of Civil Procedure governs requests for admissions. The rule states that a party may serve upon any other party a written request for the admission, for purposes of the pending action only, of the truth of any matters within the scope of the Rule. The request must set forth the admission or request for genuineness of document that relates to statements or opinions of fact or of the application of law to fact, including the genuineness of any documents described in the request. Copies of documents that are referred to in the request shall be served with the request unless they have been or are otherwise furnished or made available for inspection and copying. Each matter of which an admission is requested must be separately set forth. The matter is deemed admitted and the documents deemed genuine unless, within 30 days after service of the request (or within such shorter or longer time as the court may allow or as the parties may agree to in writing), the responding party to whom the request is directed serves upon the party requesting the admission a written answer or objection addressed to the matter, signed by the party or by the party's attorney. As in all discovery, if any objection is made, the reasons therefore shall be stated. The answer shall specifically deny the matter or set forth in detail the reasons why the answering party cannot truthfully admit or deny the matter. An answering party may not give lack of information or knowledge as a reason for failure to admit or deny unless the party states that the party has made reasonable inquiry and that the information known or readily obtainable by the party is insufficient to enable the party to admit or deny.

Exhibit 3-3 provides an example of language included in a typical request for admissions and genuineness of documents.

NEED FOR ADDITIONAL DISCOVERY, MOTIONS TO COMPEL RESPONSES

Although we will not go into great detail here, be aware that there are provisions for asking for more interrogatory responses or documents than those set forth in the rules. In addition, a responding party may move the court for additional time in which to respond to discovery. In order to achieve these ends, the party requesting

---

EXHIBIT 3-3   SAMPLE FORM LANGUAGE FOR REQUEST FOR ADMISSIONS

[Title of Court and Cause]

[Plaintiff/defendant] [*name*] requests [defendant/plaintiff] [*name*] within _____ days after service of this request make the following admissions for the purposes of this action only and subject to all pertinent objections to admissibility which may be interposed at trial:

1. Each of the following documents, exhibited with this request, is genuine.

[List the documents and describe each document.]

2. Each of the following statements is true.

[Here list the statements.]

additional questions or requests, or an extension of time in which to respond to discovery, must file a motion with the court setting forth the reasons for the request. The court will then consider the motion and make a ruling allowing or disallowing the requested relief. Typically, the motion is granted.

Likewise, if a responding party has not responded within the time allowed by the rules and has not requested an extension of time either by contacting the attorney who filed the discovery or by filing a motion for an extension of time, the requesting party may prepare and file a motion to **compel** responses. Such a motion would detail the dates the discovery was filed, efforts made to obtain responses in a timely manner, and relief sought in the form of discovery responses and monetary sanctions. The sanctions would cover the attorney and support staff time in preparing and bringing of the motion to compel. A hearing would be held on the motion and the judge would rule on the motion and the relief sought. The attorney requesting the sanctions must file a declaration detailing the time spent by attorneys and paralegals to seek the sanctions. A memorandum of points and authorities must be included, setting forth the law relied on in bringing the motion.

■ **COMPEL**
To use the authority of law to force someone to do something.

Criminal Cases

As stated in Chapter 1, in criminal cases most of the discovery will be turned over by the prosecution upon a request from the defense. In fact, the law requires that the prosecution also must turn over **exculpatory** evidence as well as damaging evidence. To obtain this evidence from the U.S. attorney or district attorney, counsel for the defendant must make a written request for it. See Exhibit 3-4 for an example of a request letter.

■ **EXCULPATORY**
Tending to or serving to excuse or clear from alleged fault or guilt.

EXHIBIT 3-4   REQUEST LETTER

Roger Shelley, District Attorney
County Government Center, Room 405
Anytown, USA

    Re: People v. Smith
          Case No. C09453-A

Dear Mr. Shelley:

On behalf of the Public Defender's Office, this is an informal discovery request. Pursuant to Penal Code §_____, it is requested that the following items be produced:

1. Names and addresses of persons the prosecutor intends to call as witnesses at trial;

2. Statements of all defendants;

(continues)

3. All physical evidence seized or obtained during the investigation of this offense;

4. The existence of a criminal conviction of any material witness;

5. Any exculpatory evidence;

6. All written or recorded statements of any witness or reports of the statements of any witness, whether or not the prosecutor intends to call that witness at trial, including the results of physical or mental examiniations, scientific tests or experiments; and

7. Any and all videotape or audiotape pertaining to the offense including, but not limited to, the 9-1-1 tape.

This discovery request is ongoing. If you have any questions, feel free to contact me. Thank you for your cooperation in this matter.

Sincerely,

IN-HOUSE ORGANIZATION OF DOCUMENTS

Now that the paperwork is beginning to flow, it can become overwhelming unless properly catalogued and filed. Every law office operates differently with regard to document management based upon the size of the firm, the size of the case, the extent that technology is used in an office, and the individual preferences of the attorney responsible for the particular case. We will address some of the more widely accepted and implemented practices of document management and control.

Every document management system should address the following areas:

organizing documents

maintaining originals

indexing documents

establishing document identifiers

separating key documents in a case

compiling documents in a searchable database

In order to manage the documents that result from your efforts of sending out letters and subpoenas, or personally obtaining documents by, for example, going to the courthouse and photocopying records, it is necessary to have a procedure in place. Initially, when the number of individual documents is relatively small, usually under 100, there may be no need to identify each page of each document separately. Binders with tabbed separations between documents, together with a logical grouping of documents may suffice. For example, all medical records would be kept together but separated by medical care provider and further separating records that pertain only to the **instant** incident from other records. A table of contents should be in the front of each binder.

Once documents and other evidence begin to be produced as a result of discovery, the control and flow of paperwork become even more crucial.

Most firms maintain the original documents separate and apart from working copies. It is important to have a pristine set of documents that no one may access unless it is to make a photocopy or perhaps to use the original at a hearing or deposition (making a copy for any actual exhibits) and then return the original to its safe place. It will be important to have the original documents available for trial. One person, preferably the paralegal, should have responsibility for and control over maintaining the originals. Anyone needing a copy for any purpose should request it from the paralegal.

Exhibit 3-5 is a simple example of how documents might be handled in the Olde case.

In the sample, the *MO* refers to documents received from our client, and *CCI* refers to documents acquired from the defendant. Other identifiers would be used to designate documents from other sources. A master list index of abbreviations should be maintained close to the documents.

> ▇ **INSTANT**
> Present or current. The "instant case" means the current lawsuit.

Document Tracking Tools

Tools for keeping track of documents include database software, spreadsheets, and word processing tables. In smaller cases where the indexing and tracking of documents is being done in-house, Microsoft® Excel® spreadsheets may be adequate. In larger cases, you may need to create a database to handle the volume and complexity of documents. A more complex database would aid in cross-referencing documents as well.

> **CAREER TIP**
>
> If you enjoy using your organizational skills and have an aptitude for technology, you may find that creating, organizing, and managing file databases is a career path.

EXHIBIT 3-5	SAMPLE DOCUMENT NUMBERING SYSTEM	
DOCUMENT IDENTIFIER	**DOCUMENT DATE**	**DOCUMENT DESCRIPTION**
MO 0001-0004	2/2/01	Hurry-Up Ambulance Service records.
MO 0018-0167	2/2/01– 2/9/01	CCI medical records.
MO 0292-0364	3/14/02	Complaint and discovery regarding Jones v. CCI, case for negligence.
CCI 010-047	3/18/02	Documents produced in response to Request for Production, Set 1.
MO 0920-1102	4/27/03	Legal Research Memo re: litigation.

■ **CLASS ACTION**

A lawsuit brought for yourself and other persons in the same situation. To bring a class action you must convince the court that there are too many persons in the class (group) to make them all individually a part of the lawsuit and that your interests are the same as theirs, so that you can adequately represent their needs.

You can create a simple database using Microsoft® Access™, for example, or purchase and use a specific software program. Document databases contain groups of fields used to organize case documents. They are customizable and searchable. Once information is entered into the software program, indexes, chronologies, witness lists, and specific reports can be created. Creating a database can be very time consuming, but it is definitely worth the time and effort in complex litigation. If the database requirements become so sophisticated as to exceed the capabilities of the attorney and paralegal, an outside vendor may be consulted to assist in providing a program to meet the needs for the particular case.

Complex litigation includes **class action** lawsuits and multiple-party lawsuits. These cases are challenging due to the numbers of parties and issues and, accordingly, the voluminous amounts of material generated by the parties. The amount of time and resources needed to adequately represent a client involved in such a case is quite large, thereby justifying a decision to have a legal team devoted to working on only the one case. Complex litigation often becomes a large project requiring constant management, coordination, and organization.

Documents generated in a simple lawsuit may be organized in a file folder with subparts. The subparts would initially include sections for correspondence, pleadings, discovery, investigation, notes, research, and experts. Over the course of time, issues may develop that would require more detailed subparts; for example, motion for summary judgment or witnesses.

Correspondence

The correspondence section of the file contains all communications. This includes, for example, letters to and from the client and opposing counsel, informal requests for records, and so forth. The correspondence is filed in date order with the most recent documents on top. If this section of the file becomes too bulky, you may choose to break it out into subparts for specific kinds of correspondence, such as correspondence with the client, correspondence with opposing counsel, and correspondence with the insurer. Hard copies of all e-mail communications should be made and filed in the correspondence section as well.

Pleadings

Pleadings include the documents that contain the formal allegations submitted by the parties in the lawsuit such as the complaint, answer, cross-complaint, and so on. Again, if these documents begin to accumulate, subparts may be created for the various types of pleadings, especially if multiple parties are involved. For example, if cross-claims or counterclaims are filed with responses, you may need to open additional subparts to the folders for the sake of organization.

Discovery

The discovery section contains formal requests for discovery and responses to the requests. Objections filed in response to discovery requests and motions regarding discovery are also included. Discovery may be broken down into subfiles for the specific kind of discovery involved, such as requests for production and responses, interrogatories, and answers. To further organize discovery in cases with several parties, it may be reasonable to create additional files containing discovery to and from those parties.

Investigation Materials

Investigation includes information acquired through witness interviews, police reports, or viewing, photographing, and mapping an accident scene. Factual investigation may consist of research regarding a particular product, corporation, medical condition, or technical issue that pertains to the case but may not be considered evidence. This is in-house research done to develop and educate the attorney and paralegal on the factual issues involved in the case. For example, in the Omniphone case, the paralegal may conduct factual research into the technology used in cellular telephones. The research would help the attorney and paralegal understand the technical issues so that they would be better able to work with expert witnesses and the client. In the Olde case, the paralegal would perform background investigation into Convalescent Care, Inc. by contacting various agencies. However, in order to perform this task competently, the paralegal may first have to educate himself concerning such issues as agency oversight of convalescent facilities and governmental rules and regulations concerning such oversight.

Notes

The notes section typically includes notes made during telephone conversations, interviews, tracking information, interoffice memoranda, telephone numbers, and contact information. It is important to maintain current contact information for all parties, attorneys, witnesses, and potential witnesses.

Research

Research includes legal research such as copies of cases, statutes, codes, or other information as a result of reviewing the law applicable to the case at hand. In addition, this section contains records of **Shepardized** cases used in points and authorities and motions filed by all parties. Besides case law, official regulations cited in court documents are kept here. For example, pleadings in the Olde case may cite

■ **SHEPARDIZE**
To use the Shepard's citation system to trace the history of a case after it is decided to see if it is followed, overruled, distinguished, etc.

specific sections from rules and regulations set out in the U.S. Code having to do with nursing homes and convalescent care facilities or Medicare provisions.

Experts

The experts section of the file includes information on persons with specialized knowledge who may be called upon to help develop the case and/or to testify at trial. This section may include articles reviewed to determine experts, conversations about potential experts, and Internet research on topics to be discussed with potential experts.

Some law offices color code files or file tabs to identify the file sections or the particular kind of matter; for example, red for personal injury, blue for domestic relations, green for probate, and so forth. The practice in other firms may be to color code file folders. Notebooks may be used to sort and identify information. It is not unusual for attorneys within firms to have preferences regarding the organization of information, although there will most likely be a standard procedure for basic filing methods. If a paralegal is working primarily on one case, she may like to keep a file or notebook with copies of current documents or documents she most frequently refers to.

Spreadsheets are useful to create document summaries, case chronologies, and time lines. Fields are entered into cells or text boxes. The cells are labeled and data pertaining to each field is entered in the cells below the field name. Most word processing programs have spreadsheet capability. See Exhibit 3-6 for a time line demonstrating events that occurred in the Olde case.

Word processing programs can be used to create tables with rows and columns containing information. Creating tables is an adequate method of making indexes. Remember that indexes will be revised frequently, so it is important to use the method that is most efficient and accessible to the person updating the lists. Use a header or footer with the date in order to identify the most recent index.

A helpful feature of all of these tracking and organization tools is that they can be easily updated, revised, and edited. Information on litigation support software is easily available on the Web and from vendors. It is a good idea to network with colleagues for recommendations, suggestions, and comparisons between document management programs.

DOCUMENT NUMBERING

Documents may be numbered in a variety of ways. It is preferable to number copies of documents rather than the originals. Original documents should be preserved as they were received with no changes, additions, marking, highlighting, numbers, or other alterations. The lowest level of technology is, of course, numbering by hand. Because the methods discussed above and the labeling programs available in word

EXHIBIT 3-6 TIME LINE

DATE	EVENT	RECORDS SUPPORTING
2/2/2001	Fell in home	Client depo, Young depo, ambulance records
2/2/2001	Admitted to hospital	Hospital Admission report, ambulance records, client depo, Young depo
2/9/2001	Discharged from hospital	Hospital Discharge report, ambulance transport records, client depo, Young depo, CCI admitting records
3/29/2001	Readmitted to hospital	Hospital Admission report, ambulance records, client depo, Young depo
4/12/2001	Discharged from hospital	Hospital Discharge report, client depo, Young depo
6/5/2001	CCI Records requested	Cover letter from Young to CCI, Young depo, copy of Young check for copy costs
7/1/2001	CCI Records received	Postmarked envelope, cover letter from CCI with records, Young depo

processing programs are easy to use, it is worth the effort to employ them in order to have a more professional appearing system. Small, unobtrusive stickers can be numbered using a word processor and then applied to the documents. Notes may be added to the stickers, if desired. The latest generation of copiers and scanners has document numbering features in the software that will print directly on the documents.

A Bates stamp is a hand-held numbering machine that applies an inked number to the document and then automatically rolls over to the next number. Bates stamping is a widely accepted system of numbering. It is easy to use and fast. Bates stamping is also a permanent marking system, so be sure documents are in the order in which they should be numbered, as the numbers can not be changed once applied.

Whatever numbering system is selected, it is important to place the number in the same place on each page of each document. If a document has very little white space available, it is appropriate to apply the number to the back of the document or on a removable label affixed to the front in order to avoid covering up any of the writing or drawing on the front of the document.

An index of the numbered documents must be created in order to facilitate locating a document. It is helpful to keep copies of the index in a couple of locations. One copy should be with the documents themselves. For example, if the documents are being stored in boxes, a copy of the index reflecting the contents of the box should be affixed to the outside of each carton. If the documents are in binders, a copy of the index should be kept in the front of each binder containing the documents listed on the index. A master set of indexes should be kept separately so that the person looking for a particular document can peruse the master list instead of having to pull out each box or binder in order to read the index.

Management systems for larger cases are similar to those outlined above. However, since there will be many more boxes of documents, the contents of each box should be summarized as well as indexed. For example, a box might be labeled "Documents produced by defendant pursuant to plaintiff's first request for production of documents." The index would then follow.

CONCLUSION

It is common for every law office to establish its own protocol for managing documents. However, you may be called upon to develop a system for either the entire office or for a particular case. Becoming familiar with the various programs, methods, and options will make you a greater asset to your firm.

■ KEY TERMS _____

class action	instant	request for production
compel	interrogatories	sanctions
contentions	jurisdiction	Shepardize
denial	object	summary judgment
deposition	product liability	verify
dispositive	propound	
exculpatory	request for admissions	

■ REVIEW QUESTIONS _____

1. What is the difference between formal and informal discovery?
2. Name four discovery tools. Provide a brief description of each.
3. What sections of the Federal Rules of Civil Procedure govern discovery?
4. What is the purpose of discovery?
5. What are six reasons to object when responding to discovery?
6. List the key components of an in-house document management system.

■ APPLYING WHAT YOU HAVE LEARNED _____

1. Create a detailed discovery plan for *Olde v. Convalescent Care, Inc.*
2. Draft 10 interrogatories from CCI to Olde.

3. Draft 10 requests for production from Olde to CCI.

4. Your attorney has requested that you prepare an outline of questions she should ask Mrs. Olde at deposition. What are the key areas that should be covered? Do not list actual questions; rather, provide an outline of topics to be covered.

ILLUSTRATIVE CASE

Read the excerpts from the following case and answer the following questions:

1. What is the rule that would allow admission into evidence of the sketches referred to in the case? Why were copies rather than originals allowed?

2. How was the immigration card determined to be relevant?

3. What was the significance of the Jell-O box? In what stage of the discovery process would the Jell-O box have been produced? What documents would have been needed to obtain the Jell-O box?

UNITED STATES V. ROSENBERG ET AL.

UNITED STATES COURT OF APPEALS SECOND CIRCUIT, 195 F.2D 583

JANUARY 10, 1952, ARGUED; FEBRUARY 25, 1952, DECIDED.

On January 31, 1951, the grand jury indicted Julius and Ethel Rosenberg, David Greenglass, Anatoli Yakolev, and Morton Sobell for conspiring between 1944 and 1950 to violate 50 U.S.C. at 32 by combining to communicate to the Union of Soviet Socialist Republics documents, writings, sketches, notes and information relating to the national defense of the United States, with intent and reason to believe that they would be used to the advantage of the Soviet Union. The indictment listed 10 overt acts done in furtherance of the conspiracy, including the receipt by Julius Rosenberg from Ruth Greenglass of a paper containing written information after a trip by Ruth to New Mexico, and the additional receipt by Julius from David Greenglass of a paper containing sketches of experiments conducted at the Los Alamos Project. . . . The trial of the defendants, Julius and Ethel Rosenberg and Morton Sobell, in the United States District Court for the Southern District of New York, lasted 14 days.

At the trial, witnesses for the government testified to the following: In November 1944, Ruth Greenglass planned a visit to her husband, David, stationed as a soldier in the Los Alamos atomic experimental station. Before her visit, Ethel and Julius Rosenberg, sister and brother-in-law of David Greenglass, urged Ruth to obtain from David specific information concerning the location, personnel, physical description, security measures, camouflage and experiments at Los Alamos. Ruth was to commit this information to memory and tell it to Julius upon her return to New York, for ultimate transmittal to the Soviet Union. David, reluctant at first, agreed to give Ruth the information Julius had requested. He told her the location and security measures of the station, and the names of leading scientists working there. When David returned to New York in 1945 on furlough, he wrote out a fuller report on the project for Julius, and sketched a lens mold used in the atomic experiment. A few nights later, at the Rosenberg home, the Greenglasses were introduced to Mrs. Sidorovich whom Julius explained might be sent as an emissary to collect information from David in New Mexico. It was agreed that whoever was sent would bear a torn half of the top of a Jell-O box which would match the

(continues)

ILLUSTRATIVE CASE *(continued)*

half retained in Ruth's possession. Ethel Rosenberg, at this time, admitted her active part in the espionage work Julius was carrying on, and her regular typing of information for him. Julius introduced David to a Russian, who questioned David about the atomic-bomb operation and formula. In June 1945, Harry Gold arrived in Albuquerque with the torn half of the Jell-O box and the salutation, 'I come from Julius.' He had been assigned to the mission by Yakolev, his Soviet superior, and had, the day before his trip, met, pursuant to Yakolev's command, with Emil Fuchs, British scientist and Russian spy working at Los Alamos. David delivered to Gold information about personnel in the project who might be recruited for espionage, and another sketch of the lens mold, showing the basic principles of implosion used in the bomb construction. Gold relayed the information to Yakolev. On a revisit of the Greenglasses to New York, David turned over a sketch of the cross-section and a 10-page exposition of the bomb to Rosenberg. Ethel typed up the report, and, during this meeting, Julius admitted he had stolen a proximity fuse from a factory, and had given it to Russia. After the war, David went into business—a small machine-shop—with Julius, and Julius several times offered to send David to college on Russian money. Julius confided to David that he was helping the Russians subsidize American students, that he had contacts in New York and Ohio, and supplied information for siphoning to Russia, that he transmitted information to Russia on microfilm equipment, and that he received rewards for his services from the Russians in money and gifts. In 1950, Julius came to David and told him to leave the country immediately, since Dr. Fuchs, one of Gold's collaborators, had been arrested; he, Julius, would supply the money and the plan to get to Russia. A month later, after Gold's arrest, Julius repeated the warning to flee, adding that he and his family intended to do likewise, and giving David $1,000. Julius said his own flight was necessitated by the fact that Jacob Golos, already exposed as a Soviet agent, and Elizabeth Bentley probably knew him. Julius said he had made several phone calls to her and that she had acted as a go-between for him and Golos. Julius gave David an additional $4,000 for the trip and Julius had passport photos taken, telling the photographer that he and his family planned to leave for France. After David's arrest for espionage, Ethel asked Ruth to make David keep quiet about Julius and take the blame alone, since Julius had been released after admitting nothing to the F.B.I. In 1944, Julius several times solicited Max Elitcher, a Navy Department engineer, to obtain anti-aircraft and fire-control secrets for Russia, and in 1948 asked him not to leave his Navy Department job because he could be of use there in espionage. A month or so later Elitcher accompanied Sobell to deliver 'valuable information' in a 35-millimeter can to Julius.

The Rosenbergs took the stand and testified as follows: They had never solicited the Greenglasses for atomic information or participated in any kind of espionage work for Russia. Julius denied stealing a proximity fuse. He did not, he said, ever know Harry Gold or call Elizabeth Bentley. He admitted that he and David went into business together after the war, but said they did not enjoy good business relations. In 1950, David, according to Julius, excited, asked Julius to get a smallpox vaccination certificate from his doctor and to find out what kind of injections were necessary for entrance into Mexico. Ruth had told Julius that David stole things while in the Army, and Julius thought David was in trouble on this account. David asked for a few thousand in cash and, when Julius refused, told Julius he would be sorry. Julius denied that he gave David any money to flee, or had any passport pictures of his own family taken preparatory to flight. He never discussed anything pertaining to espionage with either Sobell or Elitcher although he saw both socially. In short, the Rosenbergs denied any and every part of the evidence which the government introduced in so far as it connected them with Soviet espionage. Sobell did not take the stand but he pleaded not guilty. At the end of the trial, the jury found the three defendants guilty as charged. The trial judge sentenced the Rosenbergs to death, and Sobell to 30 years' imprisonment.

(continues)

ILLUSTRATIVE CASE *(continued)*

COUNSEL: Myles J. Lane, New York City (Roy M. Cohn, James B. Kilsheimer 3d and Stanley D. Robinson, all of New York City, of counsel), for United States of America.

Emanuel H. Bloch, New York City, for Julius Rosenberg and Ethel Rosenberg.

Harold M. Phillips and Edward Kuntz, New York City (Howard N. Meyer, New York City of counsel), for Morton Sobell.

JUDGES: Before SWAN, Chief Judge, and CHASE and FRANK, Circuit Judges.

OPINION BY JUDGE JEROME FRANK

Since two of the defendants must be put to death if the judgments stand, it goes without saying that we have scrutinized the record with extraordinary care to see whether it contains any of the errors asserted on this appeal.

The Rosenbergs contend that four Government exhibits (2, 6, 7 and 8), consisting of sketches made by David Greenglass of lens molds and an atom bomb were improperly admitted in evidence. Exhibits 2 and 8 are diagrams of a clover-leaf type high explosive lens mold used in atomic bomb experiments and a cross-section of an atom bomb, respectively. David Greenglass testified that these diagrams, which he reproduced for use at the trial, were accurate replicas of sketches given by him to Julius Rosenberg in 1945, and last seen by him at that time. Greenglass further testified that Exhibits 6 and 7 were accurate representations of lens mold sketches which he turned over to Harry Gold, in conjunction with a report on atomic experimentation, in June, 1945. The original sketches were allegedly delivered to Yakolev by Gold and transmitted to the Soviet Union. Greenglass explained all four exhibits to the jury and used them to illustrate his testimonial description of the information he imparted to Rosenberg and Gold. Such sketches would ordinarily be admissible under the 'map, diagram, and chart' rule which permits a witness to clarify his testimony by written illustration, so as to communicate complicated or confusing information more easily to the jury. Defendants also object because David's superiors at Los Alamos were allowed to examine these sketches and to testify that they were reasonably accurate portrayals of the lens mold and atomic mechanisms used in the experimental station. We see no error here. A witness may always comment upon the substance or import of another witness' testimony; there is no reason to differentiate between verbal and nonverbal testimony in this respect. At no time were the sketches held out as those actually transmitted by Greenglass to Russia or exact replicas or copies thereof. They represented only Greenglass' recollection of what he had given the foreign agents. Hence there was no infraction of the secondary evidence rule.

The prosecution introduced as an entry 'in the regular course of business' a card made by an Immigration Inspector at the time Sobell re-entered the United States, stating that he had been 'Deported from Mexico.' This evidence is attacked as both irrelevant and hearsay. But Sobell's forced return to the United States was certainly relevant to the government's theory that he had fled to Mexico to escape prosecution, for otherwise the jury might have inferred that he had returned voluntarily to stand trial. The hearsay objection is equally without merit. As an entry of this type is required in the case of every deportee from Mexico and was made by the border inspector in the course of his duties, it qualifies as a business entry under 28 U.S.C. at 1732, 1733. The inspector who made the entry testified at the trial, and was available for cross-examination as to the extent of his observations and his reasons for making the entry.

Affirmed.

FOOTNOTES

For additional resources, visit our Web site at www.westlegalstudies.com

4

Depositions

After studying this chapter you should be able to:

❏ describe the step-by-step procedure of taking the deposition of a party, witness, or expert witness.

❏ understand how to prepare a witness for a deposition.

❏ summarize deposition testimony.

INTRODUCTION

A deposition is another method of accumulating evidence to support or refute allegations made in a lawsuit. Depositions also preserve testimony to be later corroborated or challenged during trial. The paralegal's role in helping attorneys and witnesses prepare for deposition, assistance during deposition, and the ability to summarize deposition testimony are important to the process of gathering and using evidence.

DEFINITIONS

A deposition involves taking sworn testimony of a party or nonparty witness, or **deponent**, outside of court, in accordance with the rules of the particular court that has jurisdiction. A deposition is included in the discovery process as a method for the parties to obtain information from each other in preparation for trial. As in the other discovery tools discussed in the preceding chapter, depositions provide an opportunity for the parties and their attorneys to gain insight into the facts and allegations of the lawsuit and to avoid surprise at trial as well as to preserve testimony for use at trial. The deposition testimony may be used as a substitution for the live witness if the witness is unable to physically appear at trial due to illness or death or is otherwise unavailable to attend trial. In that case, the deposition testimony may be read into the trial court record. Deposition testimony may also be used to **impeach** a witness during trial.

A deposition is a statement made under oath by a party or witness or expert witness in response to oral examination or written questions. It is subject to cross-examination and the testimony is preserved in writing and may also be preserved on videotape or DVD. The responses to the questions are recorded by a **court reporter**. A court reporter is a specially trained person who makes a verbatim written record, or transcript, of the proceedings in a deposition or a courtroom. The person being deposed is also known as the deponent. A **transcript** is the written record of a deposition or of court proceedings. While exceedingly common in civil cases, depositions are rarely used in criminal cases. This is because of the expense involved in conducting the deposition and also because there is often little time to conduct lengthy discovery in criminal matters due to the defendant's constitutional right to a speedy trial.

A deposition allows counsel to test the memory of a witness and to observe the witness's demeanor, appearance and attitude. Those impressions may indicate how the jury may respond to the witness.

Depositions also allow counsel to obtain more specific information about the claims made or being defended in a case because the questions may be a bit broader and the follow-up questions more specific than in other discovery. Depositions also allow the questioner to review document at length in detail with the deponent.

Depositions provide the only opportunity to obtain information from non-party witnesses prior to trial testimony.

There are differing schools of thought regarding the best time to take a deposition during the pendency of a case. Some attorneys believe it is important to take the deposition or a witness early on because memories are fresher. Other attorneys like to lay groundwork with other discovery tools before incurring the costs involved in depositions. It is important not to wait until too close to the discovery cut-off date in case the deponent refuses to testify or to answer specific questions, and appropriate motions must be made to the court and ruled on.

■ **DEPONENT**

Person who gives sworn testimony out of court.

■ **IMPEACH**

To show that a witness is untruthful, either by evidence of past conduct or by showing directly that the witness is not telling the truth.

■ **COURT REPORTER**

A stenographer who records and transcribes a verbatim transcription of proceedings in a court or other legal proceeding.

■ **TRANSCRIPT**

A copy, especially the official copy, of the record of a court proceeding.

NOTICING A DEPOSITION

A deposition must be noticed by the party wishing to depose the witness. The **deposition notice** must include the date, time and place of the deposition, the name of the deponent, and the items, if any, that the deponent is required to produce at the time of the deposition. Usually, the deposition is taken at the office of one of the attorneys involved in the lawsuit, most frequently at the office of the noticing attorney. If many parties and attorneys are involved, a large conference room may be necessary. If the law firm does not have a space large enough to accommodate all those who will be present, the court reporting firm may have space or may help to arrange for a suitable location.

For the sake of convenience, if the deponent does not reside near the office of the noticing attorney, the deposition may take place at a location that is mutually convenient to the deponent and the attorneys. If the attorneys must travel to a location near the deponent, a local court reporter will most likely be able to assist in finding a place for the deposition to occur. Most firms have professional relationships with one or more court reporting firms. Court reporters or management personnel at these firms are good resources when an out-of-town court reporter is needed. It is helpful to contact someone at the office the law firm usually uses to ask for a reference to a court reporting office out of the area.

Many state and federal jurisdictions have forms for the notice of deposition and subpoena duces tecum. Be sure to check the jurisdiction of the case to determine the appropriate form, if applicable. If the jurisdiction does not have a form, the paralegal may be asked to draft a notice of deposition. Such a notice would include the language in Exhibit 4-1.

EXHIBIT 4-1   SAMPLE FORM FOR NOTICE OF TAKING DEPOSITION

[Title of Court and Cause]

To: _____

Attorney for _____

[Address]

PLEASE TAKE NOTICE that [defendant/plaintiff] [*name*] will take the deposition upon oral examination of [plaintiff/defendant], [*name and address of deponent*], before a person authorized by law to administer oaths at [*place*], on [*date*], at [*time*].

[Defendant/plaintiff] hereby requests [*name of deponent*] to appear before this oral examination at the above time and place.

(continues)

EXHIBIT 4-1   SAMPLE FORM FOR NOTICE OF TAKING DEPOSITION *(continued)*

The deposition will continue from day to day until completed, excluding Saturdays, Sundays, and legal holidays.

Dated: _____   [Name of Firm]

By: _____
Attorney for _____

With regard to taking depositions in state court cases, it is important to become familiar with the particular jurisdiction's rules regarding depositions. For example, in California state actions, a deposition notice must contain the following elements:

- deponent's name
- deponent's address, if known, or a statement that it is unknown, if not
- date of the deposition
- time of the deposition
- place of the deposition

In some instances, the deposing attorney may request the deponent to bring documents to the deposition. In that case, a notice of deposition and request for documents must be served. The documents may either be listed within the body of the notice (see Exhibit 4-2) or attached as an Exhibit A to the notice.

EXHIBIT 4-2   SAMPLE FORM FOR NOTICE OF TAKING DEPOSITION WITH RECORDS

[F.R.C.P. 30(b) (5)]

[Title of Court and Cause]

To: _____

Attorney for _____

[Address]

PLEASE TAKE NOTICE that the [defendant/plaintiff] [name] will take the deposition upon oral examination of [plaintiff/defendant], [name and address of deponent], before a person authorized by law to administer oaths at [place], on [date], at [time].

(continues)

EXHIBIT 4-2   SAMPLE FORM FOR NOTICE OF TAKING DEPOSITION WITH RECORDS *(continued)*

[Defendant/plaintiff] hereby requests [*name of deponent*] to appear before this oral examination at the above time and place and requests [*name of deponent*] to produce and to permit [defendant/plaintiff] to copy and inspect at the oral examination each of the following documents:

[*List documents individually or by category and describe each of them.*]

The deposition will continue from day to day until completed. You are at liberty to appear and examine the witness.

Dated: _____   *[Name of Firm]*

By: _____
Attorney for _____

In planning for the deposition, keep in mind that, barring permission from the court or a stipulation between the parties, the deposition day must be at least 10 days away. If the notice of deposition is served by hand, this date is acceptable. If not, add five days for mailing when calculating the deposition date. Absent special dispensation in the form of agreement among the parties or a court order, you may not schedule a deposition for Saturday or Sunday or on a holiday.

Whenever possible, in setting a date for the deposition it is considered professional courtesy to communicate with opposing counsel that you plan to depose a party or witness. The attorney representing the party will have the opportunity to contact the party to be deposed and then suggest dates and times. By contacting opposing counsel before sending out a deposition notice, a mutually agreeable date may be selected. However, it is not always possible to select a date among the attorneys and the deponent within a reasonable timeframe. In that case, it is certainly acceptable to notice the deposition as required by law.

At the deposition, the court reporter will administer an oath that is similar to that given in a court of law. Upon being sworn, the deponent will answer questions. All answers are given under penalty of perjury and there are consequences to the deponent for giving false testimony. Initially, the attorney who noticed the deposition will provide some basic instructions, or admonitions, to the deponent. These will include instructing the deponent to answer all questions verbally since the court reporter cannot record nods, gestures, or other nonverbal responses. The attorney who noticed the deposition will ask questions first (this is known as direct examination). If the deponent is a party to the proceeding, the attorney representing the deponent may wish to ask questions as well in order to clarify or expound upon questions asked by the adverse attorney. Attorneys for other parties, if any, may also question the deponent at this time (this is known as cross-examination). The first attorney may then ask more questions (redirect examination), and the others may want to ask more questions as well (re-cross examination). The court reporter will be making a verbatim transcript of the deposition as it is occurring. Many court reporters make a sound recording of the deposition as well.

Documents are often referred to during a deposition. These may be documents the deposing attorney brings or documents brought by the deponent in response a notice of deposition that included a request for production of documents. The documents will be marked as exhibits and attached to the deposition transcript.

THE DEPOSITION TRANSCRIPT

The deposition transcript appears in a Q and A, page and line numbered format similar to the following:

EXHIBIT 4-3   DEPOSITION TRANSCRIPT

1 Q. Please state your name for the record.

2 A. Mary Smith.

3 Q. What is your date of birth?

4 A. Um, I was born on January 12, 1951.

5 Q. Where were you born?

6 A. Well, I was born in Rolla, Missouri, but then we moved around a lot so I lived

7   lots of different places while I was growing up. First we lived in

8 Q. We'll get to that, Ms. Smith. Please just answer the question I ask.

9 A. Oh. Sorry. I tend to keep going once I get started.

10 Q. Mrs. Olde, you were asked to bring several documents with you to the

11   deposition today. One of those was your driver's license. Did you

12   bring that with you today?

13 A. Yes. I'm sure I did.

14 Q. May I see it, please?

15 A. It's in here somewhere. Here it is.

16 Q. I will ask that a copy of the deponent's driver's license be made. We will

17   mark it as Exhibit 1 to this deposition.

As set out above, the court reporter has transcribed every word, including "oh" and "um." It is the court reporter's job to accurately transcribe every utterance made by anyone in the room.

Under certain circumstances a deposition may be videotaped. This usually occurs when the deponent is very ill and may not be well enough for trial. It can also be done if the deponent will be out of town or otherwise unavailable during trial. A special notice is required when a deposition is to be videotaped.

Just as in the courtroom, attorneys may object to questions asked during the course of the deposition. Although there is usually no judge present to rule on any objection made, the objection will be preserved for trial. (In very unusual circumstances, such as the deposition of then-president William Jefferson Clinton, a judge may be present to rule upon issues that arise during the deposition.) Usually, the deponent will be instructed by his or her attorney to answer the question. However, between the deposition and the trial, the attorney seeking an answer to the question may ask the court to rule on the objection. If the objection is upheld, it will also be upheld at trial, and any answer given at the deposition will be excluded at trial.

TIMING OF DEPOSITIONS

In the usual sequence of discovery, depositions are taken after interrogatories, requests for production, and requests for admissions have been propounded and responded to. There are several reasons for waiting until other discovery has been thoroughly conducted before noticing depositions. The primary reason is expense. Depositions are expensive and time consuming, often involving travel on the part of the deponent and attorneys to the location of the deposition. Also, the party noticing the deposition must pay for the court reporter and for the original deposition transcript. Any other parties wishing to have a copy of the deposition transcript must pay for it.

By conducting other preliminary investigations and discovery, the attorneys will have a sense of who the most important witnesses and parties are in a lawsuit. The parties to the lawsuit will typically be deposed. At this time, the responses to other discovery may be used to form the foundation for the questions asked at deposition. The questioning attorneys will have much more information to use when questioning the parties and other witnesses as a result of prior discovery. For example, witnesses to the allegations in the complaint will have been provided, personal information about the parties will be known, and documents pertinent to the case will have been disclosed.

The length of time for conducting a deposition varies greatly. A deposition in which the deponent merely verifies the authenticity of documents may be as brief as 15 minutes. A deposition of an expert witness who is testifying as to very detailed and complex issues may last several days. Obviously, cases involving several attorneys representing several parties will take longer, as each attorney is entitled to question the deponent. It is difficult to predict the time it may take to complete a deposition and, therefore, difficult to predict the cost. The person noticing the deposition bears the cost of the court reporter and the original transcript. Any other costs associated with the deposition such as renting a room, snacks that may be provided, the fee for the videographer, must also be borne by the noticing attorney. Copies of the deposition transcript and copies of any videos of the deposition will be paid for by the person requesting them.

As with other discovery methods, it is useful at deposition to determine testimony that may be potentially damaging to your case. It is always better to learn of the pitfalls of your case before trial in order to develop a plan on how to address those weaknesses. Learning what needs to be bolstered in your case before trial provides time to do so by conducting additional discovery or research into the troubling issues.

A deposition also provides the attorney with valuable soft information. Besides factual information on the witness's knowledge of the particular issues upon which he or she is questioned, the deposition gives the attorneys the opportunity to see what kind of witness the deponent will make at court. It is at the time of deposition that attorneys often decide whether or not to have a particular witness testify at trial. If it is essential that a witness who did poorly as a deponent should testify at trial, there will be time to work with that person to make him or her a more effective witness.

Although paralegals may not conduct depositions, you may attend a deposition and assist the lawyer by taking notes and coordinating documents and exhibits. If you have been involved in a case from the outset you also provide valuable information to the attorney concerning whom to depose, potential questions to ask, and documents to request. After a deposition is completed and the transcript is received, you may be asked to summarize the deposition.

PREPARING FOR THE DEPOSITION

A paralegal can participate to a great extent in preparing for the deposition, from working with the other attorneys to facilitate scheduling, to drafting and serving the necessary notices and subpoenas as outlined above, to making arrangements with the court reporter, to preparing the witness, if applicable.

Establishing a good relationship with a court reporting firm is essential to all the scheduling, canceling, and rescheduling of depositions that occur. It can be a tricky business to work with several attorneys and nonparty deponents to schedule a mutually convenient time for a deposition. It is not unusual to have to reschedule the deposition several times before it actually occurs. Patience and a sense of humor are required. A good relationship with a reliable court reporting firm is especially useful when scheduling out-of-town depositions. Then, the local firm will work with you to locate a good firm in the location you need.

If the deposition is to be videotaped, it is necessary to have the appropriate facilities. Most likely, the court reporting firm will either have or help to obtain the necessary equipment and the technicians to use it. However, it will be up to the paralegal to make sure the deposition location has adequate space, seating arrangements, lighting, and electrical outlets needed to take a videotaped deposition.

Even when your attorney is taking the deposition of an adversarial party, it is important to provide a pleasant and comfortable setting for the deposition. The deponent will remember the way he or she was treated while in hostile territory and it will bode well to make a positive impression. You will most likely be meeting the deponent again in the courtroom, as well as opposing counsel, and it is helpful to be remembered as having been courteous and thoughtful during a perhaps unpleasant situation. Providing water, soft drinks, and coffee, checking in on breaks to see that all are comfortable, and making copies of exhibits will all make the experience run more smoothly.

You may be called upon to prepare a list of questions and to carefully review the file prior to the deposition to identify any documents and elements of pleadings that should be covered in questioning.

You may also be asked to participate in preparing the witness for deposition. This preparation may run from simple hand-holding to reviewing elements of the lawsuit with the witness and helping the witness gather and become familiar with documents that are expected to be used at the deposition.

Preparing the Witness

It is crucial that the witness be familiar with the basics of being deposed. Much of this may seem to be simply common sense to us. However, remember that this may be a very stressful situation for the deponent. He or she may feel attacked by opposing counsel. The deponent may be asked to recall the details of painful memories. Questions may seem confusing or tricky. Careful witness preparation will help the deponent understand the process and know what is expected. It is important that the witness always tell the truth. The deponent should listen carefully to the question. If he or she does not understand, the question may be repeated or rephrased. The deponent should be instructed not to answer the question until it is thoroughly understood. The deponent should not volunteer information but should answer questions briefly. It is important that the witness remain calm and request breaks when needed. If asked to look at a document, the deponent should take adequate time to be certain to understand the document.

It is useful to make a roadmap for the witness to refer to when preparing for a deposition. Exhibit 4-4 is an example of a set of guidelines that may be given to the witness when you meet to discuss the deposition.

EXHIBIT 4-4   DEPOSITION GUIDELINES

WHAT IS A DEPOSITION?

A deposition is your testimony, under oath. You will be asked questions by the opposing attorney, and the questions and your answers will be recorded by an official court reporter. There is little difference between testimony at a deposition and testimony in the courtroom, except there is no judge presiding. Rulings over inadmissible matters will be

(continues)

EXHIBIT 4-4   DEPOSITION GUIDELINES *(continued)*

made by the judge at the time of the trial, not on the taking of the deposition. The deposition transcript may be used at trial to impeach (discredit) a witness on the stand. It may also be used to take the place of a live witness who is unable to appear at trial due to illness, death, or another reason that prevents the witness from giving live testimony.

PURPOSE OF A DEPOSITION

Opposing counsel is taking your deposition for four reasons:

1. They want to find out what facts you have in your actual knowledge and possession regarding the issues in your lawsuit. They are interested in what your story is now and what it is going to be at the trial.

2. They want you to testify to a specific story so that you will have to tell the same story at the trial and they will know in advance what your story is going to be.

3. Your testimony given in a deposition may be read at trial. They hope to catch you in a lie or omission because if they were to do so, they can claim at the trial that you are not a truthful person and, therefore, your testimony should not be believed on any of the points, particularly the crucial ones.

4. A deposition may be used to narrow the issues in your case. Stipulations of fact and other agreements may be made during the course of the deposition which may substantially shorten the trial.

All of the above are very legitimate purposes and opposing counsel has every right to take your deposition for these purposes and in this fashion. Your attorney has the right to ask questions of you during the deposition; usually, however, your attorney will ask you questions only to clarify an answer that may be confusing. Likewise, we have the same right to take the deposition of the opposing party and witnesses.

If there are some issues about your case that you consider worrisome, you should discuss those matters with your attorney before the start of the deposition.

SUGGESTIONS FOR PREPARATION

The following are suggestions to help you prepare to give your deposition. Please study these suggestions carefully.

ALWAYS TELL THE TRUTH when giving your deposition. Failure to tell the truth in a deposition constitutes perjury, a crime under the Penal Code. You may assume that the attorney questioning you has the ability to make anyone who is playing fast and loose with the truth feel very uncomfortable.

LISTEN TO THE QUESTION. Do not answer any question unless you hear it completely. If you did not hear the question asked, ask the other attorney to repeat it or ask the court reporter to read it back.

(continues)

EXHIBIT 4-4   DEPOSITION GUIDELINES *(continued)*

UNDERSTAND THE QUESTION BEFORE ANSWERING. Do not hesitate to ask the other attorney to repeat or rephrase the question until you do understand it. You may ask to have the question rephrased until you understand it.

PAUSE AFTER EACH QUESTION. This gives you an opportunity to think and make an appropriate response. It also permits your attorney to formulate an objection to the question if one is appropriate. It is a good idea to wait a couple of beats before saying anything. Take the time you need to gather your thoughts.

DO NOT GUESS at any answer. If you do not know the answer to a question, even though you feel you would appear ignorant or evasive saying that you do not know, you should nevertheless do so. It is perfectly acceptable to admit that you do not know an answer to a question.

RIGHT TO CONFER WITH LAWYER. At any time during the deposition you will have the right to confer with your attorney privately regarding the question and any proposed answer. Do not hesitate to exercise this right. Simply say that you need to take a break.

DO NOT VOLUNTEER INFORMATION. Answer the question that is asked of you and then stop. Volunteering information provides an opportunity for opposing counsel to ask questions he or she may not have previously even considered pursuing. Do not do the questioning attorney's job for him or her.

NO EXPLANATIONS. Never attempt to explain or justify your answer. You are there to give the facts as you know them and you are not supposed to apologize or attempt to justify those facts. Any attempt at such would make it appear that you doubt the accuracy or authenticity of your own testimony. Again, simply answer the question asked.

BE VERBAL. Speak loudly enough so everyone can hear you. Do not nod or make gestures; these cannot be recorded by the court reporter.

QUOTING OTHERS. If you are testifying with regard to conversations, make clear whether you are paraphrasing comments made by you or other persons, or whether you are quoting exactly what was said.

REMAIN CALM AND POLITE. Do not lose your temper no matter how hard you are pressed. If you lose your temper, you may be playing into the other side's hands. Do not argue with the other attorney. Give him or her the information in the same tone of voice and manner that you do in answer to your own attorney's questions. The lawyer has the right to ask questions, and your own attorney will object to any inappropriate questions or actions by the other lawyer. Remember that the attorney on the other side has a job to do and that the job is to represent his or her client as well as possible.

BE AWARE of questions involving distances and time. If at any time you estimate distances or time in any of your answers, state that it is an estimate.

(continues)

EXHIBIT 4-4   DEPOSITION GUIDELINES *(continued)*

NEVER SAY NEVER. Eliminate adjectives and superlatives such as "never" and "always" from your vocabulary. These phrases may come back to haunt you.

DO NOT TESTIFY about documents, or about what other people know, or about your state of mind at a particular time unless you are specifically asked.

NOTES, DIARIES, ETC. Do not plan to use any notes, diaries, or any other documents to assist you during your deposition unless such document has been specifically reviewed by your attorney. Notes to refresh your memory or any other such documents may be examined by the other side.

DOCUMENTS TO BE PRODUCED. You may have been instructed to produce documents at your deposition. You should bring the originals in the event there is any question as to the accuracy of the copies. Be sure that your attorney has seen any documents you bring beforehand.

DOCUMENTS NOT PRODUCED. If information is in a document that you need to see in order to testify truthfully and accurately, request the other attorney to provide you with a copy of the document. Do not agree to supply any documents or information. If you are asked to supply documents or information, refer the other lawyer to your counsel. Do not, without the request of your attorney, reach into your pocket for a Social Security card, driver's license, or any other document. Do not ask your lawyer to produce anything that is in his or her file. Do not turn to your attorney to ask for information and do not turn to another witness, if one should be present, to ask for information. When confronted with documents, examine them carefully. If you haven't seen a particular document before or did not prepare it, don't try to guess what it means. Do not vouch for the accuracy of a document. Also, be careful not to interpret a date shown on a document as being the true date of its writing. Be sure your attorney has reviewed the documents before answering any questions pertaining to them.

MISTAKES. If at anytime during the deposition you realize you have given an erroneous answer or you have misspoken, correct your answer as soon as you recognize your error. Tell either the opposing lawyer that you misspoke, or tell your own attorney at the first available opportunity.

LISTEN. Do not let the opponent put words in your mouth. If necessary, restate or rephrase the attorney's question in your own words. Pay particular attention to introductory clauses preceding the question. Do not accept the other attorney's summary of your testimony unless it is completely accurate.

RELAX. You are not expected to know by memory all details of what was said when, by whom, and where over a long period of time. Do not offer an answer requiring you to consult records not available at the deposition or requiring you to consult your friends and associates for the answer.

(continues)

> ### EXHIBIT 4-4   DEPOSITION GUIDELINES *(continued)*
>
> **DON'T BE EMBARRASSED** about admitting that you have met and consulted with your attorney prior to giving your deposition. If asked what you talked about, simply say your attorney merely instructed you to be truthful and honest. What else you and your attorney discuss is confidential and should not be revealed to the other side.
>
> **DO NOT BE AFRAID.** There is no one who is going to harm you and there is no need to show fear or anxiety or to be afraid to answer questions truthfully. If you begin to feel anxious or confused, ask for a break.
>
> **BEWARE** of questions by the other attorney beginning with words similar to "is that all?" A good answer to such a question would include phrases such as "To the best of my recollection at the present time." Also, beware of compound questions.
>
> **NO JOKES.** Never joke in a deposition. Try to avoid wisecracks and obscenities. The humor would not be apparent on the transcript and may look crude or untruthful. Your behavior should be professional and cool. Humor usually does not come across well on the transcript.
>
> **OBJECTIONS TO QUESTIONS.** There may be one or more questions asked of you during the deposition that your attorney will find objectionable because it is not part of the proper discovery in the case. In such an instance, your attorney will instruct you not to answer the question. Occasionally, the opposing attorney will ask that such question be "certified," meaning that it will be presented to the judge at a later date to determine whether you should answer the question.
>
> **DO NOT CONVERSE WITH OPPONENT.** After the deposition is over, do not chat with your opponents or their attorney. Remember, the other attorney is your legal enemy. Do not let his or her friendly manner cause you to drop your guard or become chatty. Do not be concerned, however, if your attorney is conversing with opposing counsel. Remember that they have professional relationships.
>
> **DO NOT SPECULATE.** Do not try to figure out before you answer whether a truthful answer will help or hinder your case. Answer truthfully. Your attorney can deal with the truth effectively, but is handicapped when you answer any other way. Second-guessing the opposing attorney may lead to misunderstanding.
>
> **FINAL ADVICE.** Your deposition is being taken to provide the opponent with information to be used AGAINST you. You cannot "win" a deposition. So please answer the questions truthfully, but concisely. Do not provide more information than the other attorney has asked for. You are free to consult with your attorney during the deposition, and you should if you have any questions about how to answer.

If you are not present during the deposition and have a good relationship with the witness, check on her during breaks to see if she is comfortable and to do some of that all-important hand holding, if appropriate.

SUMMARIZING DEPOSITIONS

Within 30 days of the deposition, either the original transcript will be delivered to the attorney who noticed the deposition or the court reporting firm will contact the deponent directly and ask him or her to come to the office to review and sign the transcript. The deponent has the opportunity to make changes to the transcript in form or substance. For example, if a date is incorrect or a name is misspelled, the witness should make appropriate corrections. However, if a deponent wishes to make more critical changes, such as changing a "no" answer to a "yes" answer, he or she should consult with the attorney to determine whether such substantive changes should be made. Everyone makes mistakes, but the attorney will want to be sure any mistakes can be explained in a way that does not harm the veracity of the deponent. The witness then signs the deposition transcript under penalty of perjury.

Well-taken depositions provide a wealth of information regarding the issues, facts, and allegations of a lawsuit, but also insight into the strategies of the other parties. Because deposition transcripts are often hundreds of pages in length, it is crucial that they be summarized in great detail. In more complex cases, depositions are often summarized in more than one way. For example, a paralegal may prepare a summary that gives page and line detail of information obtained and another summary that includes information just on particular aspects of the case.

A benefit of a page and line summary is that it is easy to then refer to the transcript itself at trial. It also provides the most detailed summary. The summary is prepared while carefully reviewing the transcript. If a page and line summary is carefully prepared, the attorney may not need to refer to the actual transcript again. This will reduce greatly the amount of paper to manage during trial preparation and at trial. A several-hundred-page-long deposition transcript may be reduced to a fraction of its original length. If a witness says something quite significant, it should be quoted directly from the transcript in the summary.

After preparing a summary, you may write a separate memorandum to point out to the responsible attorney any significant findings, contradictions with other discovery, or notes regarding additional discovery or witnesses. This memorandum may also contain definitions for technical terms m phrases or terms of art that may have been used, particularly by an expert witness or a specialist percipient witness. When a technical witness, such as an expert witness or physician, is deposed, there may be a great deal of technical language or jargon or terms of art particular to the expertise of the deponent. While preparing the summary, you should be thinking how the testimony impacts the case.

Exhibit 4-5 contains sample pages from the transcript of Mrs. Olde's deposition taken May 2, 2002. The attorney for Convalescent Care, Inc. is examining Mrs. Olde.

This is a fairly straightforward examination and response. A summary of this portion of the deposition is found in Exhibit 4-6.

TIP

Software programs may be purchased to assist with summarizing depositions. Use of these programs requires specialized training but may be well worth the time and cost of the software and training if many depositions need to be summarized. These programs help with finding specific terms or words used in a deposition and organizing them, and can compare testimony from several deponents. They are very beneficial in organizing and analyzing testimony from several witnesses deposed in a single case.

EXHIBIT 4-5   SAMPLE DEPOSITION TRANSCRIPT FROM *OLDE v. CCI*

1 Q. Mrs. Olde, in what room of your house did you fall on February 2, 2001?

2 A. The living room. Well, actually, it was between the living room and the dining

3   room.

4 Q. Is there a hallway there, or what?

5 A. No. The rooms just kind of run into each other.

6 Q. What kind of floor covering was there?

7 A. Wall-to-wall carpet.

8 Q. How old was that carpet?

9 A. Well, let me think. Pretty old, I believe.

10 Q. Can you be more specific? What do you consider to be pretty old? Five

11   years old, ten years old. What is pretty old?

12 A. Well, I got it after all the children had grown up and moved out but before my

13   husband died. Let's see, that was in 1985. So it must be about twenty years

14   old.

EXHIBIT 4-6   SUMMARY OF OLDE DEPOSITION

PAGE	LINE	TESTIMONY
14	1-3	She fell between the dining room and living room.
14	6-13	The floor was covered in wall-to-wall carpet that was approximately 20 years old.

A sample transcript from the emergency room treating physician, in Exhibit 4-7, would be somewhat more complex:

EXHIBIT 4-7   TREATING PHYSICIAN DEPOSITION TRANSCRIPT

1 Q. Now, Dr. Brown, you testified that you determined that in addition to Mrs.

2   Olde's hip not healing properly, she also seemed to be suffering from

3   some other ailments, is that correct?

4 A. Yes, that's correct.

(continues)

EXHIBIT 4-7   TREATING PHYSICIAN DEPOSITION TRANSCRIPT *(continued)*

5 Q. What led you to believe that there was anything else wrong?

6 A. The patient seemed disoriented which was unusual.

7 Q. Isn't that to be expected in someone her age?

8 A. I had seen Mrs. Olde when she was in previously and she had been very

9   well oriented to her surroundings. She was lucid and responded

10   apropriately to questions.

11 Q. Was she taking any medication that would cause her to be disoriented?

12 A. She was on some medication and I took that into account. Her lack of

13   orientation combined with other symptoms made me suspicious.

14 Q. What other symptoms?

15 A. We needed to catheterize her in order to perform some tests. After several

16   hours, she had passed no urine via the catheter which suggested some

17   degree of dehydration.

18 Q. What tests did you perform?

19 A. The records indicate that a CBC, CAT scan, MRI, x-rays of the femur and

20   chest, EKG and ECG were all performed.

21 Q. How did you know her hip was not healing properly?

22 A. The patient should have been able to withstand some weight bearing on her

23   extremity by this point and she could not stand on the leg at all.

24 Q. Again, could this not be attributable, at least in part, to her age?

Page 81

1 A. It was my understanding that the patient had been quite active up until the

2   time of her fall. Had she been receiving proper physical therapy, as

3   prescribed, I would have expected to see more progress by this time.

4 Q. How do you know she was not receiving physical therapy?

5 A. I had no way of knowing at the time. Later, when I spoke with her

6   daughter, she reported that she did not believe her mother was receiving

7   physical therapy at CCI.

(continues)

EXHIBIT 4-7   TREATING PHYSICIAN DEPOSITION TRANSCRIPT *(continued)*

8 Q. What kind of physical therapy did you prescribe?

9 A. Range of motion exercises, stretching, ADL assistance, all of which are

10   the usual protocol from someone recovering from a hip fracture.

Page 82

CAREER TIP

Law firms often seek out paralegals with expertise in a particular field, such as medicine or technical fields, to review and summarize expert witness depositions as well as medical records or technical records received during the course of discovery.

The summary of the physician's deposition would include definitions of medical terms used. This may require the paralegal to do nonlegal research. It is important that the paralegal understand the terms used in depositions as she is often responsible for educating the attorney regarding nonlegal factual issues in a lawsuit. In order to successfully accomplish this, the paralegal will need to have access to and know how to use medical and scientific Web sites, dictionaries, and reference materials.

CONCLUSION

Information gathered in depositions can be of utmost importance in preparing for trial. Often, testimony garnered from a deponent may lead to fruitful settlement discussions by the attorneys. Depositions provide an opportunity to look at the lawsuit from different angles and to hear the facts from the people who witnessed or experienced them. The testimony may strengthen a case or shed light on weaknesses. Participating in depositions can be a rewarding experience for a paralegal because he will be able to put all his skills to use, synthesizing information, research and writing, and strengthening his relationship with the client and witnesses.

KEY TERMS

court reporter	deposition notice	transcript
deponent	impeach	

REVIEW QUESTIONS

1. What is the paralegal's role in the deposition process?
2. List five instructions you would give to a witness prior to his deposition.
3. How can a deposition be used to impeach a witness?
4. What is the usual timing of a deposition in the discovery process?

■ APPLYING WHAT YOU HAVE LEARNED

1. What are the contents of a deposition notice?
2. Describe direct examination, cross-examination, redirect examination, and re-cross examination.
3. What are the service requirements for a deposition notice?
4. When can a deposition be videotaped?
5. Who pays for a deposition?
6. Summarize the emergency room physician's deposition testimony as set out in the chapter.

ILLUSTRATIVE CASE

Read the excerpts from the following case and answer the following questions:

1. What is the judge's opinion regarding the importance of the deposition?
2. What rules does the judge rely upon in his opinion?
3. According to the judge, what are the purposes of the discovery and evidence rules?

150 F.R.D. 525

UNITED STATES DISTRICT COURT,

E.D. PENNSYLVANIA.

ARTHUR J. HALL, PLAINTIFF,

V.

CLIFTON PRECISION, A DIVISION OF LITTON SYSTEMS, INC.

CIV. A. NO. 92-5947.

JULY 29, 1993.

Civil action was commenced. During discovery, dispute arose regarding conduct of deposition. The District Court, Gawthrop, J., held that: (1) witness being deposed and his or her attorney may not confer during course of deposition unless conference is for purpose of determining whether privilege should be asserted, and (2) witness and counsel are not entitled to confer about document shown to witness during deposition before witness answers questions about it.

Ordered accordingly.

OPINION

GAWTHROP, District Judge.

Currently at bar is an issue on which, despite its presence in nearly every case brought under the Federal Rules of Civil Procedure, there is not a lot of case law: the conduct of lawyers at depositions. More specifically, the questions before the court are (1) to what extent may a lawyer confer with a client, off the record and outside earshot of the other lawyers, during a deposition of the client, and (2) does a lawyer have the right to inspect, before the deposition of

(continues)

ILLUSTRATIVE CASE *(continued)*

a client begins, all documents which opposing counsel intends to show the client during the deposition, so that the lawyer can review them with the client before the deposition?

In this case, Robert F. Stewart, Esquire, counsel for defendant, noticed the deposition of the plaintiff, Arthur J. Hall. Before the deposition began, Mr. Hall's counsel, Joel W. Todd, Esquire, asked Mr. Stewart for a copy of each document which Mr. Stewart intended to show Mr. Hall during the deposition so that he could review the documents with Mr. Hall before the deposition began. Mr. Stewart declined to produce the documents.

At the beginning of the deposition, Mr. Stewart described the deposition process to Mr. Hall. During that description, he told Mr. Hall, "[c]ertainly ask me to clarify any question that you do not understand. Or if you have any difficulty understanding my questions, I'll be happy to try to rephrase them to make it possible for you to be able to answer them." Deposition of Arthur J. Hall, at 5-6. Mr. Todd then interjected, "Mr. Hall, at any time if you want to stop and talk to me, all you have to do is indicate that to me." *Id.* at 6. Mr. Stewart then stated his position: "[t]his witness is here to give testimony, to be answering my questions, and not to have conferences with counsel in order to aid him in developing his responses to my questions." *Id.*

During the brief, unfinished deposition, there were two interruptions. The first occurred when, according to Mr. Todd, Mr. Hall wished to confer with him about the meaning of the word "document." Nevertheless, when the deposition resumed, Mr. Hall asked Mr. Stewart about the meaning of "document." *Id.* at 9-10. The second interruption occurred when Mr. Stewart showed a document to Mr. Hall and began to ask him a question about it. Before Mr. Stewart finished his question about the document, Mr. Todd said, "I've got to review it with my client." *Id.* at 18. Mr. Stewart stated his objection "to Mr. Todd reviewing with his client documents that Mr. Hall is about to be questioned on in this deposition." *Id.* The parties then contacted the court, which ordered that the deposition be adjourned until the question of attorney-client discussion during the deposition could be resolved. That afternoon, the court held a conference with both counsel about their conduct at the deposition. At the conference, Mr. Todd asserted that an attorney and client have the right to confer with one another at any time during the taking of the client's deposition. At the end of the conference, the court requested counsel to submit letter briefs on the issue, which they have done.

The Federal Rules of Civil Procedure give the court control over the discovery process. Rule 26(f) authorizes the court, after a discovery conference, to enter an order "setting limitations on discovery" and "determining other such matters . . . as are necessary for the proper management of discovery." Such a conference may be called by the court itself or upon a motion by one of the parties. The Advisory Committee Notes point out that Subdivision (f) was added to Rule 26 in 1980 because the Committee +believed that discovery "abuse can best be prevented by intervention by the court as soon as abuse is threatened."

Rule 30 governs oral depositions. Rule 30(c) states: "[e]xamination and cross-examination of witnesses may proceed as permitted at the trial." Rule 30(d) gives the court the power to terminate or limit the scope of a deposition "on motion of a party" if the court finds that the deposition is being conducted in "bad faith or in such manner as unreasonably to annoy, embarrass, or oppress the deponent or party." All phases of the examination are subject to the control of the court, which has discretion to make any orders necessary to prevent the abuse of the discovery and deposition process. See, 8 Charles A. Wright & Arthur R. Miller, Federal Practice and Procedure §§ 2113, 2116 (1971).

(continues)

ILLUSTRATIVE CASE *(continued)*

Rules 37(a)(2) and 37(a)(3) permit a party to seek, and the court to grant, an order which compels a deponent to respond to a question or to give a less evasive or more complete response.

Taken together, Rules 26(f), 30, and 37(a), along with Rule 16, which gives the court control over pre-trial case management, vest the court with broad authority and discretion to control discovery, including the conduct of depositions. [1] It is pursuant to that authority and discretion that I enter this Opinion and Order.

Plaintiff's counsel has submitted no citation, no case law, in support of his argument that an attorney and client may confer at their pleasure during the client's deposition. On the other hand, defendant has submitted orders from numerous courts holding that such conversations are not allowed. Those courts have held that private conferences between deponents and their attorneys during the taking of a deposition are improper unless the conferences are for the purpose of determining whether a privilege should be asserted.

The United States District Court for the Eastern District of New York has adopted a similar view in a standing order: "[a]n attorney for a deponent shall not initiate a private conference with the deponent during the actual taking of a deposition, except for the purpose of determining whether a privilege should be asserted." *Standing Orders of the Court on Effective Discovery in Civil Cases,* 102 F.R.D. 339, 351, no. 13 (E.D.N.Y. 1984). In combination with another standing order which prohibits "[o]bjections in the presence of the witness which are used to suggest an answer to the witness," *id.* at 351, no. 12, the judges of that district have attempted to insure that the testimony taken during a deposition is completely that of the deponent, rather than a version of that testimony which has been edited or glossed by the deponent's lawyer.

One of the purposes of the discovery rules in general, and the deposition rules in particular, is to elicit the facts of a case before trial. Another purpose is to even the playing field somewhat by allowing all parties access to the same information, thereby tending to prevent trial by surprise. Depositions serve another purpose as well: the memorialization, the freezing, of a witness's testimony at an early stage of the proceedings, before that witness's recollection of the events at issue either has faded or has been altered by intervening events, other discovery, or the helpful suggestions of lawyers.

The underlying purpose of a deposition is to find out what a witness saw, heard, or did—what the witness thinks. A deposition is meant to be a question-and-answer conversation between the deposing lawyer and the witness. There is no proper need for the witness's own lawyer to act as an intermediary, interpreting questions, deciding which questions the witness should answer, and helping the witness to formulate answers. The witness comes to the deposition to testify, not to indulge in a parody of Charlie McCarthy, with lawyers coaching or bending the witness's words to mold a legally convenient record. It is the witness—not the lawyer—who is the witness. As an advocate, the lawyer is free to frame those facts in a manner favorable to the client, and also to make favorable and creative arguments of law.[2] But the lawyer is not entitled to be creative with the facts. Rather, a lawyer must accept the facts as they develop. Therefore, I hold that a lawyer and client do not have an absolute right to confer during the course of the client's deposition.

Concern has been expressed as to the client's right to counsel and to due process. A lawyer, of course, has the right, if not the duty,[3] to prepare a client for a deposition. But once a deposition begins, the right to counsel is somewhat tempered by the underlying goal of our discovery rules: getting to the truth. Under Rule 30(c), depositions generally are to be conducted under the same testimonial rules as are trials. During a civil trial, a witness and his or her lawyer are

(continues)

ILLUSTRATIVE CASE *(continued)*

not permitted to confer at their pleasure during the witness's testimony.[4] Once a witness has been prepared and has taken the stand, that witness is on his or her own.

The same is true at a deposition. The fact that there is no judge in the room to prevent private conferences does not mean that such conferences should or may occur. The underlying reason for preventing private conferences is still present: they tend, at the very least, to give the appearance of obstructing the truth.

These considerations apply also to conferences initiated by the witness, as opposed to the witness's lawyer. To allow private conferences initiated by the witness would be to allow the witness to listen to the question, ask his or her lawyer for the answer, and then parrot the lawyer's response. Again, this is not what depositions are all about—or, at least, it is not what they are supposed to be all about. If the witness does not understand the question, or needs some language further defined or some documents further explained, the witness can ask the deposing lawyer to clarify or further explain the question.[5] After all, the lawyer who asked the question is in a better position to explain the question than is the witness's own lawyer. There is simply no qualitative distinction between private conferences initiated by a lawyer and those initiated by a witness. Neither should occur.

These rules also apply during recesses. Once the deposition has begun, the preparation period is over and the deposing lawyer is entitled to pursue the chosen line of inquiry without interjection by the witness's counsel. Private conferences are barred during the deposition, and the fortuitous occurrence of a coffee break, lunch break, or evening recess is no reason to change the rules. Otherwise, the same problems would persist. A clever lawyer or witness who finds that a deposition is going in an undesired or unanticipated direction could simply insist on a short recess to discuss the unanticipated yet desired answers, thereby circumventing the prohibition on private conferences. Therefore, I hold that conferences between witness and lawyer are prohibited both during the deposition and during recesses.[6]

The same reasoning applies to conferences about documents shown to the witness during the deposition. When the deposing attorney presents a document to a witness at a deposition, that attorney is entitled to have the witness, and the witness alone, answer questions about the document. The witness's lawyer should be given a copy of the document for his or her own inspection, but there is no valid reason why the lawyer and the witness should have to confer about the document before the witness answers questions about it.[7] If the witness does not recall having seen the document before or does not understand the document, the witness may ask the deposing lawyer for some additional information, or the witness may simply testify to the lack of knowledge or understanding. But there need not be an off-the-record conference between witness and lawyer in order to ascertain whether the witness understands the document or a pending question about the document.

As mentioned above, the majority of federal courts which have issued deposition guidelines have held that a private conference between witness and attorney is permissible if the purpose of the conference is to decide whether to assert a privilege. With this exception I agree. Since the assertion of a privilege is a proper, and very important, objection during a deposition, it makes sense to allow the witness the opportunity to consult with counsel about whether to assert a privilege. Further, privileges are violated not only by the admission of privileged evidence at trial, but by the very disclosures themselves. Thus, it is important that the witness be fully informed of his or her rights before making a statement which might reveal privileged information. However, when such a conference occurs, the conferring attorney should

(continues)

ILLUSTRATIVE CASE *(continued)*

place on the record the fact that the conference occurred, the subject of the conference, and the decision reached as to whether to assert a privilege.

Having discussed off-the-record witness-coaching, I now turn to a related concern: on-the-record witness-coaching through suggestive objections. Without guidelines on suggestive objections, the spirit of the prohibition against private conferences could be flouted by a lawyer's making of lengthy objections which contain information suggestive of an answer to a pending question. The Supreme Court has recently addressed the issue of suggestive objections in the Proposed Amendments to the Federal Rules of Civil Procedure and Forms, H.R.Doc. No. 74, 103rd Cong., 1st Sess., at 50-52 (Apr. 22, 1993). Proposed Amended Rule 30(d) reads:

(1) Any objection to evidence during a deposition shall be stated concisely and in a non-argumentative and non-suggestive manner. A party may instruct a deponent not to answer only when necessary to preserve a privilege, to enforce a limitation on evidence directed by the court, or to present a motion pursuant to paragraph (3).[8]

(2) By order or local rule, the court may limit the time permitted for the conduct of a deposition, but shall allow additional time consistent with Rule 26(b)(2) if needed for a fair examination of the deponent or if the deponent or another party impedes or delays the examination. If the court finds such an impediment, delay, or other conduct that has frustrated the fair examination of the deponent, it may impose upon the persons responsible an appropriate sanction, including the reasonable costs and attorney's fees incurred by any parties as a result thereof.

The Committee Notes following the proposed amended rule contain the following observations:

Depositions frequently have been unduly prolonged, if not unfairly frustrated, by lengthy objections and colloquy, often suggesting how the deponent should respond .... [O]bjections ... should be limited to those that under Rule 32(d)(3) might be waived if not made at that time .... [O]ther objections can ... be raised for the first time at trial and therefore should be kept at a minimum during a deposition.

Directions to a deponent not to answer a question can be even more disruptive than objections ....

In general, counsel should not engage in any conduct during a deposition that would not be allowed in the presence of a judicial officer. The making of an excessive number of objections may itself constitute sanctionable conduct.

Proposed Amendments, H.R.Doc. No. 74, at 261-63.

The proposed amendments and committee notes aptly observe that objections and colloquy by lawyers tend to disrupt the question-and-answer rhythm of a deposition and obstruct the witness's testimony. Since most objections, such as those grounded on relevance or materiality, are preserved for trial, they need not be made.[9] As for those few objections which would be waived if not made immediately, they should be stated pithily. See, Fed.R.Civ.P. 32(d)(3).

The Federal Rules of Evidence contain no provision allowing lawyers to interrupt the trial testimony of a witness to make a statement. Such behavior should likewise be prohibited at depositions, since it tends to obstruct the taking of the witness's testimony. It should go without saying that lawyers are strictly prohibited from making any comments, either on or off the record, which might suggest or limit a witness's answer to an unobjectionable question.

In short, depositions are to be limited to what they were and are intended to be: question-and-answer sessions between a lawyer and a witness aimed at uncovering the facts in a lawsuit. When a deposition becomes something other than that because of the strategic interruptions, suggestions, statements, and arguments of counsel, it not only

(continues)

ILLUSTRATIVE CASE *(continued)*

becomes unnecessarily long, but it ceases to serve the purpose of the Federal Rules of Civil Procedure: to find and fix[10] the truth.

Depositions are the factual battleground where the vast majority of litigation actually takes place. It may safely be said that Rule 30 has spawned a veritable cottage industry. The significance of depositions has grown geometrically over the years to the point where their pervasiveness now dwarfs both the time spent and the facts learned at the actual trial—assuming there is a trial, which there usually is not.[11] The pretrial tail now wags the trial dog. Thus, it is particularly important that this discovery device not be abused. Counsel should never forget that even though the deposition may be taking place far from a real courtroom, with no black-robed overseer peering down upon them, as long as the deposition is conducted under the caption of this court and proceeding under the authority of the rules of this court, counsel are operating as officers of this court. They should comport themselves accordingly; should they be tempted to stray, they should remember that this judge is but a phone call away.

An Order containing guidelines for the conduct of the depositions of parties and other witnesses represented by counsel in this case follows.

---

[1] Plaintiff's counsel argues that since the Rule 30(d) says "on motion of a party," the court is powerless to act absent such a motion. This argument is specious; the Federal Rules of Civil Procedure, and their overseers, the judiciary, are not so passively impotent.

[2] I note that under Rule 32(d)(3)(A), objections to the competency, relevancy, or materiality of deposition testimony generally are preserved for trial. Therefore, counsel should not repeatedly interrupt the deposition to make these objections. Of course, the witness's counsel is free to object on the ground that a question asks for an answer which is protected by a privilege, and to make objections which would be waived if not raised immediately. *See,* Fed.R.Civ.P. 32(d)(3)(B).

[3] "A lawyer shall provide competent representation to a client. Competent representation requires the legal knowledge, skill, thoroughness and preparation necessary for the representation." Pennsylvania Rule of Professional Conduct 1.1.

[4] Lawyers, of course, do not often attempt to interrupt the questioning of their clients at trial to have private conferences, probably because they think that doing so would tend to diminish the witness-client's credibility. Some district courts have ordered lawyers and witness-clients not to confer even during lunch and overnight breaks in the witness-client's testimony. In *Aiello v. City of Wilmington,* 623 F.2d 845, 858-59 (3d Cir. 1980), the district court, because of its concern over "witness coaching," ordered the plaintiff and his counsel not to communicate during breaks in the plaintiff's cross-examination. The Third Circuit did not decide, and to this court's knowledge still has not decided, whether such an order might violate the right to counsel.

[5] At the beginning of the deposition, the deposing lawyer should explain to the witness, as did Mr. Stewart here, that the witness should feel free to ask for clarification at any time during the deposition.

[6] To the extent that such conferences do occur, in violation of this Opinion and Order, I am of the view that these conferences are not covered by the attorney-client privilege, at least as to

(continues)

ILLUSTRATIVE CASE *(continued)*

what is said by the lawyer to the witness. Therefore, any such conferences are fair game for inquiry by the deposing attorney to ascertain whether there has been any coaching and, if so, what.

[7] This approach is consistent with Federal Rule of Evidence 613(a), which provides: "[i]n examining a witness concerning a prior statement made by the witness, whether written or not, the statement need not be shown nor its contents disclosed to the witness at that time, but on request the same shall be shown or disclosed to opposing counsel." The Advisory Committee Notes observe that "[t]he provision for disclosure to counsel is designed to protect against unwarranted insinuations that a statement has been made when the fact is to the contrary." Thus, the requirement that counsel be shown the document exists only to assure counsel that the document actually exists, not to allow counsel to prepare the witness to testify about it.

Rule 613(a) is contrary to the rule in *Queen Caroline's Case*, 129 Eng.Rep. 976 (1820). In that case, English judges advised that, before being cross-examined about a document, a witness must be shown the document and given the opportunity to read the relevant portion. The rule proved so obstructive that it was abolished by Parliament in 1854. 17 & 18 Vict., ch. 125, § 24 (1854) (Eng.). *See*, John W. Strong et al., 1 McCormick on Evidence § 28 (4th ed. 1992).

[8] Paragraph (3) is substantially similar to the current Rule 30(d), which governs motions to terminate or limit examination because of bad faith, unreasonableness, annoyance, embarrassment, or oppression.

[9] I also note that a favorite objection or interjection of lawyers is, "I don't understand the question; therefore the witness doesn't understand the question." This is not a proper objection. If the witness needs clarification, the witness may ask the deposing lawyer for clarification. A lawyer's purported lack of understanding is not a proper reason to interrupt a deposition. In addition, counsel is not permitted to state on the record their interpretations of questions, since those interpretations are irrelevant and often suggestive of a particularly desired answer.

[10] "Fix" in the sense of firmly stabilizing (such as a photographic image), rather than bending or muting the record to make it more factually comfy—as in to "fix" a prize fight, or a jury.

[11] From October 1, 1991, to September 30, 1992, 8,771 civil cases terminated in this judicial district. Of those, only 337, or 3.8%, actually went to trial. Annual Report of the Director of the Administrative Office of the United States Courts—1992, at Table C 4A. The reality is that what is learned at depositions becomes the factual basis upon which most cases are disposed of—not by trial, but by settlement. Thus, if those "facts" get skewed, the risk is grave that so also will the quality of justice.

For additional resources, visit our Web site at www.westlegalstudies.com

5

Reports, Tests, and Expert Witnesses

After studying this chapter you should be able to:

❑ understand the difference between pre-litigation and post-litigation reports.

❑ understand where to look for relevant pre-litigation reports.

❑ appreciate how expert witnesses are used in a case.

❑ know how to find an expert witness for your case.

❑ understand your role as a paralegal in working with a retained expert.

INTRODUCTION

An important evidence tool is what is commonly known as a report. A report may take many forms, but there are two basic categories in the litigation context. First, there are reports that are prepared during the ordinary course of business. We will call these **pre-litigation reports**. **Ordinary course of business** means that the report was prepared in the context of an everyday, routine business event, for example, during the investigation of a traffic collision, during the testing of a product for introduction into the marketplace, by a governmental agency performing a study, or during the examination of a patient by a physician.

The second type of report is that prepared by an **expert witness** hired during the course of a lawsuit. This sort of report, what we will call a **post-litigation report**, is prepared not in the ordinary course of business but with the specific purpose of helping to prove or disprove facts or allegations made in a case.

Paralegals are instrumental in gathering both types of reports and in locating and working with expert witnesses.

PRE-LITIGATION REPORTS

Reports are routinely created for a variety of purposes. One example is the incident report prepared by law enforcement personnel to describe the events that led up to a vehicle or boating accident and to make a finding of responsibility. Medical reports are very commonly used in litigation. An example is the radiology report prepared by a physician when he or she interprets the results of an X-ray, CT scan, or MRI. Someone involved in a land use case would find helpful an environmental impact report prepared by a consulting engineer to provide information on the effect a proposed new housing development will have on the water supply, air quality, and other environmental factors in a community.

An enormous amount of useful reports are prepared by the state and federal governments. One illustration of this is a report by the U.S. Department of Energy on electric and hybrid vehicle research. Many of these reports can be found in the library or online.

As stated above, pre-litigation reports are prepared during the ordinary course of business to summarize events or scientific findings. At the time they are prepared, no one is planning to sue anyone.

Once a lawsuit is under way, it falls upon the paralegal to begin locating and gathering whatever pre-litigation reports might exist that are relevant to the subject matter of the case. As a new paralegal, you may not have any idea about where to start looking. Until you have gained some experience in the field, you would be wise to get some guidance about where to begin from your supervising attorney or from other, seasoned paralegals in your office.

Case Scenario

Following is our third case scenario, a hypothetical personal injury case.

The Johnson family—Bob, Martha, and their son Daniel, age 13—rented a houseboat for a week's vacation on Lake Vista. The houseboat used by the Johnsons was manufactured by Foxfire Boat Company and was rented to them by Lake Vista Vacation Rentals.

The Johnsons boarded the houseboat on Saturday morning, accompanied by an employee of Lake Vista Vacation Rentals, who showed them how to operate the boat engine and steer, and gave them a brief lecture on boating safety and right of way rules. The Johnsons loaded their gear onto the houseboat and cast off. The day was very warm, and while Bob and Martha concentrated on navigating the lake, Daniel decided to explore the boat. After a while, Daniel began to feel a little seasick and lay down in his cabin, which was at the rear of the boat near the engine. The cabin was warm, so he opened the porthole. A few hours later, Martha began looking for Daniel when he did not respond to her calls. She found him unconscious on his bed.

Bob called ahead on his cell phone to have an ambulance waiting on shore to take Daniel to the hospital. Tests performed by the hospital showed that Daniel suffered a high level of exposure to carbon monoxide, a potentially lethal compound. Although he survived the exposure, it appears that Daniel suffered permanent brain damage.

The Johnsons filed a lawsuit against Foxfire Boat Company and Lake Vista Vacation Rentals to recover Daniel's medical expenses and to provide funds for his future care, since his cognitive and intellectual functions have been impaired. They allege that the design of the houseboat and engine were defective and that Lake Vista Vacation Rentals failed to properly warn them of the dangers.

THE SEARCH FOR PRE-LITIGATION REPORTS

Your firm is retained by Foxfire Boat Company to defend it in the Johnson action. As the paralegal assigned to the case, you will begin gathering all evidence that may be relevant to the matter. For the purposes of this chapter we will concentrate on what reports you might be able to locate.

■ **INCIDENT REPORT**
A report usually prepared by a law enforcement agency to describe a collision, accident, assault, or other incident. The report contains such information as the date and time of the incident, the weather, the names of persons who were involved in the incident or witnessed it, a description of what happened, and measurements taken at the scene.

Marine Patrol Investigation

Your first step would be to contact the sheriff's department in whose jurisdiction Lake Vista is located. The U.S. Coast Guard requires that all accidents that occur on waterways be investigated and that a report be prepared. On inland lakes, that duty often falls to the sheriff's department. The responding deputy or officer may also be required by his or her local jurisdiction to prepare an incident report in addition to the Marine Patrol Investigation Report. A copy of these reports can usually be obtained for a small fee.

An **incident report** is a wonderful starting place to begin your investigation of the case. Details about the date, time, and weather conditions are recorded. There is information about condition of the victim when found, and to which hospital he or she was taken. Witnesses to the incident are often listed, along with their contact information, and sometimes statements are taken and written down. See Exhibit 5–1 for a sample incident report.

EXHIBIT 5-1   SAMPLE INCIDENT REPORT

MARINE ACCIDENT REPORT DEPARTMENT OF BOATING & WATERWAYS   PAGE 1 OF 2

SPECIAL CONDITIONS	NO. INJURED	AGENCY			JUDICIAL DISTRICT			NUMBER	
None	1	Sheriff			Lake Co.			L14-06	
	NO. KILLED 0	CITY Lake Vista		COUNTY Lake		BEAT			

LOCATION	ACCIDENT OCCURRED ON Lake Vista				MONTH 8 DAY 10 YEAR 05	TIME (24:00) 14:30	DEW NUMBER	OFFICER NO. 684
	NEAREST LANDMARK (NAVIGATION AID) 500 feet S/E boat docks					INVESTIGATED BY Dolgren		PHONE

PARTY 1	NAME (FIRST, MIDDLE, LAST) Bob Johnson				STREET ADDRESS 1234 Main St.			
OPERATOR X	IDENTIFICATION DL N04392	BIRTH DATE 4/2/59	SEX M	RACE W	CITY Anytown USA	STATE	ZIP	PHONE
SWIMMER	VESSEL 1992 MAKE, MODEL, LENGTH Foxfire housebuat		VESSEL NUMBER 30XL29	VESSEL NAME None			VIOLATION CHARGED None	
MOORED	HULL IDENTIFICATION NO. NAR31007G		HORSEPOWER	INSURANCE YES X NO	OWNER'S NAME Lake Vista Vacation Rentals			
OTHER	DIRECTION OF TRAVEL South	ON WATERWAY Lake Vista		POB	OWNER'S ADDRESS 439 Lake Dr., Lake Vista			
	ESTIMATED SPEED 10	DISPOSITION OF VESSEL Returned to owner		BY OPERATOR	ON ORDERS OF	DAMAGE: MINOR, MOD, MAJOR, TOTAL None		LOCATION

PROPERTY	DESCRIPTION OF DAMAGE None							
	OWNER'S NAME		ADDRESS		ZIP	PHONE	NOTIFIED: YES___ NO___	

INJURED/ WITNESS	WITNESS ONLY	AGE 13	SEX M	FATAL No	EXTENT OF INJURY SEVERE WOUND OTHER VISIBLE INJURY CO poisoning	COMPLAINT OF PAIN U/C	OPERATOR	PASS	INJURED WAS SKIER	SWIMMER	OTHER X	IN VESSEL NUMBER
	NAME Daniel Johnson							PHONE 555-1015	DISAPPEARANCE YES___ NO X			
	ADDRESS 1234 Main St, Anytown USA						TAKEN TO (INJURED ONLY) St. Mary's Hospital					

INJURED/ WITNESS	WITNESS ONLY X	AGE 35	SEX F	FATAL	EXTENT OF INJURY SEVERE WOUND OTHER VISIBLE INJURY N/A	COMPLAINT OF PAIN	OPERATOR	PASS	INJURED WAS SKIER	SWIMMER	OTHER	IN VESSEL NUMBER
	NAME Martha Johnson							PHONE 555-1015	DISAPPEARANCE YES___ NO___			
	ADDRESS 1234 Main St, Anytown USA						TAKEN TO (INJURED ONLY)					

INJURED/ WITNESS	WITNESS ONLY	AGE	SEX	FATAL	EXTENT OF INJURY SEVERE WOUND OTHER VISIBLE INJURY	COMPLAINT OF PAIN	OPERATOR	PASS	INJURED WAS SKIER	SWIMMER	OTHER	IN VESSEL NUMBER
	NAME							PHONE	DISAPPEARANCE YES___ NO___			
	ADDRESS						TAKEN TO (INJURED ONLY)					

SKETCH (INCLUDE VESSEL, WIND, CURRENT DIRECTION) INDICATE TRUE NORTH	MISCELLANEOUS
	COPY OF STATE FORM A-1 GIVEN TO OPERATOR(S)
	REPORT FORWARDED TO:

(continues)

EXHIBIT 5–1   SAMPLE INCIDENT REPORT *(continued)*

Page 2

DATE OF ACCIDENT (MO, DAY, YR.): 8/10/05   TIME (24.00): 14:30

USER I.D.: _____   NUMBER: _____

PRIMARY ACCIDENT FACTOR

SECTION VIOLATION	
OTHER IMPROPER VIOLATION*	
OTHER THAN OPERATOR*	X
UNKNOWN*	

WIND

X	NONE	LIGHT (9-6 m.p.h.)
	MODERATE (7-14)	STRONG (15-25)
	STRONG (25+)	

TYPE OF ACCIDENT

SIDESWIPE	BROADSIDE
GROUNDING	CAPSIZING
FIRE/EXPLOSION	FALL OVERB'D
PERSON STR'K	BURNS
HIT OBJECT FIXED/FLOATING	
OTHER* CO poisoning	

TIDE

EBB	FLOOD
SLACK WATER	NOT APPLICABLE

TEMPERATURE ESTIMATE

AIR _____   WATER _____

VESSEL INVOLVED WITH

OTHER VESSEL	SKIER
SWIMMER	FIXED OBJECT
OTHER OBJECT	X NON-COLLISION
OTHER*	

LIGHTING

DAYLIGHT X	DUSK-DAWN
DARK	ARTIFICIAL

VISIBILITY

GOOD X	FAIR
POOR	

WEATHER

CLEAR X	CLOUDY
FOG	RAIN
SNOW	HAZY

PERSONAL FLOTATION DEVICES

Was vessel adequately equipped with Coast Guard approved PFDs?   Y   N

Were they accessible?   Y   N

Were they used?   Y   N

WATER CONDITIONS

X CALM	CHOPPY
ROUGH	VERY ROUGH
STRONG CURRENT	

FIRE EXTINGUISHERS

Was approved type fire fighting equipment aboard?   Y   N

Were they used?   Y   N

OTHER ASSOCIATED FACTORS**

WEATHER	
IMPROPER LOOKOUT	
UNFAMILIAR WITH WATER	
LOADING	
VESSEL EQUIPMENT	
VISION OBSCUREMENTS	
SPEED	
NOT LEGALLY EQUIPPED	
OPERATOR INEXPERIENCE	
OTHER*	

X	HAD NOT BEEN DRINKING
	HBD NOT UNDER THE INFLUENCE
	HBD UNDER INFLUENCE
	HBD IMPAIRMENT UNKNOWN
	UNDER DRUG INFLUENCE
	OTHER PHYSICAL IMPAIRMENT
	IMPAIRMENT UNKNOWN
	NOT APPLICABLE

MOVEMENT PRECEDING ACCIDENT

X	CRUISING
	MANEUVERING
	WATER SKIING
	TOWING/BEING TOWED
	DRIFTING
	AT ANCHOR
	TIED TO DOCK
	FUELING
	FISHING
	RACING
	OTHER

VESSEL TYPE

OPEN MOTORBOAT	
CABIN MOTORBOAT	
RAFT	
SAIL	
AUXILIARY SAIL	
ROW BOAT, KAYAK, CANOE	
HOUSEBOAT	X
RENTAL	
OTHER*	

OUTBOARD	
INBOARD/OUTBOARD	
SAIL/SAIL AND AUXILIARY	
PADDLE (Hand Propelled)	
JET DRIVE	
OTHER*	

KIND OF FUEL

X	GASOLINE
	DIESEL
	OTHER

HULL MATERIAL

WOOD	
ALUMINUM	
STEEL	
FIBERGLASS/PLASTIC	X
OTHER	

* Explain in Accident Narrative
** Check all that apply

ACCIDENT NARRATIVE

The accident occurred on a warm summer day in open water, approximately 500 feet SE of the boat docks. The weather was good with good visibility.

Statements

Bob Johnson stated that the victim, his 13 year old son, Daniel, was exploring the vessel while Mr. Johnson was navigating. Daniel reported he was feeling seasick and went to his cabin in the rear of the vessel. A few hours later he was found unconscious on his bed.

Martha Johnson declined to give a statement.

The victim will be interviewed at the hospital once approval is given by his doctors.

Conclusion

Initial hospital tests show high level of exposure by victim to carbon monoxide.

INVESTIGATED BY (Name, Rank)	ID NUMBER	INVESTIGATED BY (Name, Rank)	ID NUMBER	REVIEWED BY
Dolgren/Officer	684			Sgt. Fremont

Ambulance/Hospital Reports

Upon reviewing the incident report, you learn that Daniel Johnson was transported by Acme Ambulance Company to St. Mary's Hospital in Vista Valley. Using a business records subpoena (see Chapter 2), you can request a copy of the report generated by the ambulance crew following their delivery of Daniel to St. Mary's. The ambulance report will show what time the ambulance was called and when it arrived at the dock to meet the houseboat. The report will describe the condition Daniel was in and what life-saving measures may have been performed, both at the scene and during the ride to the hospital. Finally, the report will show when the ambulance arrived at St. Mary's. All of this information will be informative as to the level of severity of Daniel's injuries, and the quality and timeliness of the care provided by the ambulance personnel, and it will be important for your medical experts to review as the case progresses.

Another step will be to subpoena Daniel's records from St. Mary's Hospital. Among those records will be reports of various medical tests performed on Daniel during his stay. These might include oxygen saturation tests, MRIs, SPECT scans, and cognitive tests. These tests will be critical in showing the experts what level of carbon monoxide was ingested by Daniel and the level of brain damage he suffered.

School Records

In order to establish background information on Daniel, your attorney may ask you to subpoena his school records. School records may have within them reports on academic testing and other measures of skills and intelligence that can be used by your expert witnesses in defending the case. This information would be useful if Daniel's parents are claiming, as part of their damages, that Daniel was a brilliant student who had a promising career as a physicist or other highly paid professional. If it can be shown that Daniel had poor grades, was unmotivated, or had other academic problems, it may be possible to reduce the amount of damages.

Engineering Reports

You now shift your attention away from Daniel and to the houseboat and its engine. Your client, Foxfire Boat Company, may have reports from its design engineers when the plans for the houseboat were being drawn up. There may be engineering specifications and reports prepared by the manufacturer of the engine used by Foxfire on the houseboat. Either you or your attorney should request copies of these reports from the client.

Governmental or Private Industry Reports

When an issue reaches a certain level of importance, or when the safety of the public is at stake, studies are often performed by governmental agencies, professional organizations, or other industry leaders to research the problem and what can be done about it. Many of the reports written about these studies are available to the public and, with the advent of the Internet, are now very easy to locate.

Putting the words "carbon monoxide" and "carbon monoxide + houseboat" into a search engine such as Google or Yahoo! turns up an enormous amount of information. The National Park Service, for example, prints "Morning Reports" for distribution to its offices nationwide. The August 28, 2002, "Morning Report" discusses an instance of drowning due to carbon monoxide poisoning (see Exhibit 5–2 for an excerpt). The Occupational Safety and Health Administration prepared a report on January 19, 1989, which gives the results of its study on the safe limits for exposure to carbon monoxide (see Exhibit 5–3). A private group based in the United Kingdom has a Web site, <http://www.carbonmonoxidekills.com>, which acts as a clearinghouse for information on the topic. Finally, the U.S. Department of the Interior has a Watercraft Safety Working Group which, among other duties, gathers information on carbon monoxide dangers aboard houseboats. Exhibit 5–4 is a listing of some of the materials that were available on the Department of Interior's Web site at the time this textbook was written.

EXHIBIT 5–2   EXCERPT FROM NATIONAL PARK SERVICE REPORT

NATIONAL PARK SERVICE

MORNING REPORT

TO: **ALL NATIONAL PARK SERVICE AREAS AND OFFICES**

FROM: **DIVISION OF RANGER ACTIVITIES, WASHINGTON OFFICE**

DAY/DATE: **WEDNESDAY, AUGUST 28, 2002**

INCIDENTS

02-421 – Glen Canyon NRA (UT/AZ) – Drowning; Carbon Monoxide Poisoning

On the afternoon of August 17th, park dispatch received a call reporting that a nine-year-old girl had drowned in the Halls Creek Bay area of the park. Family members were conducting CPR when Halls Crossing SDR Steve Luckesen arrived on the scene, but they were not successful. The girl was reportedly washing her hair alongside a beached 26-foot Searay cabin cruiser, utilizing the warm water from the exhaust port while the generator was running. A girlfriend who was also washing her hair there left to eat lunch. The victim

(continues)

EXHIBIT 5–2   EXCERPT FROM NATIONAL PARK SERVICE REPORT (continued)

was found to be missing shortly thereafter and subsequently located in two-and-a-half feet of water next to the boat. The victim's girlfriend was later treated at the Bullfrog Clinic for carbon monoxide poisoning. An hour after oxygen therapy was begun, her monoxide level registered at 18%. The victim's blood carbon monoxide level was later found to be 39%. This brings the total known carbon monoxide related fatalities within the park since 1994 to twelve.

EXHIBIT 5–3   OCCUPATIONAL SAFETY AND HEALTH ADMINISTRATION REPORT ON CARBON MONOXIDE

OSHA comments from the January 19, 1989 Final Rule on Air Contaminants Project extracted from 54FR2332 et. seq. This rule was remanded by the U.S. Circuit Court of Appeals and the limits are not currently in force.

CARBON MONOXIDE

CAS: 630-08-0; CHEMICAL FORMULA: CO

OSHA's former limit for carbon monoxide was 50 ppm as an 8-hour TWA. The ACGIH has a TLV-TWA of 50 ppm with a TLV-STEL of 400 ppm. NIOSH (1973d/Ex. 1-237) recommends an 8-hour TWA limit of 35 ppm with a 200-ppm ceiling. The proposed PEL and ceiling were 35 ppm and 200 ppm, respectively; NIOSH (Ex. 8-47, Table N1) concurs that these limits are appropriate, and they are established in the final rule. Carbon monoxide is a flammable, colorless, practically odorless gas.

Carbon monoxide readily combines with hemoglobin to form carboxyhemoglobin (COHb). Excessive accumulations of COHb cause hypoxic stress in healthy individuals as a result of the reduced oxygen-carrying capacity of the blood. In patients with cardiovascular disease, such stress can further impair cardiovascular function. The ACGIH (1986/Ex. 1-3) cites a number of studies showing that exposure to 50 ppm TWA carbon monoxide generally results in COHb levels of 8 to 10 percent, and that such levels are not generally associated with overt signs or symptoms of health impairment in healthy individuals under nonstressful conditions. However, the ACGIH comments that a TLV of 25 ppm, which results in COHb levels of 4 percent or less, may be necessary to protect workers with cardiovascular disease, because this condition places workers at higher risk of serious cardiovascular injury (ACGIH 1986/ Ex. 1-3, p. 106). The NIOSH recommendation of 35 ppm TWA is also aimed at protecting workers with chronic heart disease; NIOSH believes that such workers should not be allowed to have carboxyhemoglobin

(continues)

**EXHIBIT 5–3   OCCUPATIONAL SAFETY AND HEALTH ADMINISTRATION
REPORT ON CARBON MONOXIDE** *(continued)*

levels that approach 5 percent. The rationale for the ACGIH's recommendation of a
400-ppm TLV-STEL for CO is not entirely clear, but may be based on a study by Schulte
(1964/Ex. 1-366), which stated that exposure to 100 ppm carbon monoxide for four
hours is excessive.

Several commenters (Exs. 133, 188, 3-675, 3-673, L3-1330, 3-902, 3-660, 3-349, 3-1123,
and 129) submitted comments on the Agency's proposed limits for carbon monoxide.
Some of these commenters (Exs. 3-675 and 3-673) were concerned that the revised limits
would have serious economic impacts on their industries (electric utilities, steel, and non-
ferrous foundries). However, OSHA has determined that it is feasible for facilities in these
sectors to comply with the proposed CO limits (see Section VII of the preamble).

Many rulemaking participants questioned the health basis for lowering the former
CO limit of 50 ppm as an 8-hour TWA to 35 ppm and supplementing this limit with a
200-ppm STEL (Exs. 133A, 188, 3-660, 3-349, 3-1123, and 129). These commenters
pointed out that the discussion of CO's health effects in the preamble to the proposal
(53 FR 21171) stated that the carboxyhemoglobin levels associated with CO exposures
of 50 ppm "are not associated with toxic effects in healthy individuals." According to the
American Iron and Steel Institute (Ex. 3-1123), whose remarks were typical of the views
of these commenters:

> The proposed PEL should not be adopted because there is not adequate evidence that
> exposure to carbon monoxide at levels of 50 ppm TWA poses a significant risk to
> workers with heart or pulmonary disease . . . (Ex. 3-1123, p. 23).

H.K. Thompson, Corporate Industrial Hygiene Manager of Caterpillar, Inc.
(Ex. 3-349), stated:

> PELs or TLVs are not set to protect individuals with chronic heart disease. In our
> industry we transfer people with disabilities to jobs where the risk for them is minimal
> (Ex. 3-349, p. 3).

In response to these commenters, OSHA quotes the ACGIH (1986/Ex. 1-3):

> Each molecule of CO combining with hemoglobin reduces the oxygen carrying capacity
> of the blood and exerts a finite stress on man. Thus, it may be reasoned that there is
> no dose of CO that is not without an effect on the body. Whether that effect is physio-
> logic or harmful depends upon the dose of CO and the state of health of the exposed
> individual. The body compensates for this hypoxic stress by increasing cardiac output
> and blood flow to specific organs, such as the brain or the heart. When this ability to
> compensate is overpowered or is limited by disease, tissue injury results [emphasis
> added]. Exposure to CO sufficient to produce COHb saturations in the 3-5% range

(continues)

**EXHIBIT 5–3   OCCUPATIONAL SAFETY AND HEALTH ADMINISTRATION
REPORT ON CARBON MONOXIDE** *(continued)*

impairs cardiovascular function in patients with cardiovascular disease and in normal
subjects . . . . The primary effect of exposure to low concentrations of CO on workmen
results from the hypoxic stress secondary to the reduction in the oxygen-carrying
capacity of blood . . . . workmen with significant disease, both detected and undetected,
may not be able to compensate adequately and are at risk of serious injury. For such
workers, a TLV of 25 ppm . . . might be necessary. Even such a concentration might be
detrimental to the health of some workers who might have far advanced cardiovascu-
lar disease . . . . It would appear to the Committee that the timeweighted TLV of 50
ppm for carbon monoxide might also be too high under conditions of heavy labor, high
temperatures, or at high elevations (ACGIH 1986/Ex. 1-3, p. 106).

Thus, the ACGIH also regards a lower limit for CO as necessary to protect workers
with cardiovascular or pulmonary disease or those working under stressful conditions.

NIOSH (Ex. 150, Comments on Carbon Monoxide) submitted a substantial amount
of posthearing evidence demonstrating the significant risk associated with CO exposure,
particularly with respect to coronary heart disease. The following studies are particularly
relevant to this issue. Atkins and Baker (1985, as cited in NIOSH/Ex. 150) report the case
of two workers with preexisting coronary artery disease who died after exposure to CO
at work. A study of firefighters in Los Angeles (Barnard and Weber 1979, as cited in
NIOSH/Ex. 150) suggests that CO exposure during firefighting may be responsible for the
high incidence of heart disease in firefighters; peak exposures during fire fighting were as
high as 3000 ppm CO, with 40 percent of peak values in the 100- to 500-ppm CO range.
A prevalence study by Hernberg et al. (1976, as cited in NIOSH/ Ex. 150) reports a clear
dose-response relationship between CO exposure and angina pectoris in foundry workers. Stern and co-workers (1981, as cited in NIOSH/Ex. 150) suggest that the slight overall excess of deaths in motor vehicle examiners caused by cardiovascular disease is
attributable to chronic exposure to low levels of CO (10 to 24 ppm as an 8-hour TWA).
The AFL-CIO's posthearing comment (Ex. 194) agrees that the comments submitted by
NIOSH are persuasive evidence of the need to reduce the 8-hour TWA for CO.

NIOSH also submitted recent data on carbon monoxide's reproductive effects and
on its neurotoxic/behavioral effects. Based on a review of all of these studies, NIOSH
concludes that "[t]he new data suggest a reevaluation of the REL and strongly support
the inference that there is a significant risk of material impairment to health at the . . .
[former] 50-ppm PEL which will be reduced by the proposed 35-ppm PEL" (Ex. 150,
Comments on Carbon Monoxide).

OSHA notes that cardiovascular disease (detected or undetected) and pulmonary
impairment are widespread in the general population in this country, and that workers

(continues)

EXHIBIT 5–3   OCCUPATIONAL SAFETY AND HEALTH ADMINISTRATION
REPORT ON CARBON MONOXIDE *(continued)*

constitute a significant part of this general population. In addition, workers regularly encounter complex and stressful situations at work, including heat stress, jobs demanding heavy exertion, and tasks requiring both judgment and motor coordination.

The AISI (Ex. 129) submitted an article (Redmond, Emes, Mazumdar et al. 1977, "Mortality of Steelworkers Employed in Hot Jobs") to OSHA which, in the opinion of the AISI, demonstrates that steelworkers who are exposed to high heat (and ostensibly also to CO) do not have coronary heart disease. Based on this article, the AISI asks that the steel industry be exempted from the revised PEL for CO. OSHA finds the article submitted by the AISI unconvincing on the point at issue; the article is not primarily concerned with CO exposures but with heat stress and, further, does not include a large enough sample to demonstrate the absence of an effect. Moreover, OSHA is establishing limits that will apply to all of general industry; the Agency does not customarily set standards based on the particular conditions prevailing in a specific operation or industry.

However, some evidence has been submitted by the AISI (Ex. 129) to the effect that the ceiling limit cannot regularly be achieved with engineering and work practice controls in specific operations in SIC 33. These operations are: blast furnace operations, vessel blowing at basic oxygen furnaces, and sinter plant operations. There is no evidence to the contrary in the record. For these operations, OSHA will therefore permit more flexibility in the use of respirators. The burden of proof will not be on employers to demonstrate that compliance with the ceiling by means of engineering and work practice controls is infeasible in any compliance action involving these operations in SIC 33.

There may be a few other operations that fall into this same category; however, the record is unclear on this point. Based on an appropriate showing pursuant to the OSH Act, OSHA will favorably consider requests for variances for specific operations in SIC 33 involving methods of compliance for the ceiling limit. Of course, all requests for variances or any other matters will be considered based on their merits.

OSHA thus finds that the reduced 8-hour TWA of 35 ppm for carbon monoxide is needed to reduce the significant risk of serious injury that has repeatedly been demonstrated to result from overexposure to CO in a host of occupational environments. The Agency concludes that a ceiling of 200 ppm is necessary to ensure that peak CO exposures do not reach levels demonstrated to be hazardous and that overall full-shift exposures remain under good control. In the absence of a ceiling, concentrations approaching the Immediately-Dangerous-to-Life-or-Health (IDLH) level of 1500 ppm could occur.

(continues)

EXHIBIT 5–3   OCCUPATIONAL SAFETY AND HEALTH ADMINISTRATION REPORT ON CARBON MONOXIDE *(continued)*

In the final rule, OSHA is establishing an 8-hour TWA of 35 ppm and a ceiling of 200 ppm as the PELs for carbon monoxide to ensure that employee COHb levels are maintained at or below 5 percent, in order to protect those workers at greater risk because of cardiovascular or pulmonary impairment. In addition, these revised limits will protect healthy workers who must work in environments involving exertion, heat stress, or other strenuous conditions. The Agency has determined that these limits will substantially reduce the significant occupational risk associated with both chronic and peak CO exposures in the workplace. OSHA concludes that the hypoxic stress associated with overexposures to carbon monoxide clearly constitutes a material impairment of health and functional capacity.

While reports of this type may not be specifically related to the facts of your case, it is important that you and your attorney educate yourselves about the prevalence and severity of the issue. Attorneys will use this type of background information to make decisions about such concerns as whether the case should be settled early on, whether the client can get a fair trial in the venue where the complaint was filed, and whether a jury would be predisposed against the client.

EXHIBIT 5-4   RESOURCES AVAILABLE ON U.S. DEPARTMENT OF THE INTERIOR WEB SITE

Boat-Related CO Poisonings on U.S. Waters, National Case Listing, (Adobe .pdf format) Updated October 2003.

U.S. Congress, Subcommittee on Coast Guard and Maritime Transportation, Testimony. Hearings on Recreational Boating Safety focused on carbon monoxide poisonings on houseboats, May 15, 2001.

January 2004 – NIOSH Report (EPHB 171-34a), An Evaluation of Factors that Might Influence Exhaust Stack Performance to Prevent Carbon Monoxide Poisonings from Houseboat Generator Exhaust.

American Society of Safety Engineers, November 2003, Journal article titled "Carbon Monoxide and Houseboats: An evaluation of a stack exhaust system to reduce poisonings from generator exhaust."

April 2003 – NIOSH Report (EPHB 171-31a), Carbon Monoxide Emissions and Exposures on 16 Recreational Boats Under Various Operating Conditions at Lake Norman, NC.

This is not an exhaustive list of every type of pre-litigation report that may be available, but it gives you an idea of where to start looking. It is important for the paralegal to be alert to potential leads. For instance, one report may include in its appendix a list of other reports used as references, any of which may need to be gathered and reviewed for relevant information. An MRI report for a patient may mention that the current images are being compared to an MRI performed years before, which you may not have known existed. The more information you can gather, the better. Of course, you must always be cognizant of the litigation budget that has been set for the case. Always obtain the attorney's permission before pursuing additional lines of investigation.

As each report is obtained, your supervising attorney may ask you to review it and prepare a summary of the contents and their relevance to your case. The reports should be safely stored and indexed for later retrieval.

EXPERT WITNESSES AND POST-LITIGATION REPORTS

The complexity of modern lawsuits sometimes makes it difficult for a judge and jury to understand and interpret facts. How can a group of lay people make a decision about liability or guilt when faced with such daunting issues as whether a hotel balcony that collapsed had been properly constructed? Whether the partial fingerprint on a murder weapon really belongs to the defendant? What a doctor's standard of care is when operating on a patient? Parties to a lawsuit (or the prosecutor or defense counsel in a criminal case) often retain expert witnesses to assist them in a variety of ways.

Unlike a regular or lay witness, an expert witness possesses special knowledge or experience on a particular subject. Lay witnesses are normally allowed to testify only about the facts of a case, that is, what they observed, what actions they took. The expert witness is allowed to testify at trial not only about facts, but also about the professional conclusions he or she draws from these facts.

Expert witnesses perform many functions during the life of the case. They can be called upon to act as consultants at the outset of a case to give advice as to the party's culpability and make recommendations for settlement. Expert witnesses can also advise the attorney on types of discovery to pursue and specific questions to ask during depositions to elicit the information necessary to prove the case. They are often asked to review documents and reports gathered by the paralegal and give opinions about strengths and weaknesses in the client's case.

Often the expert witness will perform independent research on issues and testing on persons or objects central to the lawsuit and prepare expert opinions and reports. It is this latter function that we will focus on for this chapter.

LOCATING AND SELECTING EXPERT WITNESSES

The more complicated or technical the case, the more likely an expert will be needed to provide opinions to the judge and jury. The specialized knowledge of an expert can assist the judge and jury in understanding the evidence and in making sense of the facts in a case. Basically an expert witness is someone who has knowledge of a particular subject beyond what the average person knows, and who obtained that knowledge through either education, training, skill, or experience. The expert then uses that advanced knowledge to give **opinion evidence** about facts, causation, damages, or whatever area the expert is asked to testify about. As stated above, ordinary or lay witnesses, on the other hand, are not allowed to give their opinions, only to state the facts.

Locating potential experts is a task that is often assigned to the paralegal on the case. The Federal Rules of Evidence, Rules 701–706 (see Appendix A) discuss the use of and rules relating to expert witness testimony.

When one first thinks of an expert witness, such as a doctor or engineer, one immediately thinks of a university-trained individual with an abundance of letters after his or her name. While that is often the case, sometimes lawsuits involve issues for which no formal degree can be obtained. For example, in our Case Scenario No. 3, there is probably no university that gives a degree in houseboat rental operations. Where would you look for an expert in that field?

Although your client may be an expert on his or her business, or has an employee with credentials who could testify, it may be necessary to find an independent person to evaluate the case and render an opinion. Someone who is an actual party to the lawsuit may be too emotionally involved to be objective, and even if he can be objective, the jury may not be swayed by his opinion because they feel he might be biased. There are many ways to locate experts in a particular field.

The best way to find a tried and true expert witness is by word of mouth. The expert will be someone who has experience and who already has done a good job for the person making the recommendation to you. You may be able to obtain a referral from fellow paralegals in the community or your attorney may have attorney peers she can call.

All of the studies and pre-litigation reports you have been accumulating will act as another source for potential expert witnesses. Often the studies and reports will contain bibliographies, listings of papers upon which the author of the report relied in his research. If you find a particular study that is right on point to your case issues, the author may be a candidate as an expert.

There are nationwide services that report on trial outcomes and jury verdicts. They often list the names of the experts who testified on a particular topic during the trial. This is not only a good way to get a lead on a possible expert, but you can also check the expert's track record by seeing how many times she was on the winning or losing side.

■ **OPINION EVIDENCE**
Evidence of what a witness thinks, believes, or concludes about facts, rather than what the witness saw, heard, etc. Opinion evidence is usually accepted only from an expert witness.

TIP

Attorneys often wait until the middle or end of a case, when they have started trial preparation, to locate and hire an expert witness. This is often a mistake, as an expert can be extremely useful in evaluating the value of the case and the exposure to the client, and giving guidance during the early discovery phase.

University professors can make excellent experts because they can translate their teaching skills from the classroom to the courtroom. They often publish articles in their areas of expertise as required by university policy. Telephoning the department of your local university for the field of study in which you are interested may turn up some names of potential experts.

Another source of potential experts is an expert referral service. Companies such as TASA (Technical Advisory Service for Attorneys) register thousands of experts in all types of fields and will match you with one that you need for a fee. Some expert witnesses will advertise in legal periodicals for attorneys that are published by bar associations or other law-oriented organizations. These periodicals often contain articles authored by experts on areas of interest to attorneys. The periodical may be able to put you in contact with an author who has expertise in an area in which you are interested.

When your topic of interest is not mainstream, such as the rental of houseboats by Lake Vista Vacation Rentals in Case Scenario No. 3, you may have to approach a respected business owner who has a lot of experience in that field to be your expert.

Once you have compiled a list of potential experts for your attorney, the attorney will probably want to interview them before selecting one who will be brought onto the legal team. When choosing an expert witness, the attorney will be looking at several criteria including the expert's education and credentials; what experience the expert has with lawsuits, including the number of times the expert has been deposed or testified in the courtroom; whether the expert has a preference for plaintiff or defense cases; and the expert's demeanor and appearance. The latter measures are nearly as important as an expert's background. A person may be the most educated individual on a particular topic, but if he cannot explain the issues in layman's terms that will be understood by a jury, or if he comes across as arrogant and dismissive, thereby alienating the jury, he will be of no use whatsoever.

WORKING WITH THE EXPERT WITNESS

Once an expert witness has been selected, it often falls upon the paralegal to be a liaison to the expert and the conduit of information back and forth between the expert and the attorney. You may be asked to supply documents and reports that have already been gathered in the case to the expert and answer questions about facts that come up during the expert's review of the case.

One thing is important to keep in mind during this process. Whatever you tell the expert or give to the expert may be discoverable by the opposing party. That means no document that could fall under the **attorney-client privilege** or the **attorney work-product doctrine** should be turned over to an expert witness without your supervising attorney's approval. Further, you should never reveal confidential client matters or case strategy to the expert without attorney approval. When the expert witness is eventually deposed, you can rest assured she will be asked to provide copies of all documents received from your office and she will be asked about all communications with anyone at your office.

■ **ATTORNEY-CLIENT PRIVILEGE**

The right of a client, and the duty of that client's lawyer, to keep confidential the contents of almost all communication between them.

■ **ATTORNEY WORK-PRODUCT DOCTRINE**

An attorney's right to withhold from discovery all documents or things gathered and prepared in preparation for or during the course of litigation, including any notes or memos that reflect the attorney's impressions or conclusions about the lawsuit.

If the expert will be performing any inspection or testing of materials or products, it will be the paralegal's job to make the necessary arrangements. You need to obtain the materials or access to them, arrange the date, time, and place for the testing or inspection, and give the proper notices (see Chapter 8 for more information and forms for inspecting physical evidence). If the testing involves what is known as **destructive testing**, the necessary authorization must be given by the owner of the product or else a court order must be obtained. Destructive testing involves dismantling or demolishing either the physical evidence itself or surrounding materials in order to reach the evidence. Examples of destructive testing include opening up the wall of a home to inspect potentially faulty wiring, taking apart the steering mechanism of a vehicle to show how an accident occurred, or performing chemical testing on children's pajamas to determine whether factory-applied fire retardant was effective.

Often medical experts may want to examine the plaintiff to determine the validity and extent of the injuries complained of, whether they will be acute or chronic, and the extent to which remedial measures could be taken.

An important new tool used by accident reconstruction experts is the data that is downloaded from a vehicle's Event Data Recorder (EDR). In the mid-1990s, the National Highway Traffic Safety Administration asked that all automobile manufacturers gather retrievable data on crashes where air bags were deployed. Today, virtually every new vehicle sold in the United States is equipped with crash data recording capabilities, although only certain manufacturers make EDR data generally available to the public. The EDR monitors various operational aspects of the vehicle, such as engine speed, vehicle speed, throttle position, brake switch, and driver seat belt circuit. These data are recorded in one-second intervals and stored for five seconds. When a crash occurs that is sufficient to cause air bag deployment, the data from the five-second interval preceding the crash is locked into memory and can be retrieved by an accident reconstruction expert who has the proper training and equipment. The data can be used as a good scientific starting point for analyzing a collision and evaluating the injury potential of a crash.

There are many types of inspection or testing that expert witnesses in our Case Scenario No. 3 may perform. For example, plaintiffs may have a boating expert who wants to examine the layout of the cabins in the Foxfire houseboat and measure the proximity of Daniel's cabin to the engine exhaust port. Plaintiffs may also have an engineering expert who wants to take apart the engine to see if it was operating properly (this would be an example of destructive testing). On the defense side of the case, Foxfire Boat Company may wish to retain a neuropsychologist to examine Daniel and test his cognitive functions to determine the extent of his impairment.

It will be up to the attorney to decide whether the expert will be asked to provide a written report of her findings. There are various strategies involved in making this decision. Keep in mind that any paperwork generated or gathered by the expert may be discoverable by the opposing party, including not only formal reports but written correspondence or memos regarding her findings, photographs, and research materials reviewed and considered. If the expert's research ultimately produces an opinion that is critical of your client, the attorney may not want that put on paper, but instead to be given as an oral report by the expert. If the expert prepares a written

■ **DESTRUCTIVE TESTING**

Examination and testing, usually by an expert witness, of physical evidence in a case that will result in the permanent or temporary destruction of that evidence. Examples of temporary destructive testing are disassembling a motor or knocking out the wall of a house to look for mold infestation. Permanent destructive testing includes the analysis of blood samples or chemical testing of defective fire retardant.

report, it must be carefully preserved in the case file for later production and use at trial. See Exhibit 5–5 for examples of reports that might be generated in the Johnson v. Foxfire case.

Finally, the paralegal is often asked to work with the expert in scheduling his or her deposition and in clearing dates on the expert's calendar for trial. The paralegal should immediately inform the expert witnesses when a case has settled or a trial is continued so that they can open up their calendars for other matters.

THE OPPOSING PARTIES' EXPERTS

The paralegal's work with experts extends beyond interacting with the client's retained experts. The opposing party will also be hiring and disclosing expert witnesses, who will need to be deposed. A valuable task that the paralegal can perform is background research on the opposition's designated expert witnesses. All sorts of damaging information can be learned about them. Some experts have claimed they graduated from a university that never heard of them. Others have written papers in the past that arrived at conclusions diametrically opposed to the opinions they are now attempting to put forth in your case. All sorts of useful information can be unearthed about an opposing party's expert by doing a little investigation in the case files published by nationwide jury verdict publications, by checking items in the expert's resume, or performing an Internet search using a search engine such as Google.

CONCLUSION

The hunt for pre-litigation reports is a typical type of nonlegal research in which paralegals can be actively involved and is a critical part of the discovery process. With knowledge of subpoena preparation and good Internet research skills, a paralegal can locate a wealth of reports and evidence relevant and critical to the case. Helping to locate, select, and interface with expert witnesses is both interesting and informative work for a paralegal.

EXHIBIT 5–5   ALLEGATIONS AND POSSIBLE REPORTS FOR CASE SCENARIO NO. 3

FOR PLAINTIFF

1. Daniel Johnson suffered carbon monoxide exposure while aboard a houseboat manufactured by Foxfire Boat Co.	Incident report (pre-litigation) Hospital and ambulance reports (pre-litigation)

(continues)

**EXHIBIT 5–5   ALLEGATIONS AND POSSIBLE REPORTS FOR CASE
SCENARIO NO. 3** *(continued)*

2. Daniel has suffered permanent brain damage from the carbon monoxide exposure.	Cognitive and brain function test reports (pre- and post-litigation) Government reports re:results from exposure to carbon monoxide (pre-litigation)
3. The houseboat engine installed in the subject houseboat was defective.	Mechanical engineering expert reports (post-litigation)
4. The design of the houseboat was defective in that it allowed carbon monoxide to be drawn into open portholes.	Design engineering expert reports (post- litigation)
5. Daniel will be unable to be gainfully employed or provide for himself in the future.	Medical expert reports (post-litigation) Economics expert reports (post-litigation)

FOR DEFENDANT FOXFIRE BOAT COMPANY

1. Daniel was a poor student who had exhibited cognitive and intellectual impairment at an early age.	School test reports (pre-litigation) Medical expert reports (post-litigation)
2. The engine installed on the houseboat was functioning properly.	Engineering and maintenance reports (pre- and post-litigation)
3. Defendant Lake Vista Vacation Rentals was negligent in its policies about instructing boat renters in the proper operation of the houseboats and the potential dangers of carbon monoxide poisoning.	Opinion reached by person experienced in vessel rental operations.

KEY TERMS

attorney-client privilege

attorney work-product doctrine

destructive testing

expert witness

incident report

opinion evidence

ordinary course of business

pre-litigation report

post-litigation report

REVIEW QUESTIONS

1. Explain the difference between pre- and post-litigation reports.
2. What type of information might be found in an incident report?
3. What types of legal documents would be required to request copies of an injured party's records from the hospital?

4. What is an expert witness and what functions does he or she serve?

5. Describe three ways to locate a potential expert witness.

6. What are some of the criteria used in choosing an expert witness?

7. Why must you be careful about what information is shared with an expert witness?

8. What is destructive testing?

■ APPLYING WHAT YOU HAVE LEARNED

1. In the Johnson v. Foxfire case your client, Foxfire Boat Company, wants to have Daniel Johnson examined by a child psychologist, and your attorney has passed this assignment on to you. Locate the name of a child psychologist who could serve as an expert witness in your case. Describe how you located him or her.

2. Develop a discovery plan for defendant in the Johnson v. Foxfire case. What documents would you like to see, who would you want to depose, and what else would you like to do?

3. Your contact at Foxfire Boat Company informs you that the company has reports prepared by its engineers at the time the houseboat was being designed. The reports say that there was a risk of carbon monoxide exposure in the aft cabins under certain conditions. What should you do with this information? Should you provide copies of the reports to the expert witness? Why or why not?

4. Compare the evidentiary rules of your own state with Rules 701–706 of the Federal Rules of Evidence relating to expert witness testimony. Are they similar or different? Describe the differences, if any.

ILLUSTRATIVE CASE

Read the following case, excerpted from the U.S. Supreme Court's opinion, and answer the following questions:

1. The expert witness for Western Air Lines came to a different conclusion than the expert witness for Captain Criswell and his coplaintiffs. Describe the differences in their opinions. Which expert did the jury believe?

2. The Court makes a strong statement about allowing the trier of fact (the jury) to weigh the validity of expert opinion testimony rather than simply deferring to the expert. Why is this important?

EXCERPT FROM WESTERN AIR LINES, INC. V. CRISWELL, ET AL.

472 U.S. 400 (1985)

CERTIORARI TO THE UNITED STATES COURT OF APPEALS FOR THE NINTH CIRCUIT, CASE NO. 83-1545

STEVENS, J., DELIVERED THE OPINION OF THE COURT.

The petitioner Western Air Lines, Inc., requires that its flight engineers retire at age 60. Although the Age Discrimination in Employment Act of 1967 (ADEA) generally prohibits mandatory retirement before age 70, the Act provides an exception "where age is a bona fide occupational qualification [BFOQ] reasonably necessary to the normal operation of the

(continues)

ILLUSTRATIVE CASE (continued)

particular business." A jury concluded that Western's mandatory retirement rule did not qualify as a BFOQ even though it purportedly was adopted for safety reasons. The question here is whether the jury was properly instructed on the elements of the BFOQ defense.

In its commercial airline operations Western operates a variety of aircraft, including the Boeing 727 and the McDonnell-Douglas DC-10. These aircraft require three crew members in the cockpit: a captain, a first officer, and a flight engineer. "The 'captain' is the pilot and controls the aircraft. He is responsible for all phases of its operation. The 'first officer' is the copilot and assists the caption. The 'flight engineer' usually monitors a side-facing instrument panel. He does not operate the flight controls unless the captain and the first officer become incapacitated." (*Trans World Airlines, Inc. v. Thurston*, 469 U.S. 111, 114).

A regulation of the Federal Aviation Administration (FAA) prohibits any person from serving as a pilot or first officer on a commercial flight "if that person has reached his 60th birthday." (14 CFR 121.383(c) (1986)) The FAA has justified the retention of mandatory retirement for pilots on the theory that "incapacitating medical events" and "adverse psychological, emotional and physical changes" occur as a consequence of aging. "The inability to detect or predict with precision an individual's risk of sudden or subtle incapacitation, in the face of known age-related risks, counsels against relaxation of the rule."

At the same time, the FAA has refused to establish a mandatory retirement age for flight engineers. "While a flight engineer has important duties which contribute to the safe operation of the airplane, he or she may not assume the responsibilities of the pilot in command." Moreover, available statistics establish that flight engineers have rarely been a contributing cause or factor in commercial aircraft "accidents" or "incidents."

In 1978 respondents Criswell and Starley were captains operating DC-10s for Western. Both men celebrated their 60th birthdays in July 1978. Under the collective-bargaining agreement in effect between Western and the union, cockpit crew members could obtain open positions by bidding in order of seniority. In order to avoid mandatory retirement under the FAA's under-age-60 rule for pilots, Criswell and Starley applied for reassignment as flight engineers. Western denied both requests, ostensibly on the ground that both employees were members of the company's retirement plan which required all crew members to retire at age 60. For the same reason, respondent Ron, a career flight engineer, was also retired in 1978 after his 60th birthday . . . .

Criswell, Starley and Ron brought this action against Western, contending that the under-age-60 qualification for the position of flight engineer violated the ADEA. In the District Court, Western defended, in part, on the theory that the age-60 rule is a BFOQ "reasonably necessary" to the safe operation of the airline. All parties submitted evidence concerning the nature of the flight engineer's tasks, the physiological and psychological traits required to perform them, and the availability of those traits among persons over age 60.

As the District Court summarized, the evidence at trial established that the flight engineer's "normal duties are less critical to the safety of flight than those of a pilot." The flight engineer, however, does have critical functions in emergency situations and, of course, might cause considerable disruption in the event of his own medical emergency.

The actual capabilities of persons over age 60, and the ability to detect disease or a precipitous decline in their faculties, were the subject of conflicting medical testimony. Western's expert witness, a former FAA Deputy Federal Air Surgeon, was especially concerned about the possibility of a "cardiovascular event" such as a heart attack. He testified

(continues)

ILLUSTRATIVE CASE *(continued)*

that "with advancing age the likelihood of onset of disease increases and that in persons over age 60 it could not be predicted whether and when such diseases would occur."

The plaintiffs' experts on the other hand, testified that physiological deterioration is caused by disease, not aging, and "it was feasible to determine on the basis of individual medical examinations whether flight deck crew members, including those over age 60, were physically qualified to continue. These conclusions were corroborated by the nonmedical evidence."

"The record also reveals that both the FAA and the airlines have been able to deal with the health problems of pilots on an individualized basis. Pilots who have been grounded because of alcoholism or cardiovascular disease have been recertified by the FAA and allowed to resume flying. Pilots who were unable to pass the necessary examination to maintain their FAA first class medical certificates, but who continued to qualify for second class medical certificates were allowed to 'down-grade' from pilot to [flight engineer]. There is nothing in the record to indicate that these flight deck crew members are physically better able to perform their duties than flight engineers over age 60 who have not experienced such events or that they are less likely to become incapacitated." . . .

The jury was instructed that the "BFOQ defense is available only if it is reasonably necessary to the normal operation or essence of the defendant's business." The jury was informed that "the essence of Western's business is the safe transportation of their passengers." The jury was also instructed:

"One method by which defendant Western may establish a BFOQ in this case is to prove:

(1) That in 1978, when these plaintiffs were retired, it was highly impractical for Western to deal with each second officer over age 60 on an individualized basis to determine his particular ability to perform his job safely; and

(2) That some second officers over age 60 possess traits of physiological, psychological or other nature which preclude safe and efficient job performance that cannot be ascertained by means other than knowing their age.

"In evaluating the practicability to defendant Western of dealing with second officers over age 60 on an individualized basis, with respect to the medical testimony, you should consider the state of the medical art as it existed in July 1978."

The jury rendered a verdict for plaintiffs, and awarded damages. After the trial, the District Court granted equitable relief, explaining in a written opinion why it found no merit in Western's BFOQ defense to the mandatory retirement rule.

On appeal, Western made various arguments attacking the verdict and judgment below, but the Court of Appeals affirmed in all respects. In particular, the Court of Appeals rejected Western's contentions that the instruction of the BFOQ defense was insufficiently deferential to the airline's legitimate concern for the safety of its passengers. We granted certiorari to consider the merits of this question . . . .

Age as a Proxy for Job Qualifications

Western contended below that the ADEA only requires that the employer establish "a rational basis in fact" for believing that identification of those persons lacking suitable qualifications cannot occur on an individualized basis. This "rational basis in fact" standard would have been tantamount to an instruction to return a verdict in the defendant's favor. Because that standard conveys a meaning that is significantly different from that conveyed by the statutory phrase "reasonably necessary," it was correctly rejected by the trial court.

(continues)

ILLUSTRATIVE CASE *(continued)*

Western argues that a "rational basis" standard should be adopted because medical disputes can never be proved "to a certainty" and because juries should not be permitted "to resolve bona fide conflicts among medical experts respecting the adequacy of individualized testing." The jury, however, need not be convinced beyond all doubt that medical testing is impossible, but only that the proposition is true "on a preponderance of the evidence." Moreover, Western's attack on the wisdom of assigning the resolution of complex questions to 12 laypersons is inconsistent with the structure of the ADEA. Congress expressly decided that problems involving age discrimination in employment should be resolved on a "case-by-case" basis by proof to a jury.

The "rational basis" standard is also inconsistent with the preference for individual evaluation expressed in the language and legislative history of the ADEA. Under the Act, employers are to evaluate employees between the ages of 40 and 70 on their merits, not their age. In the BFOQ defense, Congress provided a limited exception to this general principle, but required that employers validate any discrimination as "reasonably necessary to the normal operation of the particular business." It might well be "rational" to require mandatory retirement at any age less than 70, but that result would not comply with Congress' direction that employers must justify the rationale for the age chosen. Unless an employer can establish a substantial basis for believing that all or nearly all employees above an age lack the qualifications required for the position, the age selected for mandatory retirement less than 70 must be an age at which it is highly impractical for the employer to insure by individual testing that its employees will have the necessary qualifications for the job.

Western argues that its lenient standard is necessary because "where qualified experts disagree as to whether persons over a certain age can be dealt with on an individual basis, an employer must be allowed to resolve that controversy in a conservative manner." This argument incorrectly assumes that all expert opinion is entitled to equal weight, and virtually ignores the function of the trier of fact in evaluating conflicting testimony. In this case, the jury may well have attached little weight to the testimony of Western's expert witness. A rule that would require the jury to defer to the judgment of any expert witness testifying for the employer, no matter how unpersuasive, would allow some employers to give free reign to the stereotype of older workers that Congress decried in the legislative history of the ADEA.

When an employee covered by the Act is able to point to reputable businesses in the same industry that choose to eschew reliance on mandatory retirement earlier than age 70, when the employer itself relies on individualized testing in similar circumstances, and when the administrative agency with primary responsibility for maintaining airline safety has determined that individualized testing is not impractical for the relevant position, the employer's attempt to justify its decision on the basis of the contrary opinion of experts – solicited for the purposes of litigation – is hardly convincing on any objective standard short of complete deference. Even in cases involving public safety, the ADEA plainly does not permit the trier of fact to give complete deference to the employer's decision.

The judgment of the court of Appeals is affirmed.

For additional resources, visit our Web site at www.westlegalstudies.com

6

Video and Audio Recordings

OBJECTIVES _____

After studying this chapter you should be able to:

❏ know the Federal Rules of Evidence relating to recordings.

❏ understand the difference between pre-litigation videos and demonstration videos.

❏ describe the different types of pre-litigation videos.

❏ describe the different types of demonstrative videos and know how to obtain them.

❏ know what types of audiotaped evidence are available.

INTRODUCTION

Everyone from baby boomers on (and therefore most of today's jury pool) was essentially raised on television. Trial experts agree that the easiest way to reach jurors and deliver your client's message in an easily understandable fashion is by the use of video images. (Note: the term video is a blanket term that includes videotape as well as digitally recorded images.) The old adage "a picture is worth a thousand words" applies dramatically in the legal profession, especially during jury trials. Opportunities abound for paralegals to obtain videotaped evidence in anticipation of trial. Although used much less frequently in the civil arena, audiotapes can also be a resource available to litigants. Audiotapes are sometimes used in criminal matters when wiretaps have been performed on suspects.

RULES RELATING TO RECORDINGS

Rule 901(a) of the Federal Rules of Evidence states: "The requirement of authentication or identification as a condition precedent to admissibility is satisfied by evidence sufficient to support a finding that the matter in question is what its proponent claims." In their commentary on Rule 901 in the United States Code Service, Lawyers Edition (Federal Rules of Evidence, 1998), Stephen A. Saltzburg, Daniel J. Capra, and Michael M. Martin interpret the liberal standard of Rule 901 as it relates to tape recordings. They cite *United States v. Branch*, 970 F.2d 1368 (4th Cir. 1992) as an example of the approach taken toward tape recordings in most federal courts. "The Court held that the proponent was generally required to show that:

(1) the recording device was capable of recording the conversation;

(2) the operator was competent to operate the machine;

(3) the recording is a correct rendition of the occurrence;

(4) no changes, additions or deletions have been made;

(5) the recording has been preserved in a manner shown to the Court;

(6) the speakers are identified; and

(7) there was no impermissible inducement."

Courts are very concerned about the risks of alteration of tape recordings and the impact of such recordings on the jury. In *United States v. Faurote*, 749 F.2d 40 (7th Cir. 1984), the court states, "It is a well-settled principle of law that the party attempting to admit a tape recording into evidence must prove, by clear and convincing evidence, that the tape is a true, accurate and authentic recording. . . ."

TYPES OF VIDEOTAPED EVIDENCE

Video recordings that can be used as evidence in a lawsuit fall into two categories, much like pre- and post-litigation reports (see Chapter 5). Some recordings were made before a lawsuit was ever anticipated, such as television newscasts, surveillance videos from businesses, and "how-to" videos relating to specific products. These will be called **pre-litigation videos**. Others are made after the lawsuit is filed and for the purpose of creating demonstrative evidence specifically to show a judge or jury during a trial or for settlement purposes. Types of video recordings that fall into this category are videotaped depositions (discussed in Chapter 4), sub-rosa videos, day-in-the-life videos, and demonstrations or experiments upon or operation of tangible evidence. We will call these **demonstrative videos**. Each of these types of video evidence, and how to obtain and preserve it, will be discussed in detail.

■ **PRE-LITIGATION VIDEO**
Video recordings made before a lawsuit was ever anticipated, such as television newscasts, surveillance videos from businesses, and "how-to" videos relating to specific products.

■ **DEMONSTRATIVE VIDEO**
Video made for the purpose of creating demonstrative evidence, specifically to show a judge or jury during a trial or for settlement purposes. Types of video recordings that fall into this category are videotaped depositions, sub-rosa videos, and day-in-the-life videos.

PRE-LITIGATION VIDEOS

Pre-litigation videotaped evidence requires more investigative effort on the part of the paralegal. Since you were not involved in the creation of pre-litigation videos, some sleuthing is required to determine if any, in fact, exist, and whether they might be helpful to your case.

Newscasts

Television stations employ roving reporters and camera people who cover all types of newsworthy events. These events range from press conferences to car accidents, from live coverage of sporting events to people attending or speaking at public hearings. The footage shot by the cameraperson is edited down to a few seconds of video shown in conjunction with a newscaster's spoken coverage of the event. The piece actually shown during the newscast and the unused portion of the videotape can sometimes be subpoenaed by a party for use during a lawsuit. Why or when would this be beneficial to a case?

Suppose you are defending a woman being charged with burglary. The police report estimates the crime was committed sometime between 6:00 p.m. and 7:00 p.m. on a Tuesday night. Your client insists she was attending a school board meeting during that time period. The local television station had camera people present who videotaped the crowd, and your client was easily visible in the shots, thereby establishing an alibi (proof of your client's presence somewhere other than the crime scene at the relevant time).

Another example of the use of newscast videos would occur when your firm is representing a defendant in a personal injury lawsuit involving an automobile accident. The plaintiff insists she was terribly injured and her vehicle was demolished. It was turned over to a scrap yard and is no longer available for inspection. You learn that news camera people had come to the accident scene and videotaped it for the evening news. The footage shows both vehicles, and plaintiff's vehicle was only slightly damaged.

Suppose your firm's client is being prosecuted for the murder of a high-profile, local businesswoman. Your attorney wants to bring a change of venue motion because all the pretrial publicity will taint the jury pool. The attorney will be asking the court to move the case to another county where the circumstances are less well known. To support that motion, and prove to the court the extent of the pretrial publicity, you may be asked to round up all television and newspaper coverage of the murder itself and the arrest and prosecution of the client.

To obtain videotapes of newscasts or other footage during discovery, a deposition subpoena duces tecum directed to the television station is normally used, much the same way as documents are requested from third parties (see Chapter 2). If the requested materials are still available, the television station will charge a fee to duplicate the video, and copies must be made for all parties who request them. It is important to move quickly on this, as some television stations destroy old video soon after the newscast.

Surveillance Videos

Many gas stations, banks, and convenience stores have security cameras mounted in strategic places around the building and surrounding public areas. Besides being potential evidence for criminal activities, such as robberies, the images from security cameras may also be useful in civil cases. For example, your firm represents a woman who was injured when she stopped to purchase gasoline for her vehicle. She had walked from the pump island to the cashier to pay for the gas and was walking back to her vehicle when she was struck by another vehicle pulling up to the island. Your client and the driver of the vehicle are disputing the severity of the impact. Fortunately for you, the whole scene was caught on the gas station's surveillance video camera, which shows your client being knocked to the ground by the defendant's vehicle.

As with television news footage, the videos from a surveillance camera can be obtained from the owner of the property or camera via the subpoena process.

Home Videos

Sometimes in personal injury or wrongful death cases the attorney representing the plaintiff will show the jury home videos of the injured person or decedent to garner sympathy. The paralegal will work with plaintiff or plaintiff's family to obtain and view the videos and help the attorney decide what portion, if any, would be suitable evidence to show during the trial.

Another type of common home video that is useful in litigation is videotape of damage to a home after a flood or earthquake.

Product Videos

Some product manufacturers create videos about how to properly or safely use their products. For example, take a look again at Case Scenario No. 3 in Chapter 5, the Johnson v. Foxfire Boat Company litigation. Suppose Foxfire Boat Company had created a videotape entitled "Safe Operation of Your New Houseboat," which discussed the dangers of carbon monoxide poisoning and how it could be avoided. During discovery, you learn that your client, Foxfire, provided Lake Vista Vacation Rentals with a copy of the video at the time the subject houseboat was purchased, and told Lake Vista that the video should be shown to all rental customers. You further learn that Lake Vista Vacation Rentals failed to show the Johnsons (or any other rental customers) the video. This failure to warn may legally shift liability from Foxfire to Lake Vista Vacation Rentals, and "Safe Operation of Your New Houseboat" may quickly rise to the level of critical evidence.

These are just a few ideas of the common types of videotaped information that might be available to the parties in the lawsuit. It is important that the paralegal keep an open mind to the possibility that videotaped footage may exist and know how to quickly secure a copy.

Demonstrative Videos

Paralegals may enjoy flexing their creative muscles when it comes to planning and producing demonstrative videos. Remember, demonstrative videos are created after the litigation has commenced as a tool to help the trier of fact grasp the evidence.

Sub-rosa Videos

Let us imagine your firm represents a defendant in a personal injury lawsuit. After taking the plaintiff's deposition, your attorney is extremely suspicious that the plaintiff is not really hurt and is faking or exaggerating her injuries to extort a settlement out of the defendant. As part of the evidence gathering for the lawsuit, you may be asked to contact a private investigator (PI) and have a sub-rosa investigation performed.

During the sub-rosa investigation, the PI will trail the plaintiff with a hidden video camera and attempt to catch her in a physical act that contradicts her alleged injury complaints. For example, the plaintiff may be claiming that the injury has made her stiff and unable to lift heavy objects. What would jurors think if they were shown videos of the plaintiff cheerfully helping unload furniture from a friend's truck or delivering perfect strikes in a bowling alley? Many fraudulent plaintiffs are foolish enough to engage in everyday activities despite the fact they are claiming to be injured. It is up to the clever paralegal and investigator to expose the plaintiff's wrongdoing. When faced with such damaging evidence, plaintiffs' attorneys will often quickly settle or be convinced to dismiss their lawsuits.

Sub-rosa videos are often used to put a stop to insurance fraud or workers' compensation fraud. They are sometimes used in criminal cases, such as catching employees stealing from employers. Usually the videotaping must be done while the subject is in a public place. It is not proper to tape an individual in her house or backyard or any other place where there is an expectation of privacy, and videos taken this way will probably be excluded as evidence.

Paralegals can assist the investigator by providing a description of the subject to be videotaped; work, home, or other addresses where the subject can be found; a description of the subject's vehicle; and information about hobbies in which the subject participates. Another good place to ambush a fraudulent plaintiff is at the doctor's office. Some plaintiffs will limp to their appointments but forget the charade and stroll normally out to their vehicles after the doctor visit is over.

Copies of the sub-rosa video are made for the person hiring the PI. The original tape is kept safely by the PI, who will bring it to the courthouse personally at the time of trial to ensure that it has not been tampered with and that the chain of custody is intact.

Day-in-the-Life Videos

A day-in-the-life video is most often used in connection with plaintiffs who have suffered severe and debilitating injuries that permanently affect the way they live their lives. While most jurors will have sympathy for the traumatically injured, it is impossible to truly comprehend the impact that, for example, paraplegia or quadriplegia has on a person's activities. The paralegal may be asked to make arrangements for a videographer to literally follow the injured plaintiff around for a day or more, showing how difficult it is for her to dress herself, how she may need people to help her eat or take her to the toilet. With this tool, a jury will have greater understanding and empathy for the injured plaintiff and her caregivers, and be more likely to award damages that will help defray the plaintiff's pain, suffering, and medical costs.

As in sub-rosa videos, a copy will be made for plaintiff's counsel and the original will be maintained by the videographer for use at trial.

Demonstration Video

When it is not possible to bring actual physical evidence into the courtroom, a demonstration video may be just the ticket to get the idea across to the judge and jury. Demonstration videos are used in a variety of ways. For example, suppose your firm's client owned a commercial building in which a special brand of fireproof insulation was used during construction. A fire erupted and the building burned to the ground, despite the fireproofing. The client is in the process of suing the manufacturer of the insulation, which has been determined to have come from a faulty batch. During discovery, you obtain a bag of the faulty insulation from the manufacturer. Your client also goes out and purchases a good bag of the insulation. Your expert witness conducts an experiment, wherein she applies a blowtorch to the good fireproof insulation and nothing happens. She then turns the torch on the faulty insulation, which goes up in flames. Of course, an experiment with blowtorches could not be conducted in the courtroom for the jury. The best way to display this information is to videotape the experiment and show it at the time of trial.

Suppose your firm's client is injured on a carnival ride at the local fair. In order to explain to the jury the dynamics of the ride, it would be helpful to videotape the ride in action, showing the movement and location of the passengers.

Another example of how a demonstration video could be used is if your firm is representing a child who was injured while trying to cross a busy intersection near her school. There are few pedestrian warnings there and the speed limit is very high. You may wish to obtain videotape of the intersection demonstrating the high speed of the vehicles traveling through it.

TIP

When selecting a videographer to create a video that may eventually be used in a courtroom, it is essential to retain the services of a company that is familiar with litigation and court requirements. Do not have a friend or family member with a spare camera show up to do the taping. A trained videographer who is familiar with evidentiary rules will know how to prepare the lighting, tape usable audio, preserve the original tape until it is time for trial, and help you edit the video later. Get the name of a respected videographer from other paralegals or attorneys in the community or from your local court reporter.

The paralegal is limited only by her imagination in arriving at an idea for a useful illustration of a concept or fact via a demonstration video. The paralegal's mind should always be open to the best way to portray the information to the jury.

AUDIOTAPED EVIDENCE

We have all seen television shows and movies where phone taps or wiretaps were used to convict persons of crimes. While this method of obtaining audio evidence is certainly useful, a court order is usually required and paralegals are not often involved in this process. The focus of this chapter will be on the use of audiotapes in civil lawsuits.

Witness Statements

During the investigation of accidents, insurance investigators will often obtain taped **witness statements**. Witness statements are important for several reasons. First, they are usually made shortly after the accident took place, while the memories of the witnesses are fresh. As time goes by, the details of the incident tend to blur or fade. Second, there is a chance that a witness's true memory could, over time, be replaced by suggestions from other people about what happened or by what the witness reads in the newspaper. A third reason why a witness statement is important is that party witnesses (those eventually involved in any lawsuit that is filed) may be more honest at first, and then later color their stories to make them appear more favorable. A taped statement can be used to impeach later slanted testimony. Finally, a great deal of time (sometimes years) elapses between the date of the accident and the commencement of a trial. Witnesses may move away or die, leaving only their taped statements as evidence.

Paralegals should always remember to request copies of witness statement audiotapes during discovery in the lawsuit. It is important to insist on receiving an actual copy of the recording itself, not simply a typed transcript of what is on the tape. The skills of transcriptionists vary, and what you see on paper may not be an accurate representation of the words spoken on the tape. It is best to obtain a copy of the tape and have a trusted person make a transcript for you.

Recorded Meetings

The governing or official bodies of some public agencies will audiotape their public meetings as the official records of those meetings. These could include city councils, boards of supervisors, planning commissions, school boards, or services districts. During certain lawsuits, the actions taken by these public agencies and the discussion that led up to the making of the decisions can be critical evidence.

■ **WITNESS STATEMENT**
A written or oral statement made by a witness to an investigator, law enforcement personnel, or other third party, either informally or under oath, that sets forth the witness's knowledge of facts she observed.

There is a special procedure to obtain official documents and other records, including tapes, from a public entity. If it is a federal agency, a request can be made pursuant to the Freedom of Information Act (see Chapter 2). If it is a state or local agency, a state law similar to the Freedom of Information Act can be used instead. For example, California has the Public Records Act and Florida has the Sunshine Act. Sometimes these agencies videotape their proceedings in addition to or instead of audiotaping them. If so, the method of obtaining copies of videotapes is the same as obtaining an audiotape from a public agency.

As with other audiotapes that may be used as evidence, it is important to have a reliable transcript prepared and certified of either the entire tape or at least the portion that is of interest in the lawsuit. If the court requests a transcript of a tape introduced as evidence, it will be ready to submit.

CONCLUSION

In the search for evidence, paralegals must always keep in mind the possibility that video or audio recordings of a certain event connected with the lawsuit may exist. Paralegals must know the proper method for obtaining the recordings and how to properly preserve them until trial. Finally, a good trial paralegal will consider the option of demonstrative videotapes to impart to a jury information that is too cumbersome for words.

> **CAREER TIP**
>
> Public entities get many requests for their documents, recordings, and other materials every day. Paralegals can often find work as deputy clerks or fill other semi management positions overseeing the selection and duplication of public records responsive to the requests and the maintenance and organization of those records.

■ KEY TERMS

demonstrative videos   pre-litigation videos   witness statements

■ REVIEW QUESTIONS

1. What is a sub-rosa investigation and when would one be started?
2. What Federal Rule of Evidence allows for the introduction of videotapes as evidence?
3. Why is a written transcript of an audiotaped interview necessary?
4. How is a day-in-the-life video helpful to a plaintiff?
5. What discovery method should you use to obtain news footage from a local television station?
6. What discovery method is used to obtain the audiotapes of a public meeting from the U.S. Department of Energy?

■ APPLYING WHAT YOU HAVE LEARNED _____

1. If you were representing the plaintiff in the Johnson v. Foxfire case (see Chapter 5), what types of videos, either pre-litigation or demonstrative, might be helpful for your case?

2. In the Cellutronics v. Microcell case (see Chapter 1), you see an advertisement on television for the Pictophone boasting that it is a much better product than the Omniphone. Your attorney wants to obtain a copy of the advertisement as possible evidence. How would you go about it? (Hint: does the video of the advertisement belong to the television station or to the owner of the product?)

3. Find the citation in your state's codes for its equivalent of the Freedom of Information Act.

4. Find a private investigator in your area that will perform a sub-rosa investigation and find out the charges.

ILLUSTRATIVE CASE

Read the following case, excerpted from the U.S. Supreme Court's opinion, and answer the following questions:

1. Do you agree or disagree with the Court's decision that Mr. Muniz's Fifth Amendment rights were not violated by the failure of the officers to give him his Miranda warnings before videotaping him performing sobriety tests? Explain your answer.

2. Anyone who watches police-oriented television shows is familiar with the common rights read to persons under arrest, which begins, "You have the right to remain silent, anything you say can and will be used against you. . ." What many people don't know is that this police procedure arose from a 1966 U.S. Supreme Court decision involving Ernesto Miranda, a defendant in a kidnapping and rape case. Research and write a brief one-page paper about Miranda and what happened to him after his celebrated case.

EXCERPT FROM PENNSYLVANIA V. MUNIZ

496 U.S. 582 (1990)

CERTIORARI TO THE SUPERIOR COURT OF PENNSYLVANIA, CASE NO. 89-213

JUSTICE BRENNAN DELIVERED THE OPINION OF THE COURT. . . .

We must decide in this case whether various incriminating utterances of a drunken-driving suspect, made while performing a series of sobriety tests, constitute testimonial responses to custodial interrogation for purposes of the Self-Incrimination Clause of the Fifth Amendment.

(continues)

ILLUSTRATIVE CASE *(continued)*

During the early morning hours of November 30, 1986, a patrol officer spotted Inocencio Muniz and a passenger parked in a car on the shoulder of a highway. When the officer inquired whether Muniz needed assistance, Muniz replied that he had stopped the car so he could urinate. The officer smelled alcohol on Muniz's breath and observed that Muniz's eyes were glazed and bloodshot and his face was flushed. The officer then directed Muniz to remain parked until his condition improved, and Muniz gave assurances that he would do so. But as the officer returned to his vehicle, Muniz drove off. After the officer pursued Muniz down the highway and pulled him over, the officer asked Muniz to perform three standard field sobriety tests: a "horizontal gaze nystagmus" test, a "walk and turn" test, and a "one leg stand" test. Muniz performed these tests poorly, and he informed the officer that he had failed the tests because he had been drinking.

The patrol officer arrested Muniz and transported him to the West Shore facility of the Cumberland County Central Booking Center. Following its routine practice for receiving persons suspected of driving while intoxicated, the booking center videotaped the ensuing proceedings. Muniz was informed that his actions and voice were being recorded, but he was not at this time (nor had he been previously) advised of his rights under *Miranda v. Arizona*. Officer Hosterman next requested Muniz to perform each of the three sobriety tests that Muniz had been asked to perform earlier during the initial roadside stop. The videotape reveals that his eyes jerked noticeably during the gaze test, that he did not walk a very straight line, and that he could not balance himself on one leg for more than several seconds. During the latter two tests, he did not complete the requested verbal counts from 1 to 9 and from 1 to 30. Moreover, while performing these tests, Muniz "attempted to explain his difficulties in performing the various tasks, and often requested further clarification of the tasks he was to perform."

Finally, Officer Deyo asked Muniz to submit to a breathalyzer test designed to measure the alcohol content of his expelled breath. Officer Deyo read to Muniz the Commonwealth's Implied Consent Law, and explained that under the law his refusal to take the test would result in automatic suspension of his driver's license for one year. Muniz asked a number of questions about the law, commenting on the process about his state of inebriation. Muniz ultimately refused to take the breath test. At this point, Muniz was for the first time advised of his Miranda rights. Muniz then signed a statement waiving his rights and admitted in response to further questioning that he had been driving while intoxicated.

Both the video and audio portions of the videotape were admitted into evidence at Muniz's bench trial, along with the arresting officer's testimony that Muniz failed the roadside sobriety tests and made incriminating remarks at that time. Muniz was convicted of driving under the influence of alcohol. . . . Muniz filed a motion for new trial, contending that the court should have excluded the testimony relating to the field sobriety tests and the videotape taken at the booking center "because they were incriminating and completed prior to [Muniz's] receiving his Miranda warnings." The trial court denied the motion, holding that "requesting a driver suspected of driving under the influence of alcohol to perform physical tests or take a breath analysis does not violate [his] privilege against self-incrimination because [the] evidence procured is of a physical nature rather than testimonial, and therefore no Miranda warnings are required."

On appeal, the Superior Court of Pennsylvania reversed. The appellate court agreed that when Muniz was asked "to submit to a field sobriety test, and later performed these tests before the videotape camera, no Miranda warnings were required" because such sobriety tests elicit physical, rather than testimonial evidence within the meaning of the Fifth Amendment. The court concluded, however, that "when the physical nature of the tests begins to yield testimonial and

(continues)

ILLUSTRATIVE CASE (continued)

communicative statements . . . the protections afforded by Miranda are invoked." The court explained that Muniz's answers to the question regarding his sixth birthday and the statement and inquiries he made while performing the physical dexterity tests and discussing the breathalyzer test "are precisely the sort of testimonial evidence that we expressly protect in [previous cases] because they "reveal[ed] his thought processes." The court further explained: "[N]one of Muniz's utterances were spontaneous, voluntary verbalizations. Rather, they were clearly compelled by the questions and instructions presented to him during his detention at the Booking Center. Since the . . . responses and communications were elicited before Muniz received his Miranda warnings, they should have been excluded as evidence." Concluding that the audio portion of the videotape should have been suppressed in its entirety, the court reversed Muniz's conviction and remanded the case for a new trial. After the Pennsylvania Supreme Court denied the Commonwealth's application for review, we granted certiorari.

The Self Incrimination Clause of the Fifth Amendment provides that no "person . . . shall be compelled in any criminal case to be a witness against himself." . . . In *Miranda v. Arizona*, 384 U.S. 436 (1966), we reaffirmed our previous understanding that the privilege against self-incrimination protects individuals not only from legal compulsion to testify in a criminal courtroom, but also from "informal compulsion exerted by law-enforcement officers during in-custody questioning." . . . This case implicates both the "testimonial" and "compulsion" components of the privilege against self-incrimination in the context of pre-trial questioning. Because Muniz was not advised of his Miranda rights until after the videotaped proceedings at the booking center were completed, any verbal statements that were both testimonial in nature and elicited during custodial interrogation should have been suppressed.

In the initial phase of the recorded proceedings, Officer Hosterman asked Muniz his name, address, height, weight, eye color, date of birth, current age and the date of his sixth birthday. Both the delivery and content of Muniz's answers were incriminating. As the state court found, "Muniz's videotaped responses . . . certainly led the finder of fact to infer that his confusion and failure to speak clearly indicated a state of drunkenness that prohibited him from safely operating his vehicle." The Commonwealth argues, however, that admission of Muniz's answers to these questions does not contravene Fifth Amendment principles because Muniz's statement regarding his sixth birthday was not "testimonial" and his answers to the prior questions were not elicited by custodial interrogation.

. . . Muniz's answer to the sixth birthday question was incriminating, not just because of his delivery, but also because of his answer's content; the trier of fact could infer from Muniz's answer (that he did not know the proper date) that his mental state was confused. . . . The state court held that the sixth birthday question constituted an unwarranted interrogation for purposes of the privilege against self-incrimination and that Muniz's answer was incriminating. The Commonwealth does not question either conclusion. Therefore, because we conclude that Muniz's response to the sixth birthday question was testimonial, the response should have been suppressed.

During the second phase of the videotaped proceedings, Officer Hosterman asked Muniz to perform the same three sobriety tests that he had earlier performed at roadside prior to his arrest. . . . While Muniz was attempting to comprehend Officer Hosterman's instructions and then perform the requested sobriety tests, Muniz made several audible and incriminating statements. Muniz argued to the state court that both the videotaped performance of the physical tests themselves and the audio recorded verbal statements were introduced in violation of Miranda.

(continues)

ILLUSTRATIVE CASE   *(continued)*

The court refused to suppress the videotaped evidence of Muniz's paltry performance on the physical sobriety tests, reasoning that "[r]equiring a driver to perform physical [sobriety] tests . . . does not violate the privilege against self-incrimination because the evidence procured is of a physical nature rather than testimonial." With respect to Muniz's verbal statements, however, the court concluded that "none of Muniz's utterances were spontaneous, voluntary verbalizations," and because they were "elicited before Muniz received his Miranda warnings, they should have been excluded as evidence."

We disagree. Officer Hosterman's dialogue with Muniz concerning the physical sobriety tests consisted primarily of carefully scripted instructions as to how the tests were to be performed. These instructions were not likely to be perceived as calling for any verbal response and therefore were not "words or actions" constituting custodial interrogation . . . . Hence, Muniz's incriminating utterances during this phase of the videotaped proceedings were "voluntary" in the sense that they were not elicited in response to custodial interrogation.

Similarly, we conclude that Miranda does not require suppression of the statements Muniz made when asked to submit to a breathalyzer examination. Officer Deyo read Muniz a prepared script explaining how the test worked, the nature of Pennsylvania's Implied Consent Law, and the legal consequences that would ensue should he refuse. Officer Deyo then asked Muniz whether he understood the nature of the test and the law and whether he would like to submit to the test. Muniz asked Officer Deyo several questions concerning the legal consequences of refusal, which Deyo answered directly, and Muniz then commented upon his state of inebriation. . . . We believe that Muniz's statements were not prompted by interrogation within the meaning of Miranda, and therefore the absence of Miranda warnings does not require suppression of these statements at trial . . . .

We agree with the state court's conclusion that Miranda requires suppression of Muniz's response to the question regarding the date of his sixth birthday, but we do not agree that the entire audio portion of the videotape must be suppressed. Accordingly, the court's judgment reversing Muniz's conviction is vacated, and the case is remanded for further proceedings not inconsistent with this opinion.

For additional resources, visit our Web site at www.westlegalstudies.com

CHAPTER 7

Electronic Evidence

■ OBJECTIVES

After studying this chapter, you should be able to:

❑ give examples of electronic evidence.

❑ understand the federal rules governing electronic evidence.

❑ understand the discovery tools used to gather electronic evidence.

INTRODUCTION

The advent of technology in the everyday workplace and home has provided new challenges in gathering and managing documents. The kind of high-powered machinery that was once considered the domain of large corporations is now ubiquitous. It was not too many years ago that small to medium-sized businesses had just one or two computers and the only mobile telephones were in automobiles. Many of us remember a high-tech law office as one equipped with IBM Selectric correcting typewriters, although correcting the carbon copies was still done by hand! The boom of technology use by individuals both within and outside the office has been extraordinary and continues to expand.

When paralegals seek evidence and conduct discovery, they should always consider electronic information. Most jurisdictions consider "documents" to include electronically generated and stored information as well as the more traditional paper documents, but it has been just in the last few years that firms have specifically included such documents in document requests. Examples of these documents are e-mail, PowerPoint® presentations, spreadsheets, and electronically generated diagrams, charts, and flowsheets. Electronic information also includes telephone answering records and data, digital film, personal electronic calendaring and e-mail (Palm® organizer and **BlackBerry®** wireless device), and so-called black boxes from automobiles. Information stored on any device by means of a **computer chip** or other data storage device may be requested during the discovery process. In the past, seeking such evidence has been primarily in the purview of larger firms; however, it is becoming more common for firms of all sizes to include this kind of information in specific requests. Lack of sophistication and up-to-date knowledge concerning **electronic evidence** may have discouraged attorneys from gathering it in the past, but the fact that such information is so common means that it can no longer be ignored.

PREVALENCE OF ELECTRONIC EVIDENCE

Electronic evidence is a new and exciting area of discovery. It is still a rather confusing term. During the past 25 years or so, electronic evidence has usually referred more to the management side of evidence gathering. As computers became more widespread and legal professionals discovered they had more functions than word processors, evidence began to be managed electronically. The information on various documents could be entered into databases, cross-referenced, and pulled off when needed. Computers were a great boon to law offices previously drowning in paper and continue to be critical to the smooth operation of a law office today. However, the term *electronic evidence* does not pertain to the management of paper in a law office by using a computer.

As technology has become ever more prevalent in our everyday lives, the average person now uses computers, handheld electronic devices, telephone answering machines, cell phones, computer chips in television sets, and so forth to create and store information. Accessing this information can be a crucial part of gathering evidence. The same devices that have simplified our lives in so many ways have become the target of the thorough paralegal gathering evidence to support her client's case.

Over 50 percent of homes in the United States and virtually every business have computers today. Although current statistics are not available, it is estimated that nearly two-thirds of those homes with computers and nearly 88 percent of businesses have access to the World Wide Web. Over 3 *trillion* e-mail messages are sent via the Internet and intranets every day. The sheer amount of information we access on a daily basis has become difficult to comprehend.

■ **BLACKBERRY**
A handheld wireless device providing e-mail, telephone, text messaging, and Web browsing services.

■ **COMPUTER CHIP**
(Electronics) a circuit fabricated in one piece on a small, thin substrate.

■ **ELECTRONIC EVIDENCE**
Data and information with investigative value stored on or transmitted by any electronic device.

The word *computer* refers to network servers, desktops, laptops, notebook computers, mainframes, personal digital assistants, and other communication devices. The **hard drive** is the primary hardware that a computer uses to store information.

In the business world, nearly all documents are now prepared electronically. As a result of the Internet and in-house intranet systems, many communications transpire electronically and are never reduced to paper. In the realm of the legal profession, these facts present new challenges to gathering, organizing, and managing data and information.

Electronic discovery requires specific strategies, knowledge, skills, and techniques. Because technology continues to advance and change at such a rapid pace, many businesses hire outside companies to assist in gathering, managing, and preserving electronic evidence. This is perfectly acceptable and perhaps often desirable, as they can recognize savings and assure the preservation of fragile evidence.

COMPUTER FORENSICS

Computer forensics is the science of recovering deleted, erased, or hidden information. For purposes of computer forensics, the computer or other technology is considered to be a "crime scene" and the forensics expert gathers information regarding computer-related conduct and actions. The business of computer forensics has emerged in response to the growing need to identify and locate information stored on computer systems. In order to understand the importance of electronic discovery, one must realize the extent of information contained on computers. Asking for documents and other information on a computer does not require that the answering party provide the physical computer used to produce the information. Images of entire hard drives and backup tapes can be obtained. If a responding party states that information requested has been erased from the computer, a computer forensics scientist can restore the data. In addition, through forensics, it can be determined not only that the information exists but that it was erased at one time, perhaps raising red flags concerning spoliation of evidence and anticipation of litigation that will be beneficial to the asking party in the development of the case.

The computer **forensic technologist** has the skill and training to examine the image of the hard drive or other media and identify the relevant evidence as determined by the attorney. The relevant evidence is then extracted into a format that can be used by the paralegal or attorney to examine it in detail. If the evidence is voluminous, it may be sorted by type (e-mail, PowerPoint presentations, financial data, etc.), indexed, and/or imported into management software in order to be of more use to the persons needing to access the information. Whenever using others to gather information for you, remember that the attorney has ultimate responsibility for the evidence and its use. The requesting party is responsible for thoroughly educating the forensic technologist on the information to be gathered and how it is to be extracted, sorted, and distilled. The forensic technologist may well be called upon to testify

---

■ **HARD DRIVE**

A nonremovable disk in a computer that stores and reads data. It is the primary storage device on a computer.

■ **COMPUTER FORENSICS**

The science of recovering deleted, erased, or hidden information. For purposes of computer forensics, the computer or other technology is considered to be a "crime scene" and the forensics expert gathers information regarding computer-related conduct and actions.

■ **FORENSIC TECHNOLOGIST**

A person trained to use scientifically proven methods to gather, process, interpret, and use digital evidence to provide a conclusive description of activities.

regarding instructions given and methods used to retrieve data. The evidence-gathering techniques may be questioned in court.

Data recovery experts can also restore information from hard drives that have been physically damaged, either intentionally or unintentionally. For example, data from a hard drive that has been dropped into water can be restored.

Electronic discovery is also used by regulatory agencies and federal investigators to obtain information for purposes of antitrust investigations, for example. Corporations may need to conduct internal investigations of employees suspected of sharing trade secrets or other proprietary information.

Many new legal issues have been raised by the use of computers by so many in the workplace including issues involving workers' rights to privacy, sending and receiving e-mail on company-owned computers and company time, use of cell phones in the workplace to conduct conversations as well as to take photographs, use of company-owned technology to conduct personal business, to name some examples. On a larger scale, employees or corporate officers have been accused of changing financial records stored on computers and accessing employees' personal information for non-business-related purposes. Computer security is a rapidly growing and lucrative business.

RULES GOVERNING ELECTRONIC EVIDENCE

The federal judiciary has created a proposed set of rules to govern electronic discovery, and several federal district courts have already adopted local rules. State court rules are being promulgated to specifically address the subject. Many other jurisdictions are working to develop rules to apply to electronic discovery as well as guidelines for imposing sanctions for deletion of electronic information. The development of these rules is in its infancy, and many revisions and modifications are certain to occur as they are put into practice.

Examples of rules adopted by various courts follow. Note the differences in requirements regarding the use of electronic discovery.

United States District Court for the District of Wyoming

Local Rule 26.1 Discovery (excerpts)

(3) Prior to a Fed.R.Civ.P. 26(f) conference, counsel should carefully investigate their client's information management system so that they are knowledgeable as to its operation, including how information is stored and how it can be retrieved. Likewise, counsel shall reasonably review the client's computer files to ascertain the contents thereof, including archival and legacy data (outdated formats or media), and disclose in initial discovery (self-executing routine discovery) the computer based evidence which may be used to support claims or defenses.

TIP

Always keep in mind that this is currently the most rapidly evolving area of the law. It is crucial not only to remain on the lookout for changes in local, state, and federal laws, but to also take advantage of any legal and technology magazines and newsletters your firm may subscribe to. Making your best effort to stay abreast of developments will provide you with an opportunity to shine.

■ MEET AND CONFER
A requirement of courts that before certain types of motions and/or petitions will be heard by the judge, the lawyers (and sometimes their clients) must "meet and confer" to try to resolve the matter or determine the points of conflict. The benefit is that it may resolve many matters, reducing the time for arguments and making the lawyers and clients face up to the realities of their positions.

■ BACKUP DATA
Information not presently used and stored separately in order to free up data space on the hard drive and permit recovery.

(a) Duty to notify. A party seeking discovery of computer-based information shall notify the opposing party immediately, but no later than the Fed.R.Civ.P. 26(f) conference of that fact and identify as clearly as possible the categories of information which may be sought.

(b) Duty to **meet and confer**. The parties shall meet and confer regarding the following matters during the Fed.R.Civ.P. 26(f) conference:

(i) Computer-based information (in general). Counsel shall attempt to agree on steps the parties will take to segregate and preserve computer-based information in order to avoid accusations of spoliation;

(ii) E-mail information. Counsel shall attempt to agree as to the scope of e-mail discovery and attempt to agree upon an e-mail search protocol. This should include an agreement regarding inadvertent production of privileged e-mail messages;

(iii) Deleted information. Counsel shall confer and attempt to agree whether or not restoration of deleted information may be necessary, the extent to which restoration of deleted information is needed, and who will bear the costs of restoration; and

(iv) **Back-up data**. Counsel shall attempt to agree whether or not back-up data may be necessary, the extent to which back-up data is needed and who will bear the cost of obtaining back-up data.

(4) Counsel may either submit a written report or report orally on their discovery plan at the initial pretrial conference.

[Adopted November 30, 1996; amended February 10, 1998; amended effective August 20, 2001.]

United States District Court for the Eastern District of Arkansas

Local Rule 26.1

Outline for Fed. R. Civ. P. 26(f) Report

The Fed.R.Civ.P. 26(f) report filed with the court must contain the parties' views and proposals regarding the following:

. . . .

(3) Subjects on which discovery may be needed.

(4) Whether any party will likely be requested to disclose or produce information from electronic or computer-based media. If so:

(a) whether disclosure or production will be limited to data reasonably available to the parties in the ordinary course of business;

(b) the anticipated scope, cost and time required for disclosure or production of data beyond what is reasonably available to the parties in the ordinary course of business;

(c) the format and media agreed to by the parties for the production of such data as well as agreed procedures for such production;

(d) whether reasonable measures have been taken to preserve potentially discoverable data from alteration or destruction in the ordinary course of business or otherwise;

(e) other problems which the parties anticipate may arise in connection with electronic or computer-based discovery.

Effective December 1, 2000.

State courts, as well, are adopting rules that specifically address electronic evidence. See the following rule enacted by the State of Mississippi.

State of Mississippi
RULE 26. General Provisions Governing Discovery

(5) Electronic Data. To obtain discovery of data or information that exists in electronic or magnetic form, the requesting party must specifically request production of electronic or magnetic data and specify the form in which the requesting party wants it produced. The responding party must produce the electronic or magnetic data that is responsive to the request and is reasonably available to the responding party in its ordinary course of business. If the responding party cannot–through reasonable efforts–retrieve the data or information requested or produce it in the form requested, the responding party must state an objection complying with these rules. If the court orders the responding party to comply with the request, the court may also order that the requesting party pay the reasonable expenses of any extraordinary steps required to retrieve and produce the information.

From reading the three examples you will see that the Wyoming district court addresses the responsibility of an attorney regarding knowledge of the client's information management system. The Arkansas district court and Mississippi state court make no mention of that in the rules cited. The Arkansas rules want the parties to look at the time and cost involved to produce electronic data in a more direct fashion than those in Mississippi or Wyoming. Mississippi's rules apply more to the procedural issues of obtaining electronic documents. The importance of checking the rules on electronic evidence cannot be overemphasized. These rules are frequently updated and revised and new rules are enacted governing this rapidly changing topic.

The Texas state rule addresses a responding party's objection to the production due to inability to retrieve data or information requested. Further, the rule states that the requesting party must pay the reasonable expenses of any extraordinary steps required to retrieve and produce the information.

---

*Texas Rules of Civil Procedure_*

Rule 196.4 Electronic or Magnetic Data.

To obtain discovery of data or information that exists in electronic or magnetic form, the requesting party must specifically request production of electronic or magnetic data and specify the form in which the requesting party wants it produced. The responding party must produce the electronic or magnetic data that is responsive to the request and is reasonably available to the responding party in its ordinary course of business. If the responding party cannot–through reasonable efforts–retrieve the data or information requested or produce it in the form requested, the responding party must state an objection complying with these rules. If the court orders the responding party to comply with the request, the court must also order that the requesting party pay the reasonable expenses of any extraordinary steps required to retrieve and produce the information.

In the earlier years of producing electronic evidence, the requesting party frequently had to bear the expenses of retrieving the requested information. After all, the thinking at the time went, if the requesting party wanted the information, the requesting party should pay for it. However, in recent years the trend has shifted to either the producing party paying for the requested evidence or to a sharing of the costs. The federal judiciary is considering adopting rules on costs involved in electronic discovery.

Proposed Model Rule Regarding Production of Data or Information in Electronic Form; Cost-Shifting and Safe Harbor

proposal July, 2002

[Electronic Discovery; Provisions for]

(a) General. To obtain discovery of data or information that exists in electronic, digital or magnetic form, a requesting party must specifically request production of such data or information and specify the form in which it should be produced. The responding party must produce the data or information that is responsive to the request and is reasonably available to the responding party in the ordinary course of business. If the responding party cannot–through reasonable efforts–retrieve the data or information requested or produce it in the form requested, the responding party must state an objection complying with these rules.

(b) Cost-Shifting For Extraordinary Steps. A court may order, upon showing of substantial need, production of data or information that is otherwise subject to production but is not reasonably available in the ordinary course of business. If the court orders production of such data or information in the requested or other form, the court shall also order that the requesting party pay the reasonable expenses of any extraordinary steps required to retrieve and produce the information.

(c) **Safe-Harbor**; Sanctions. Nothing in these rules shall require the responding party to suspend or alter the operation in good faith of disaster recovery or document retention systems absent a preservation order issued upon good cause shown, which shall not issue unless the standards applicable to obtaining injunctive relief are met. No sanctions or other relief predicated upon a failure to maintain or preserve documents or data shall be entered in the absence of a discovery request or preservation order that describes with particularity the specific documents or data requested and evidence that the party upon whom the request or order was served willfully failed to preserve such documents or data. Evidence that reasonable steps were undertaken to notify relevant custodians of preservation obligations shall be prima facie evidence of compliance with obligations under such discovery requests or preservation orders.

■ **SAFE HARBOR**
A statement in a statute or regulation that a good faith attempt to comply is sufficient, even if the attempt has failed.

Many attorneys are still somewhat undereducated regarding technology and its uses and rely on others to bring new developments to their attention. It is vital that paralegals remain vigilant regarding the development of these new rules and guidelines as well as to when they are adopted. The ramifications of electronic discovery on the gathering and management of evidence are far-reaching. A valuable resource for every paralegal and attorney involved in electronic discovery is The Sedona Conference® (<*http://www.thesedonaconference.org*>). This organization consists of jurists, lawyers, academics, experts, and others who are interested in the role of technology (among many other issues) in the law. The Sedona Conference has developed white papers addressing topics having to do with electronic evidence.

CASE SCENARIO

In order to provide examples of gathering electronic evidence, we will introduce a new case scenario for a fictional criminal action.

In September 2003, Henri Madsen contacted Attorney Suzanne Green because he had been arrested and charged with the theft of a famous stolen painting. Earlier in the week, the police came to Henri's apartment with a search warrant. The painting Henri was accused of stealing was hanging on the wall in plain sight and Henri willingly gave it to the police, explaining that it had been a gift from his ex-girlfriend, Georgia. Georgia had told Henri that she had purchased the painting at a yard sale. Three days later, the police returned to Henri's home and charged him with the theft of the painting.

Attorney Green obtained a copy of the police report. Apparently, in July 2003 the police had received a tip that the painting had been purchased from an Internet auction site and had opened an investigation based upon this information. Henri stated that his ex-girlfriend was often in the room with him when he turned the computer on and logged on to the Internet. It would not have been difficult for her to see his log-in information, including his password. Georgia also had a key to Henri's apartment and came and went at will, whether or not Henri was present. Attorney Green informed the prosecuting attorney of this information.

Further, Henri divulged to his attorney that he knew few of Georgia's friends. Although she received telephone calls at his home, she usually took the telephone into a room out of Henri's earshot to have extended conversations. Although Henri had questioned Georgia about this when they were still a couple, Georgia indicated that she needed her privacy and felt she could speak more freely to her friends without Henri overhearing their conversations. Henri was aware, from answering the telephone, that some of these friends of Georgia's were males, but he trusted her and felt that she was, indeed, entitled to have friends separate from his relationship with her.

However, as time went on, Georgia began to spend more time with her friends than with Henri and the frequency of secretive telephone conversations increased. Eventually, Henri became uneasy with this and broke off the relationship with Georgia. The breakup occurred in August 2003.

In a criminal matter, the Federal Rules of Evidence apply, together with the Federal Rules of Criminal Procedure. Excerpts from the Federal Rules of Criminal Procedure are in Appendix C. The particular rules covering discovery are covered in Rules 15 and 16. You will note that these rules refer to the Federal Rules of Evidence. As in civil procedure, the appropriate subpoena must be issued in order to obtain evidence from nonparties. Formal discovery proceeds with requests for production, depositions, and interrogatories between the parties.

Keep in mind that when a governmental entity (a state or the United States or any agency thereof) is the plaintiff, as in our fact pattern here (or indeed, in a civil matter), the discovery process may be more arduous. The plaintiff in these circumstances will generally have more resources, both in terms of finances and manpower, at its disposal than the defendant. When representing a criminal defendant, the attorney may rely heavily on informally gathered discovery by using investigators and taking statements. However, the procedure for formal discovery is similar in both civil and criminal cases.

USING DISCOVERY TOOLS TO GATHER ELECTRONIC EVIDENCE

When a firm is retained by a client with a lawsuit involving electronic data, the client must be immediately advised not to destroy, tamper with, hide, or otherwise interfere in any way with the storage or retrieval of data that may be requested by the opposing party. The client should be instructed to begin the process of identifying and gathering all electronic evidence so that the paralegal and attorney can analyze the data. Besides educating themselves about the nature of the lawsuit and the sorts of records and documents available, they may identify documents as work product, irrelevant to the lawsuit at hand, or privileged. In the scenario presented above, Henri should be instructed not to destroy any electronic documents or records that may exist on his computer or telephone. In other cases, corporate clients would be advised not to destroy any documents on the corporate main servers or individual computers, including backup drives and storage drives. In addition, electronic security system records and telephone messages stored on answering and messaging equipment must be retained and preserved.

In this day of multibillion-dollar corporations with offices scattered throughout the world and all communicating electronically with one another as well as with outside businesses and individuals, an attorney representing a client who is considering legal action against the corporation will notify the corporation not to destroy or tamper with any electronic evidence, pending litigation. This document is referred to as a "**spoliation** letter." The purpose of the letter is to put opposing counsel on notice that you will be requesting electronic data and that the destruction of any data would be considered spoliation. In the scenario outlined above, the prosecutor may send a spoliation letter to Henri. A sample spoliation letter appears in Exhibit 7–1.

■ **SPOLIATION**
Destruction of evidence.

EXHIBIT 7–1   SAMPLE SPOLIATION LETTER

Re: Name of Case

Dear   :

Please be advised that notice is hereby given not to destroy or alter any paper or electronic files or documents or other data generated by your client or stored on your
client's computer or any other storage media, including but not limited to, hard drives,
floppy disks, CDs, backup tapes or any and all electronic devices used to conduct corporate business or containing business information of any nature must be retained and not
destroyed or altered. This notice also includes voice mail, personal data assistants (such as
Palm Pilots), and laptops, notebook computers, or other portable computers as well as
digital cameras. Your failure to comply with this notice may result in the imposition of
sanctions for spoliation of evidence.

Please instruct your client to preserve all passwords, network access codes, ID names,
software, decryption procedures, and other information necessary to access electronic
data through discovery.

Sincerely,

As in any form of discovery, a scattershot approach is not desirable and will only
lead to delay when the responding party objects for lack of specificity. The purpose
of discovery is to find evidence in the possession of the opposing side to weaken its
case or to help prove yours. Before involving an information technology specialist,
you may be wise to use interrogatories to determine the extent of electronic discovery available to you. Instead of simply requesting "all electronic records" by using a
subpoena duces tecum or request for production, you must obtain information about
the responding party's data creation and management methods.

In requesting electronic evidence, be aware that in most cases this information is as
discoverable as paper documents or other tangible evidence. In order to avoid confusion, and because many attorneys still do not automatically include electronic evidence
with paper evidence when responding to discovery, it is useful to specifically request
electronic data and information either within the body of more general requests or as
specifically numbered items. Computer systems used by one company often exist in var-

ious geographical locations, and requests must make clear that you are seeking electronic information from all locations or from specific locations.

Interrogatories inquiring into the nature and extent of an opposing party's technology should include the following areas:

- number of computers, size of memory on each computer, location
- number of workstations and technology situated at each workstation
- operating system, including name, version, etc.
- any other operating systems used in the past
- hardware and software applications used now or in the past with the particular computer
- backup system and location of backup tapes with the particular computer or by the particular user
- whether or not employees conduct business from computers at home or on laptops instead of or in addition to the company location
- type of network and configuration
- whether a digital copier is hooked up to any computers
- brands and information concerning handheld devices, cell phones, pagers and other personal electronic devices
- whether an in-house server exists
- information regarding the systems administrator
- information regarding firewalls
- type of e-mail
- information regarding network provider
- standards on preservation and storage of all electronically generated information

After the background information has been obtained through interrogatories, requests for production or deposition, the propounding party will be in a better position to make specific requests for production of electronic discovery. A forensic technologist may then be retained to collect the evidence asked for in the discovery demands. After obtaining the evidence, the information will then be extracted and restored by either the hired vendor or an in-house information technology specialist. The information may be produced via disk, **PDF** files, or other electronic media. Or, if the production is not too voluminous, it may simply be printed out. However, it is wise for the requesting party to require the information on disk to see if additional information exists. For example, the printed document will not contain the codes and a history of revisions that may exist on the hard drive.

■ **PDF (PORTABLE DOCUMENT FORMAT)**
The native file format for Adobe Systems' Acrobat. PDF is the file format for representing documents in a manner that is independent of the original application software, hardware, and operating system used to create those documents. A PDF file can describe documents containing any combination of text, graphics, and images in a device-independent and resolution-independent format.

THE VALUE OF METADATA

Metadata may best be described as "data about data." A metadata record consists of a set of elements, often referred to as fields or attributes, which describe different parts of a resource. For example, a legal memorandum typically contains author, title, and publisher elements on its face. Metadata placed in electronic documents provides the same basic information except that it is not visible to the viewer except by examining the document source.

Viewing the metadata imbedded in a document provides valuable information that may not be found in the text, for example, subject headings, levels and dates of revisions, author of the revisions, and the actual changes made each time as well as who accessed the document, with or without making changes to it.

This metadata is very useful for determining when documents were created, modified, and accessed. It may also be used to determine who accessed each document. With regard to e-mail messages, the metadata reveals message tracking information such as the sender's Internet Protocol address and mail client as well as information regarding the original author of the message, to whom it was forwarded and when it was forwarded, and revisions that may have been made along the way.

REQUESTING ELECTRONIC DISCOVERY

As in other discovery, the requesting party is responsible for bearing any costs associated with compliance by the responding party, subject to any cost sharing rules that may apply within the particular jurisdiction. The requesting party will most likely hire a computer data specialist to go to the responding party's location to gather the data and ensure its integrity. The forensic technologist may then be asked to prepare a summary of the data. A knowledgeable forensic technologist will be able to pull out information such as who authored documents; who e-mails were sent to and from, and whether attachments were included and what they are; and what changes, revisions, or alterations were made to particular documents. Depending upon the nature and volume of information sought, producing electronic evidence can be a costly undertaking.

As you can probably surmise, electronic data is usually much more voluminous than paper data. In most cases, the only paper version of a document produced in-house is the final rendition, or perhaps a marked-up draft. The final document may indicate who signed it but certainly will not show who initially created it and when, who looked at it and made revisions and when, who reviewed and approved it and when, and on and on. If any of the reviews, suggestions, and revisions were made on any computer, it will be shown in the metadata.

Exhibit 7–2 shows a sample request for production that includes some of the electronic evidence.

EXHIBIT 7–2   SAMPLE FORM REQUEST FOR ELECTRONIC EVIDENCE

[usual preamble]

Definitions:

[*Depending on the nature of the case, insert the definitions for the items you are seeking, for example:*]

Backup: A copy of data used in restoration of data and documents.

Image: A bit-by-bit copy of a hard drive. Also known as a "**ghost image**" or "mirror image."

Network: A group of connected computers that allow users to share information and equipment. Examples of networks include, but are not limited to: Local area network (**LAN**), client-server network, and wide area network (**WAN**).

Operating system: the software that directs the activity of a computer.

1. Please produce copies of any and all written policies regarding the retention of documents from _____ to _____.

2. Please produce all backup media for the period from _____ to _____.

3. Please produce all computers, together with their magnetic or optical storage media.

4. Please produce copies of the operating system software pertaining to the operating systems installed on all computers.

5. Please produce any and all voice message records for the period from _____ to _____.

6. Please produce any and all e-mail, including but not limited to current and archived programs, accounts, server-based e-mail, Web-based e-mail, dial-up e-mail, wireless e-mail, domain names, e-mail messages, attachments, and mailing lists.

■ **GHOST IMAGE**
An exact replica of the contents of a storage device such as a hard disk drive or CD-ROM that is stored on a second storage device.

■ **LAN**
Local area network for communication between computers within one or more offices within one location.

■ **WAN**
Wide Area Network. A communications network or system, including electronic devices such as telephone lines, satellite dishes, and/or radio waves, that covers a wide geographic system such as a city, county, or state.

All of the objections regarding other kinds of discovery apply to electronic discovery. The requesting party has an additional ethical responsibility as a result of the risk of inadvertent disclosure of sensitive material. This is of particular concern regarding the vast amounts of e-mail communications a party may produce. As in paper discovery, the ethics rules apply, requiring an attorney or paralegal to stop reading if he or she realizes the document being read was inadvertently produced. The producing party needs to prepare a privilege log so that assertions of privilege can be challenged in court.

TYPES OF ELECTRONIC EVIDENCE

■ **ACTIVE DATA**

Information on computer hard drives that is readily accessible and visible to the operating system and/or application software used to create it. It is readily accessible to users without deletion, modification, or reconstruction.

■ **ARCHIVAL DATA**

Information that an organization maintains for long-term storage and record keeping. The information is usually not subject to change, such as medical records or completed reports. Archival data may be written to electronic storage devices such as CDs, backup tapes, or other electronic media. It may also be maintained on hard drives, usually in a compressed format.

Active data includes documents that sit on the user's or custodian's hard drive or other storage device. Active data can be accessed by looking at the file manager or hard drive explorer tools. Office documents, spreadsheets, e-mail, and presentation materials are examples of active data. These kinds of data are generally easy to collect. However, because of the large volume that may be involved, the producing party may wish to hire a third-party company to retrieve it.

Archival data is typically found on backup tapes, floppies, CDs, or other storage devices. The information may be in a compressed format. These documents often need to be restored. Archived documents present another challenge because they may be in old formats and may not be organized in an easily accessible manner. In order to restore them, it may be necessary to utilize the software used to originally create the documents. Also, as data is backed up again and again over time, there is the need to de-duplicate. The most efficient and economical way to retrieve archival documents may be to hire a company that specializes in this type of restoration. A good forensic technologist will have access to many now-obsolete software applications, operating systems and hardware.

Forensic documents include those that have been damaged, erased, or hidden and reside on storage devices or in active files. Some documents may be retrieved reliably only by using forensic techniques. These include files on PDA devices and cell phones. A specialist will need to retrieve documents using forensic methods. The methods used will not render the electronic devices unusable.

DETERMINING THE NEED FOR AND SELECTING A FORENSIC TECHNOLOGIST OR INFORMATION TECHNOLOGIST

The technology field is changing every day. New equipment is introduced quickly; systems are constantly upgraded to meet the needs of businesses and individuals wishing to access greater amounts of information at greater speed. In order to thoroughly conduct an investigation of discoverable material that has been generated on computers, and then to present and explain the methods used to collect the information, it may very likely be necessary to hire an expert.

In most cases, electronic discovery may be conducted by a trained information technology specialist. If there are questions of spoliation, data corruption, bad faith, or intellectual property issues, a forensic technologist may be called upon. No matter what level of expertise is determined to be needed, selection of a qualified, competent vendor is crucial for the successful gathering of desired information.

If there is most likely a relatively small volume of electronic information, few custodians of information, and a long timeline, the decision may be made to handle the discovery in-house. However, in today's fast-moving business climate with ever-changing technology, this is rarely the case. Many businesses specialize in gathering, restoring, analyzing, organizing, and distilling electronically generated documents. No matter who conducts the investigation and gathering of electronic information, it is important that he or she be able to effectively testify before a jury regarding the methodologies employed in language and in a manner that the jury will understand. When researching various vendors, the paralegal should keep a few key points in mind:

- A forensic technologist should have certificates proving training in a variety of systems, that is, network administration, systems administration, internet professional training.
- The expert should be able to prove that he or she is keeping current in the field by attending conferences, seminars, additional trainings, and so on.
- The expert should have prior legal experience and be familiar with the rules of evidence and how they apply to electronic discovery.
- The expert must have the appropriate demeanor and communication skills to testify at trial on behalf of the client.
- The expert must have proven mechanisms and practices in place to maintain a continuing chain of custody for electronic material.
- The vendor must own state-of-the art equipment to perform sophisticated and comprehensive analysis.
- The law firm must check the expert's references.

> **! TIP**
>
> Information technology vendors specializing in computer storage and retrieval often hire paralegals to work with law firms because they have hands-on knowledge of how the products are used in the law office environment.

AUTHENTICATING ELECTRONIC EVIDENCE

The federal courts have thus far addressed the authentication of computer-generated evidence based upon Rule 901, particularly 901(a) of the Federal Rules of Evidence (see Exhibit 7–3). As noted above, however, the courts are in the process of developing rules that will specifically address electronic evidence.

EXHIBIT 7–3   RULE 901 OF THE FEDERAL RULES OF EVIDENCE

RULE 901. REQUIREMENT OF AUTHENTICATION OR IDENTIFICATION

(a) General provision.

The requirement of authentication or identification as a condition precedent to admissibility is satisfied by evidence sufficient to support a finding that the matter in question is what its proponent claims.

(b) Illustrations.

By way of illustration only, and not by way of limitation, the following are examples of authentication or identification conforming to the requirements of this rule:

(1) *Testimony of witness with knowledge.* Testimony that a matter is what it is claimed to be.

(continues)

EXHIBIT 7–3   RULE 901 OF THE FEDERAL RULES OF EVIDENCE (continued)

(2) *Nonexpert opinion on handwriting.* Nonexpert opinion as to the genuineness of handwriting, based upon familiarity not acquired for purposes of the litigation.

(3) *Comparison by trier or expert witness.* Comparison by the trier of fact or by expert witnesses with specimens which have been authenticated.

(4) *Distinctive characteristics and the like.* Appearance, contents, substance, internal patterns, or other distinctive characteristics, taken in conjunction with circumstances.

(5) *Voice identification.* Identification of a voice, whether heard firsthand or through mechanical or electronic transmission or recording, by opinion based upon hearing the voice at any time under circumstances connecting it with the alleged speaker.

(6) *Telephone conversations.* Telephone conversations, by evidence that a call was made to the number assigned at the time by the telephone company to a particular person or business, if (A) in the case of a person, circumstances, including self-identification, show the person answering to be the one called, or (B) in the case of a business, the call was made to a place of business and the conversation related to business reasonably transacted over the telephone.

(7) *Public records or reports.* Evidence that a writing authorized by law to be recorded or filed and in fact recorded or filed in a public office, or a purported public record, report, statement, or data compilation, in any form, is from the public office where items of this nature are kept.

(8) *Ancient documents or data compilation.* Evidence that a document or data compilation, in any form, (A) is in such condition as to create no suspicion concerning its authenticity, (B) was in a place where it, if authentic, would likely be, and (C) has been in existence 20 years or more at the time it is offered.

(9) *Process or system.* Evidence describing a process or system used to produce a result and showing that the process or system produces an accurate result.

(10) *Methods provided by statute or rule.* Any method of authentication or identification provided by Act of Congress or by other rules prescribed by the Supreme Court pursuant to statutory authority.

An experienced, competent information technologist or forensics technologist will testify in court as to the methods used in gathering the evidence, the chain of custody, and the authenticity of the evidence.

In our scenario, Henri's evidence will be proven by examining the electronic evidence. Based on Henri's insistence that he had no idea that the painting had been stolen, the paralegal for Henri's attorney hired a technology information specialist to examine Henri's computer. By retrieving data, it was found that the communications with the Internet auction site occurred at times of the day when Henri said he was at work. An examination of his timecards from his employer, obtained by subpoena, proved this to be the case. In addition to Henri's computer, his telephone answering machine was also examined. Although the tape had been recorded over since Georgia and Henri had broken up, a forensic technologist was able to retrieve the previous recordings. These recordings included messages from Georgia's friends making references to the need to get together to discuss the painting.

The forensic technologist retrieved the data, indexed it, made it searchable, and presented it in a format that could be converted from electronic to print. As the documents were retrieved, they were Bates stamped for easier identification. Henri's attorneys were then able to identify the documents they needed to mount Henri's defense and present them in a way that would be understandable to the jury. Because the retrieval had been performed following the guidelines for electronic discovery in the governing rules, authenticity was not an issue. As a result of the evidence, charges against Henri were dropped and Georgia was arrested.

This scenario demonstrates that, with good client cooperation and investigation by the attorneys and paralegals involved, some cases never have to go to trial. Henri's attorney contacted the prosecuting attorney and advised her of the results of the investigation by the forensic technologist. The prosecuting attorney was given all reports and data prepared by the technologist. Henri had been open and cooperative with all law enforcement officials, the prosecuting attorney, his attorney, and the paralegal employed by his attorney. The result was that, because of the informal discovery conducted by Henri's legal team, all charges against Henri were dropped.

KEEPING UP WITH NEW DEVELOPMENTS

As in all areas of evidence law, revisions are always in the works. When it comes to the topic of electronic evidence, changes are occurring more frequently as federal, state, and local jurisdictions struggle to gain a better grasp of the impact technology is having on the discovery process and, indeed, in all areas of substantive law and legal procedures involved with it. Be sure to stay up to date concerning changes by reading legal journals and articles, talking with colleagues, and participating in continuing education.

Not surprisingly, this area makes good use of the Internet for providing information and forms to the legal professional as well as the general public. A source for research of computer-based disclosure and discovery in civil litigation is <http://www.kenwithers.com>. For white papers and samples of forms, try <http://www.discoveryresources.org> and <http://www.fiosinc.com>. Many vendors have Web sites that contain a wealth of information on electronic discovery, including <http://www.krollontrack.com> and <http://www.attenex.com>. To keep up with the creation of standards, visit <http://www.thesedonaconference.org>.

CONCLUSION

The rapidly evolving field of electronic evidence is fascinating and exciting and will play a larger and larger role in evidence law. The paralegal may often be in the unique position of being able to educate the supervising attorney and other members of the legal team regarding developments in the law, local rules and procedures regarding electronic evidence.

■ KEY TERMS

active data	electronic evidence	metadata
archival data	forensic technologist	PDF
backup data	ghost image	safe harbor
BlackBerry	hard drive	spoliation
computer chip	LAN	WAN
computer forensics	meet and confer	

■ REVIEW QUESTIONS

1. What is the purpose of a spoliation letter?
2. Name 10 areas that should be included when inquiring into the nature and extent of an opposing party's technology.
3. Name six sources of electronic information.
4. How are the costs of producing electronic discovery determined?
5. What is data recovery?

■ APPLYING WHAT YOU HAVE LEARNED

1. List five examples of sources of electronic information.
2. What does a forensic technology scientist do?
3. What should be considered when deciding whether or not to hire a computer forensics expert to retrieve electronic information?
4. Find electronic evidence rules from two states or jurisdictions other than those used in this chapter. Compare and contrast them.

ILLUSTRATIVE CASE

Read the following case and answer the following questions:

1. What was the court's ruling regarding production of information in hard copy documentary form versus electronic form? What rules were applied in making that decision?

2. Who will pay for the discovery?

ANTI-MONOPOLY, INC., PLAINTIFF, -AGAINST- HASBRO, INC., ET AL., DEFENDANTS.

94 CIV. 2120 (LMM) (AJP)

UNITED STATES DISTRICT COURT FOR THE SOUTHERN DISTRICT OF NEW YORK

1995 U.S. DIST. LEXIS 16355; 1995-2 TRADE CAS. (CCH) P71,218

CASE SUMMARY:

PROCEDURAL POSTURE: Defendant company objected to plaintiff anti-monopoly company's motion to compel production of certain data processing files from defendant, on the grounds that it was producing the information in hard copy format and that it would have to create the information in electronic format.

OVERVIEW: Plaintiff anti-monopoly company brought a motion to compel production of certain data processing files from defendant company. Defendant company objected to the motion, on the grounds that it was producing the information in hard copy format and that it would have to create the information in electronic format. The court rejected defendant's first argument that all of the information plaintiff requested was already being produced by defendant as part of its document response. The court held that the rule was clear that the production of information in hard copy documentary form did not preclude a party from receiving that same information in computerized or electronic form. The court concluded that defendant's contention that nothing in the federal rules required it to create new documents that it did not maintain in the ordinary course of business was not consistent with the federal rule's goal of securing the just, speedy, and inexpensive determination of every action. The court noted that further rulings could depend on plaintiff's willingness to pay defendant's costs in creating the required computer program.

OUTCOME: The court held that defendant company's production of information in hard copy documentary form did not preclude plaintiff anti-monopoly company from receiving that same information in computerized or electronic form. The court noted that further rulings could depend on plaintiff's willingness to pay defendant's costs in creating the required computer program.

JUDGES: Andrew J. Peck, United States Magistrate Judge

OPINION BY: Andrew J. Peck

OPINION:

OPINION AND ORDER

(continues)

ILLUSTRATIVE CASE *(continued)*

ANDREW J. PECK, United States Magistrate Judge:

By letter motion dated October 13, 1995 (supplemented by letter dated October 31, 1995), plaintiff Anti-Monopoly, Inc. moves to compel production of certain data processing files (that is, computerized data) from defendants. The relevance of the material for discovery purposes is conceded. Defendants object largely on two grounds: (1) that they are producing the information in hard copy format, and (2) that they would have to "create" the information in electronic format.

The law is clear that data in computerized form is discoverable even if paper "hard copies" of the information have been produced, and that the producing party can be required to design a computer program to extract the data from its computerized business records, subject to the Court's discretion as to the allocation of the costs of designing such a computer program. The application of these principles to the facts of this case, however, requires further negotiation by the parties.

ANALYSIS

Rule 34(a) of the Federal Rules of Civil Procedure clearly authorizes a party to request production of computerized data:

Any party may serve on any other party a request (1) to produce . . . any designated documents (including writings, . . . and other data compilations from which information can be obtained, translated, if necessary, by the respondent through detection devices into reasonably usable form) . . . .

The 1970 Advisory Committee Notes to Rule 34 emphasize that Rule 34 applies to computer technology:

The inclusive description of "documents" is revised to accord with changing technology. It makes clear that Rule 34 applies to electronic data compilations from which information can be obtained only with the use of detection devices, and that when the data can as a practical matter be made usable by the discovering party only through respondent's devices, respondent may be required to use his devices to translate the data into usable form. In many instances, this means that respondent will have to supply a printout of computer data. The burden thus placed on respondent will vary from case to case, and the courts have ample power under Rule 26(c) to protect respondent against undue burden or expense, either by restricting discovery or requiring that the discovering party pay costs. Similarly, if the discovering party needs to check the electronic source itself, the court may protect respondent with respect to preservation of his records, confidentiality of nondiscoverable matters, and costs.

See also Sanders v. Levy, 558 F.2d 636, 648-49 (2d Cir. 1976) *(en banc) ("The 1970 amendments to the Federal Rules rendered Rule 34 specifically applicable to the discovery of computerized information."), rev'd on other grounds sub nom.* Oppenheimer Fund, Inc. v. Sanders, 437 U.S. 340, 98 S. Ct. 2380, 57 L. Ed. 2d 253 (1978) *(Rule 23 rather than Rule 34 governs identification of class members; production of computer tape proper but district court erred in imposing cost of doing so on defendants);* Santiago v. Miles, 121 F.R.D. 636, 640 (W.D.N.Y. 1988) *("A request for raw information in computer banks is proper and the information is obtainable under the discovery rules.");* Daewoo Electronics Co. v. United States, 10 C.I.T. 754, 650 F.Supp. 1003 (C.I.T. 1986) *(Rule 34 "is intended to keep pace with changing technology");* 8A C. Wright, A. Miller & R. Marcus, Federal Practice and Procedure *§ 2218 at 450 (1994) (1970 amendment of Rule 34 "brought the federal rules . . . into the computer age").*

(continues)

ILLUSTRATIVE CASE *(continued)*

As Professors Wright and Miller have noted:

> It has become evident that computers are central to modern life and consequently also to much civil litigation. As one district court put it in 1985, "computers have become so commonplace that most court battles now involve discovery of some computer-stored information."

Id. § 2218 at 449 (quoting *Bills v. Kennecott Corp., 108 F.R.D. 459, 462 (D. Utah 1985)*); see generally Manual for Complex Litigation (Third) § 21.446 (1995).

Thus, today it is black letter law that computerized data is discoverable if relevant.

Turning to defendants' objections, defendants first contend that "all of the information plaintiff requests is already being produced by [defendants] as part of [their] document response." (Defendants' 10/20/95 letter at p. 3.) That argument was rejected fifteen years ago by the court in *National Union Electric Corp. v. Matsushita Electric Industrial Co., 494 F. Supp. 1257, 1261 (E.D. Pa. 1980)* (citing, inter alia, *United States v. Davey, 543 F.2d 996, 1000 (2d Cir. 1976)*). See also 8A C. Wright, A. Miller & R. Marcus, Federal Practice and Procedure § 2218 at 452 & n.13 (citing cases). As in the present case, Matsushita involved the need for computerized sales and price information to allow analysis in an antitrust case. Thus, the rule is clear: [HN4] production of information in "hard copy" documentary form does not preclude a party from receiving that same information in computerized/electronic form.

Second, defendants contend that "nothing in the Federal rules requires Defendants to create new documents that they do not maintain in the ordinary course of business" and "Plaintiff's motion would require [defendants] to create a new electronic format, solely to ease plaintiff's review of documents." (Defendants' 10/20/95 letter at p. 1, 3.) The court rejected this same argument in Matsushita, at least where the requesting party offered to pay the cost of creating the computer program. *494 F. Supp. at 1258-62; accord, In re Air Crash Disaster at Detroit Metropolitan Airport, 130 F.R.D. 634, 635 (E.D. Mich. 1989)*. The Matsushita court further noted:

> We suspect that by the year 2000 virtually all data will be stored in some form of computer memory. To interpret the Federal Rules which, after all, are to be construed to "secure the just, speedy and inexpensive determination of every action," *F.R. Civ. P. 1* (emphasis added), in a manner which would preclude the production of material such as is requested here, would eventually defeat their purpose.

Matsushita, 494 F. Supp. at 1262-63.

In its letter dated October 30, 1995, defendants claim that:

> The documents that Hasbro has agreed to produce present the requested sales and discount data in various aggregate forms — broken down by item, customer, year or month. These are the reports that Hasbro generated for use by its management in the normal course of business during the period in question. Hasbro is not seeking to withhold electronic versions of these reports. The fact of the matter is that these reports no longer exist in electronic form. Accordingly, Hasbro can produce nothing more than the hard copy versions that it has agreed to produce.
>
>   What is at issue here, then, is not sales and discount data, but electronic versions of each and every invoice and credit memo generated by Hasbro over a four year period. The burden to Hasbro of collecting all

(continues)

ILLUSTRATIVE CASE   *(continued)*

of these electronic invoices is substantial and certain: weeks of programming and computer time to collect the invoices followed by substantial attorney review time to ensure that they are responsive. It would be impossible to complete production by the Court's November 30 deadline. The benefit to plaintiff, however, is entirely speculative. Plaintiff has made no showing as to why it is necessary or even helpful to examine individual invoices to substantiate allegations of discriminatory pricing, especially when Hasbro has already agreed to produce documents sufficient to show the terms of sale with all its customers.

If the "aggregating" reports referred to in the first paragraph truly "no longer exist in electronic form," obviously that moots the issue. n1

n1 Defendants will need to represent not just that the reports are not available electronically but that it is not possible to electronically re-create the reports by running a specially-written computer program over existing computerized business data.

As to the second quoted paragraph, the Court does not have sufficient information as to plaintiff's need for "electronic" invoices in light of other available discovery data or of the real costs (in time and money) to defendants to create a program to "collect" that data. The Court leaves it to the parties to further discuss the issue in light of the Court's ruling.

The Court further notes that, as in Matsushita, further Court rulings may depend on plaintiff's willingness to pay defendants' costs in creating the required computer program. See also, e.g., *In re Air Crash Disaster at Detroit Metropolitan Airport, 130 F.R.D. at 636* (ordering requesting party to pay costs of manufacturing computerized information); *Williams v. E.I. du Pont de Nemours & Co., 119 F.R.D. 648, 651 (W.D. Ky. 1987)* (same); *Bills v. Kennecott Corp., 108 F.R.D. at 462-64* (same).

If the parties are not able to resolve the issue, plaintiff is to submit a follow-up letter motion by November 17, 1995 (with defendants' response due November 29, 1995 and plaintiff's reply due by December 4, 1995). As appropriate, affidavits from computer personnel or computer experts should be submitted.

SO ORDERED.

For additional resources, visit our Web site at www.westlegalstudies.com

CHAPTER 8

Physical Evidence

■ OBJECTIVES

After studying this chapter you should be able to:

❏ know the Federal Rules of Civil Procedure that relate to physical evidence.

❏ understand the importance of preserving physical evidence and how to preserve it.

❏ know how to prepare a request for inspection of physical evidence.

❏ know how to conduct an inspection.

INTRODUCTION

As discussed in Chapter 1, physical (or tangible) evidence is evidence with physical substance that is related to the incident that gave rise to the case. This evidence is separate from documentary evidence (see Chapter 2) in that it represents *objects* rather than paper. An example of physical evidence would be samples of the Omniphone and Pictophone discussed in the hypothetical case in Chapter 1. Another example would be the Foxfire Boat Company houseboat used by the Johnsons in the hypothetical case described in Chapter 3 (or the engine from that houseboat). A third example would be the painting allegedly stolen by Henri in the hypothetical case in Chapter 7. As with obtaining documentary or witness evidence, the paralegal must be familiar with methods used to preserve, obtain, and inspect physical evidence during the discovery phase of the lawsuit.

RULES RELATING TO PHYSICAL EVIDENCE

Rule 34 of the Federal Rules of Civil Procedure provides for the inspection of physical evidence. Rule 34(a) states:

Any party may serve on any other party a request (1) to produce and permit the party making the request, or someone acting on the requestor's behalf, to inspect and copy, any designated documents (including writings, drawings, graphs, charts, photographs, phonorecords, and other data compilations from which information can be obtained, translated, if necessary, by the respondent through the detection devices into reasonably useable form), or to inspect and copy, test, or sample any tangible things which constitute or contain matters within the scope of Rule 26(b) and which are in the possession, custody or control of the party upon whom the request is served; or (2) to permit entry upon designated land or other property in the possession or control of the party upon whom the request is served for the purpose of inspection and measuring, surveying, photographing, testing, or sampling the property or any designated object or operation thereon, within the scope of Rule 26(b).

As with requesting the production of records, discussed in Chapter 2, a party wishing to see tangible things in the possession of another party may simply serve a formal written request to that effect (see Exhibit 8–2). If the physical evidence is in the possession, custody, or control of a nonparty, however, a subpoena pursuant to Rule 45 of the Federal Rules of Civil Procedure must be served in order to gain access.

THE FIRST STEP: PRESERVATION

It would certainly seem easier to misplace a piece of paper than a houseboat; however, spoliation of physical evidence can and does occur. While documents can be photocopied or imaged and stored in separate places, thereby assuring their safety, it is not possible to duplicate tangible evidence.

Not all spoliation is intentional. Stories abound of carelessness that led to the loss of key evidence. In one instance, a client brought an attorney an empty soda pop can with a ragged edge on which she had severely cut her lip. In his haste to leave the office that evening, the attorney left the can sitting on his credenza, only to learn in the morning that the janitorial staff had crushed the can and dumped it in the office recycle bin during their nightly cleanup.

Another illustration of unintentional spoliation involved a speedboat that was being stored by the manufacturer in a storage unit. A person had been injured by the propeller on the speedboat and the boat was being stored pending trial of the matter. The speedboat was mixed in with discarded company items, including old desks, filing cabinets, and other discontinued boat models. An energetic employee of the manufacturer, unaware of the significance of the speedboat, decided to clean out the storage unit to make space for new items, and the boat was sold.

If your firm is representing a client who has been or may be sued and a piece of physical evidence is involved, you must take immediate steps to preserve and protect that evidence. Smaller items should be labeled as to their significance, with warnings in plain view not to dispose of them. They should be locked in a storage or filing cabinet under the firm's control until needed for production or inspection. Larger items, such as speedboats, present a different problem. In bigger cities there are companies that specialize in the storage of large tangible items in litigation matters, especially vehicles that have been involved in accidents. If that option is not available to you, the firm may have to rent a storage unit big enough to house the evidence. Again, clearly label the evidence as such, with a warning not to destroy, dispose of, or alter it in any way.

If you are on the other side of the case, most often the plaintiff, there are two steps you can take to ensure that physical evidence will be preserved. The first is what is known as a **preservation of evidence letter**. This is most often sent to a defendant prior to the actual filing of the lawsuit and puts the defendant on notice that litigation is contemplated. See Exhibit 8–1 for a sample preservation of evidence letter.

> **! TIP**
>
> It is always preferable to have the piece of evidence either at your firm and under your control, or in the control of a neutral third party, such as a storage facility, rather than in the possession of the client. This will help to reduce the possibility of future claims of spoliation by the opposing party.

■ **PRESERVATION OF EVIDENCE LETTER**
A letter sent to an opposing party who is in possession of key evidence, putting the party on notice that litigation is contemplated and instructing the party to preserve the evidence.

EXHIBIT 8–1   SAMPLE PRESERVATION OF EVIDENCE LETTER

Main Street Motel
1234 Main Street
Anytown, USA

    Re: Injured Guest

Gentlepersons:

On April 18, 2002, our client, Sandra Michaels, sustained serious burn injuries caused by a defective coffeemaker located in room 102 of your motel. As you know, our office intends to file a lawsuit arising from this incident.

(continues)

EXHIBIT 8–1   SAMPLE PRESERVATION OF EVIDENCE LETTER *(continued)*

Obviously the coffeemaker and all of its component parts are critical evidence in this case. Therefore, we request that you preserve as evidence the coffeemaker and all component parts, including all the base, controls, electrical cord, and glass carafe. Please also retain any parts that have been removed or replaced and all repair or purchase records related to the coffeemaker.

We request that you allow a representative from our office, accompanied by an appropriate expert, immediate access onto the property to inspect the coffeemaker in its current condition and location. Until we have an opportunity to inspect the coffeemaker, we request that it not be removed, repaired, or altered in any manner.

Thank you.

Sincerely,

CAREER TIP

Throughout your career you will create useful forms and also run across interesting forms created by opposing counsel that are served upon you. Begin a form file in which you keep copies of the best examples, so that you do not have to reinvent the wheel when the same situation arises.

This letter serves two purposes. First, it will hopefully prevent the unintentional spoliation of evidence by a defendant who is not aware that a lawsuit is pending. Second, if the defendant does persist in destroying the evidence despite the warning, the plaintiff will be in a better position to seek sanctions from the court.

Once the lawsuit is filed, a second and even stronger step is to ask the court early in the case to enter an order requiring the parties to preserve and retain tangible evidence.

A special situation exists when the party who was the original owner of the evidence no longer has possession of it. You should serve interrogatories on the party as soon as you learn he or she no longer has the physical item to ascertain its current location. For example, if you wish to inspect the vehicle that was involved in an accident, and the party has sold it to someone else, you may be able to obtain the name and address of the new owner. It is then possible to serve the new owner with a subpoena in order to require him or her to allow the inspection of the vehicle. If there is concern that the new owner may be intending to resell or otherwise dispose of the vehicle, and the evidence is critical to the case, attorneys have been known to actually purchase the vehicle themselves in order to preserve it for trial. This would be an option for any type of physical evidence, if the case budget allows.

THE SECOND STEP: REQUESTING INSPECTION

Once the physical evidence is secure, the next thing the parties will want to do is inspect it. If the evidence is in the possession of a third party, a subpoena will be necessary in order to require the third party to make the evidence available. If the evidence is in the possession of an opposing party, a request for inspection is required.

Please see Exhibit 8–2 for a sample of a request for inspection of a boat that was involved in an accident.

EXHIBIT 8–2   SAMPLE REQUEST FOR INSPECTION

Josephine Attorney
Briggs and Briggs
853 Central Street
Tulsa, Oklahoma
(918) 555-1840

Attorney for Plaintiff

UNITED STATES DISTRICT COURT

Eastern District of Oklahoma

SUSIE RIDE,	)	
	)	Civil Action No. 00587
Plaintiff,	)	
	)	PLAINTIFF'S REQUEST FOR
v.	)	INSPECTION
	)	
ROGER FLOYD; HAPPYWAKE	)	
BOAT MANUFACTURING, INC.	)	
	)	
Defendants.	)	
————————————————	)	

PROPOUNDING PARTY: Plaintiff SUSIE RIDE

RESPONDING PARTY: Defendant ROGER FLOYD

SET NO.:   One

Susie Ride, Plaintiff herein, makes the following request pursuant to Rule 34 of the Federal Rules of Civil Procedure. Under Rule 34(b), you are required to serve a written response to this request, indicating whether you will comply with each request listed below, no later than 30 days from the date this Request was served upon you.

(continues)

EXHIBIT 8–2 SAMPLE REQUEST FOR INSPECTION *(continued)*

OBJECTS REQUESTED

You are requested to make available and provide access to the 1994 Happywake Speedster vessel, bearing Vessel Identification No. B47849G74800Y, said boat being involved in the accident which is the subject of this lawsuit, within the meaning of Federal Rules of Civil Procedure, Rule 34(a), for inspection, photographing, measuring and testing.

Said inspection will take place on January 30, 2006, at 10:00 a.m., at a place mutually convenient to the parties.

Dated: December 20, 2005

BRIGGS & BRIGGS

By: _____

Josephine Attorney
Counsel for Plaintiff

If destructive testing is going to be conducted at the inspection (see Chapter 5 regarding experts and destructive testing), it must be so noted in the request.

CONDUCTING THE INSPECTION

Paralegals are often asked to accompany attorneys to the inspection, to be a second set of eyes and ears and to assist the attorney in photographing or videotaping the evidence. Find out from your attorney ahead of time whether she will want you to take photographs or videotapes of the physical evidence, or arrange for an expert witness to accompany you. Often the client will want to attend the inspection also. Absent a court order, you will usually have only one chance to inspect the evidence prior to trial, so be prepared and thorough.

Make sure cameras are in good working order and there is plenty of film or memory available. Be sure that batteries are charged up the night before. If an expert witness is being asked to attend, be sure to send her a courtesy copy of the request or subpoena, so that the inspection can be placed on her calendar. You should also either telephone or write to the expert to see if she needs anything from you in advance to prepare for the inspection, or wants you to bring something to the inspection to assist her. If there is a possibility that videotape may be introduced as evidence during the trial of the matter, you may wish to retain the services of a professional videographer (see Chapter 6).

The opposing party and her attorney are usually present at the inspection. Respect confidentiality rules and be careful about discussing the case or the results of the inspection in their presence. Your own client must also be cautioned not to discuss strategy or other confidential information in a place where it could be overheard by the opposition.

CRIMINAL EVIDENCE

Inspection of physical evidence in a criminal matter is a less formal process. The prosecution must make available to the defense nearly all evidence that has been gathered by law enforcement and investigators. All that is usually required to inspect tangible evidence is for the defense counsel to contact the prosecutor either by telephone or by letter and set a time when the evidence can be inspected.

The prosecution must also make the physical evidence available so that the defense can conduct its own testing at a laboratory of its own choice. This could include a blood sample taken in a driving under the influence (DUI) matter, DNA evidence in a rape case, or a urine sample for drug testing. A request for discovery or similar document, depending on the jurisdiction, must be used to request release of the physical evidence for testing purposes.

Especially in criminal cases, paralegals must follow chain of custody rules scrupulously so that there is no question of the authenticity of the evidence or the resulting tests (see Chapter 1 for discussion of chain of custody issues).

CONCLUSION

As with other types of evidence, paralegals play a key role in gathering and inspecting physical evidence. Preservation and the prevention of spoliation of tangible evidence and chain of custody issues are even more vital here than with other types of evidence. A well-trained paralegal must be aware of the rules governing these areas and follow them to the letter so that valuable evidence is not lost forever.

■ KEY TERMS

preservation of evidence letter

■ REVIEW QUESTIONS

1. What procedure is used to inspect tangible evidence in the possession of a nonparty?
2. How can you protect a client's tangible evidence from accidental spoliation?
3. What is a preservation of evidence letter and when should it be used?
4. How does the process of arranging for inspection of physical evidence in a criminal matter differ from a civil matter?

■ APPLYING WHAT YOU HAVE LEARNED

1. Using the sample preservation of evidence letter in Exhibit 8–1, prepare a letter to Microcell Manufacturing on behalf of Cellutronics, Inc., asking Microcell to preserve all physical evidence you think they might have that would be important to the case (see Chapter 1 for case scenario).
2. Review the form books for your state in your local library and find a form for a court order requiring the preservation of evidence.
3. Review Case 2 in Chapter 9 regarding the accidental spraying of a farmer's pistachio orchard with defoliant. Your firm represents the defendant, the neighboring farmer, and the hired expert on pistachio trees wishes to inspect the sickened orchard. Using the form in Exhibit 8–2, prepare a request for an inspection of the pistachio orchard. Your expert wishes to remove samples from the trees, so be sure to add language to that effect in your draft request.

ILLUSTRATIVE CASE

Read the following case and answer the following questions:

1. Give some possible reasons why Chrysler decided to withdraw its request for destructive testing of the handbrake assembly.

2. As the paralegal in charge of arranging for the functional testing of the handbrake once the order has been signed, what steps would you take to make the necessary arrangements? Who would you contact? How would you document the testing?

JOHN P. QUINN, JR. V. CHRYSLER CORPORATION

35 F.R.D. 34 (1964)

UNITED STATES DISTRICT COURT FOR THE WESTERN DISTRICT OF PENNSYLVANIA

CASE NO. 63-344

(continues)

ILLUSTRATIVE CASE *(continued)*

Judge MARSH delivered the opinion of the Court.

In this personal injury diversity action the plaintiffs allege negligence and breach of warranties on the part of the defendants with respect to an allegedly defective handbraking system installed in the 1958 Plymouth station wagon manufactured by defendant Chrysler. The defendant Chrysler has moved pursuant to Rule 34, Fed. R. Civ.P., for the production of the handbrake assembly presently in possession of the plaintiffs or their expert, A.J. McKelvey. It avers that photographing, X-ray examination, inspection and testing of this assembly are essential to the preparation of a defense; specifically, it asks for an order to disassemble the handbrake assembly in order to secure a complete expert inspection. After argument, by letter to the court, counsel for Chrysler withdrew its request to disassemble the handbrake assembly, which was vigorously opposed by the plaintiffs. See affidavit of A.J. McKelvey. Accordingly, we consider here only the requests for production for the purposes of photographing, X-ray examination, and testing the handbrake assembly. In its brief, Chrysler limits its request for testing the handbrake assembly to installing it in another vehicle of similar make, model, and year, in order that a functional test thereof may be conducted.

In our opinion, the scope of Rule 34 encompasses the type of discovery herein sought by Chrysler . . . and good cause has been shown since the plaintiffs, who contend that the injuries sustained by them were caused by the defective handbrake assembly, have possession thereof, and the movant cannot test and photograph the mechanism without an order. The affidavit submitted by plaintiffs does not suggest that the allegedly patent defects of the handbrake assembly will be disturbed by installation and functional testing thereof in a similar vehicle, but addresses itself only to the request of Chrysler, now withdrawn, for *disassembling* of the mechanism. Accordingly, defendant Chrysler's motion for production will be granted, consistent with this opinion.

For additional resources, visit our Web site at www.westlegalstudies.com

9

Demonstrative Evidence

■ OBJECTIVES

After studying this chapter you should be able to:

❑ know the Federal Rules of Evidence relating to demonstrative evidence.

❑ explain the different types of demonstrative evidence and their uses.

❑ know the steps for planning the use of demonstrative evidence.

❑ understand the difference between real and demonstrative evidence.

INTRODUCTION

The complexity of today's lawsuits could not have been imagined even a decade ago. The trial team is faced with several challenges, including making a jury familiar enough with complicated concepts to render a meaningful verdict and keeping a judge and jury alert and interested through a long, sometimes drawn-out trial. It has been scientifically proven that people tend to retain facts more readily when they are provided with a mixture of verbal and nonverbal information. One method of accomplishing these goals is through the use of demonstrative evidence. Planning and creating demonstrative evidence often falls within the paralegal's job description.

THE USE OF DEMONSTRATIVE EVIDENCE

Demonstrative evidence is generally described as visual aids used for illustrative purposes. Demonstrative evidence is not real evidence, in that it was not part of the event or transaction that is the subject of the lawsuit. It is created specifically to illustrate or demonstrate a key point or issue during a trial. Examples of demonstrative evidence include blowups, photographs, charts, graphs, drawings, models, demonstrative videos (see Chapter 5), computer animation, and multimedia presentations. These and other types of demonstrative evidence and their uses will be discussed later in this chapter.

Rule 1006 of the Federal Rules of Evidence opened the door to a wide variety of demonstrative evidence now used at trial. Rule 1006 permits the admission of secondary evidence in the form of charts, summaries, or compilations as proof of the contents of voluminous writings that cannot practically or conveniently be produced in court.

Rule 1006. Summaries

The contents of voluminous writings, recordings, or photographs which cannot conveniently be examined in court may be presented in the form of a chart, summary or calculation. The original, or duplicates, shall be made available for examination or copying, or both, by other parties at reasonable time and place. The court may order that they be produced in court.

The use of demonstrative evidence is also governed by two other evidentiary rules, Rule 403 and Rule 611(a). The purpose of these rules is to allow the judge leeway to permit forms of summary evidence in the interest of promoting a fair trial or to disallow what is irrelevant, unnecessary, or apt to create a serious misimpression as to how an event might have occurred.

Rule 403. Exclusion of Relevant Evidence on Grounds of Prejudice, Confusion, or Waste of Time.

Although relevant, evidence may be excluded if its probative value is substantially outweighed by the danger of unfair prejudice, confusion of the issues, or misleading the jury, or by considerations of undue delay, waste of time, or needless presentation of cumulative evidence.

Rule 611. Mode and Order of Interrogation and Presentation.

(a) Control by Court. The court shall exercise reasonable control over the mode and order of interrogating witnesses and presenting evidence so as to (1) make the interrogation and presentation effective for the ascertainment of the truth, (2) avoid needless consumption of time, and (3) protect witnesses from harassment or undue embarrassment.

■ **PROBATIVE**

Tending to prove or actually proving something.

It is important to remember that demonstrative evidence has no **probative** value in and of itself. This means that since it is not real evidence, it cannot be used to prove a matter but only to illustrate a point or concept. Because it is not probative, demonstrative evidence will be admitted to the jury room to be used during deliberation only at the discretion of the trial judge.

During trial preparation, the trial team will decide what evidence will be used to prove the client's case and disprove the opponent's case. The evidence chosen will be marked as trial exhibits. At that time, the trial team should brainstorm whether demonstrative evidence may be needed to more simply explain or more clearly illustrate a complicated issue to the jury. Depending upon the type of demonstrative evidence needed, its creation could be handled in-house by the paralegal; however, it may be necessary to contact an outside vendor for more complicated projects. A significant benefit of Rule 1006 is that it does not require that the demonstrative evidence be created by persons with special expertise, only that it accurately reflects the underlying data and does not misrepresent the information to the trier of fact.

One of the most important factors in determining whether demonstrative evidence can or will be utilized is cost. While a photograph or graph will be relatively inexpensive to create, a computer-animated re-creation of a multiple-vehicle accident will cost many thousands of dollars. The attorney usually works with the client in creating a trial budget and will then let the paralegal know how much can be spent on demonstrative evidence. Paralegals often must be creative in crafting effective demonstrative evidence within the parameters of the client's budget.

TYPES OF DEMONSTRATIVE EVIDENCE

Following is a discussion of the most common types of demonstrative evidence.

■ **BLOWUP**

An enlargement of a document, photograph, or piece of demonstrative evidence for use at trial or pretrial; used as a method to draw attention to key information.

Blowups

One of the least expensive and most effective ways to draw attention to key information is by making an enlargement, or what is commonly known as a **blowup**. A copy service or graphics company will take a photocopy of a document, photograph, or electronic image and increase it in size to two feet by three feet, or larger, and then mount the document on poster board or foam-core board. The graphics company can even add such features as the highlighting of certain text on the blowup, thereby accentuating exactly what is important about that particular document. The attorney then displays the blowup in the courtroom on an easel to assist him in making a specific point. This technique is effective in drawing the jurors' attention simultaneously to a particular piece of evidence and making certain, as the saying goes, that "everyone is on the same page."

One type of document that would be suitable for a blowup is a page from a witness's deposition transcript containing damaging testimony. If the witness then tries to change what he said while on the witness stand, the attorney can display the blowup and catch him in the contradiction (a technique known as impeaching a witness). It is also possible to blow up another piece of demonstrative evidence, such as a chart or graph, that the attorney wishes to discuss with a witness while the jury follows along.

You may prepare a blowup of a key medical record that contains an important diagnosis of the client or a page from a report that concludes the opposing party was responsible for an accident. Sometimes trial attorneys will leave such damaging evidence sitting on the easel throughout the trial as a constant reminder to the jury.

The most important rule to remember about blowups is to not overuse them. They are designed to create heightened impact for the jury. If nearly every documentary exhibit is enlarged, the jury will quickly grow used to seeing large documents, and key pieces of evidence will no longer be underscored. Remember that the underlying document from which the blowup is made must be admitted into evidence by the judge before the blowup can be displayed to the jury.

Graphs/Charts

Graphs and charts are useful in assisting the judge and jury in following complicated time sequences, relationships in events, or mathematical evidence, such as summaries of accounting data. Great care must be taken in creating the chart to be certain that it accurately reflects the underlying data. Federal Rule 1006 requires that the original evidence be made available by the party introducing the chart or summary if there is a dispute as to the accuracy of the summary. Following are some illustrations of the use of these important tools.

Case 1 — A woman was injured during a motor vehicle accident and sued the driver of the vehicle that hit her. In the normal course of discovery, the paralegal representing the defendant subpoenaed the woman's medical records. While preparing a time line showing the dates and types of treatment, the paralegal noticed there was a long period of inactivity, followed by a sudden cluster of appointments and treatment, followed by another long period of inactivity, and so on. Curious about this unusual pattern of medical treatment, the paralegal looked at the case files to observe the dates of activity in the lawsuit. The paralegal noticed an exact correlation between the woman's treatments and important events in the lawsuit, such as responding to discovery, the taking of depositions, and so on. The paralegal used this information to create a line graph that illustrated the overlapping relationship between the woman's treatment and the activity in the lawsuit. The graph made it very clear to the jury that the woman was manipulating her treatment to build a case, and that her injuries were probably not as severe as she alleged.

Case 2 — The firm's client is a pistachio farmer. One windy day, the neighboring farmer hired a helicopter to spray a defoliant on a weed-infested field next to the client's healthy orchard. The wind carried the defoliant onto the leaves of the pistachio trees. While it did not kill the trees outright, it sickened them to the point where the production levels of pistachios dropped for several years. In proving the damages for the case, the client has a variety of different records such as harvest data, processing data, weight tags showing tonnage, and other information. It would take half a day to plow through these records during the trial to show the production levels before the accidental spraying of defoliant and the years of substandard production. Nothing will put a jury to sleep faster than the monotonous recitation of figures. The creative paralegal can prepare a bar graph from the underlying records, illustrating the high production levels before the spraying and then showing the bars dropping for several years after the spraying before rising again.

Case 3 — Tools such as time lines can be used to show the jury exactly when a complicated string of events occurred. They can illustrate actions that occurred over many years or only minutes, and can instill a sense of the urgency of an incident. Such a time line was used in a wrongful death case. The estate of a woman who purchased a personal alarm system sued the alarm manufacturer for failing to respond to a choking emergency that resulted in the woman's death. A time line created by the paralegal began with the time the woman first began choking, to the time her daughter activated the personal alarm system, to the time the daughter began administering the Heimlich maneuver while waiting for a response from the alarm company. The time line then tracked the continued attempts to resuscitate the woman, the daughter's call to 911 when the alarm company failed to respond, the arrival of the ambulance, and attempted cardiopulmonary resuscitation. The time line ended when the woman was pronounced dead. Total elapsed time: 40 minutes. Drama can be heightened with the use of color. The beginning of the chart showing the time line was colored a serene green. As the choking continued and the woman's situation became more serious, the color of the chart changed to an alarming red color. It ended with black as the woman was pronounced dead.

Paralegals can use standard computer software, such as Microsoft Excel® or Harvard Graphics, to create bar charts, pie charts, and other number-based graphs. For more complicated charts, graphic art companies that specialize in legal-related products can be hired to help the paralegal conceive a design for a colorful, illustrative piece of demonstrative evidence that will capture and hold the jury's attention. See Exhibit 9-1.

CAREER TIP

Former paralegals with graphic arts skills have opened their own companies specializing in the creation of graphs, charts, and other types of demonstrative evidence.

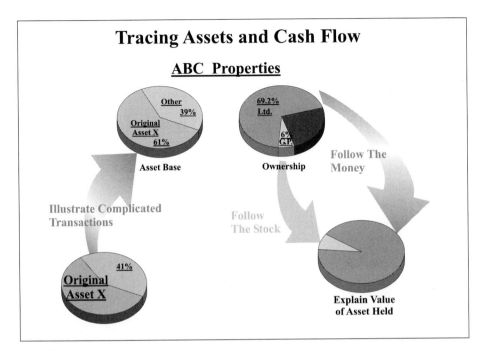

EXHIBIT 9-1   Sample chart.

Photographs

The old adage that a picture is worth a thousand words is particularly applicable in a courtroom, where the trial attorney is under the pressure of time to put on his case quickly without boring the jury or irritating the judge. Photographs have a wide variety of uses at trial. They can be used to freeze an issue in time, for example, a farmer's field flooded by a levee break, a building burned by arson, or injuries that would be healed by the time the case goes to trial.

Aerial photographs can be used to show scale or perspective to a jury to help them understand a particular issue. See Exhibit 9-2. For example, suppose your firm represents a property owner involved in a boundary dispute with a neighbor whose new fence has been built over the property line. Many cities have mapped their neighborhoods with the use of aerial photographs. It is possible for the paralegal to obtain from the assessor's office a photograph of the city block containing the two houses involved in the lawsuit and prepare an overlay showing where the surveyed boundary is between the properties.

EXHIBIT 9-2   Aerial photograph.

Historical aerial photographs are also very useful in showing changes in features on land over periods of time. In a dispute over riparian rights, for example, photographs over several years can show the change in the course of a stream. When a subdivision of homeowners complained that oil was coming up in the ground of their backyards, historical photographs from the 1920s showed that oil wells and sumps had once existed near the property. In another situation, a homeowner fenced his backyard, cutting off an unofficial public pathway through his property to the beach. Neighbors brought a lawsuit claiming that the path had been there for many years. Historical aerial photos were used to show when the path first appeared and where. These types of photographs can often be purchased from online companies. Sometimes local universities will have libraries of old photographs.

In wrongful death cases it is sometimes difficult for the attorney to create any sort of empathy with the decedent on the part of the jury. When the person is only mentioned by name, he becomes more of an abstract concept than a living, breathing human being. To overcome this, attorneys will often show the jury photographs of the decedent laughing with family members, holding a newborn baby, or celebrating a birthday, in an attempt to establish an emotional connection.

In a personal injury lawsuit, showing the jury a photograph of the mangled vehicle in which the injured person had been riding will speak volumes about the severity of the injuries. An example is shown in Exhibit 9-3.

Paralegals can be of great help, suggesting areas where photographs would be helpful, hiring a photographer to obtain photographs if they do not already exist, and having blowups made if necessary.

Drawings/Illustrations

These types of demonstrative evidence can be used when photographs are not available or will not suffice. Drawings and illustrations can be expensive for the client, as they must usually be prepared by an expert in a particular field. A drawing or illustration might be useful in a situation where your client's hand was injured at work when it was crushed in a drill press whose guard had been improperly removed by the employer. An engineer or draftsperson can be hired to make a drawing of the machine with a cutaway view of the drill underneath the guard, showing the position of the client's hand during the injury and how it would have been protected had the guard been properly in place. Trial graphics companies also have three dimensional modeling software that can be used to create drawings and cutaways, both still and animated.

Reproduced by permission. Collison Analysis and Reconstruction

EXHIBIT 9-3 Photograph of wrecked vehicle.

From X-rays, medical illustrators can make drawings showing a fractured ankle, which the medical expert can use to describe how the injury incurred. A drawing of a normal ankle can be shown next to the broken one so that the jury can compare and get a sense of the extent of the injury. Exhibit 9-4 is an example of a medical illustration.

Models

A valuable tool for a more hands-on demonstration is a model. These are most effective to demonstrate movement or scale. Virtually anything can be made into a model if it will assist the jury in understanding a particular issue. A medical expert witness commonly uses a model in demonstrating the movement of a particular part of the human body. Full-size plastic recreations of knee joints or shoulder joints can be used by the expert to show the jury how movement is impaired following an injury.

Another use of a movement type of model is to recreate an intersection or street where a motor vehicle accident occurred. The intersection can be pictured from the air and small model cars mounted with Velcro® or magnets can be moved around by witnesses or attorneys to illustrate how the vehicles entered the intersection and collided. Models such as these can be prepared with the help of accident reconstruction experts and graphics artists. See Exhibits 9-5 and 9-6.

ACCIDENT 4-6-99
Open Left Tibula-Fibula Fracture

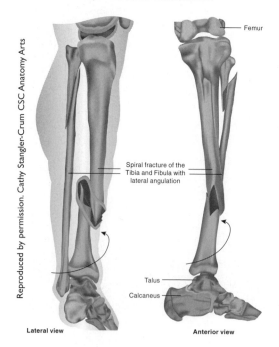

Reproduced by permission. Cathy Stangler-Crum CSC Anatomy Arts

Femur

Spiral fracture of the
Tibia and Fibula with
lateral angulation

Talus

Calcaneus

Lateral view

Anterior view

EXHIBIT 9-4 Medical illustration.

EXHIBIT 9-5   Photograph of model #1.

EXHIBIT 9-6   Photograph of model #2.

Sometimes models can be used where juries really need a three-dimensional image, rather than a photograph, to understand distance and proximity relationships. For example, suppose your firm represents a homeowner who lives on the side of a hill. The local power company cut a swath across the hill above the client's home, creating a trench in which to bury power lines. This destabilized the hill, causing a large landslide during the rainy season, which buried part of the client's house and property. Although photographs were taken, it was difficult in two dimensions to show the scale of what happened. You can have a model of the hillside and house created, much like the familiar large-scale model train sets, and the jury will be better able to understand the distances from the trench to the property and how far the landslide traveled.

Sometimes it is impossible to get an idea across to the jury short of re-creating an exact replica of what happened. In one case, a woman who was shopping in a store was severely injured by a toy rocking horse, which fell off of a tall shelf above her and struck her on the head. The trial team for the woman had the rocking horse itself as real evidence, but it appeared lightweight and flimsy. The team was concerned that the jury would not believe that such an object could cause the injuries of which the woman complained. The paralegal arranged for a replica of the store shelf to be constructed to scale at the correct height and set up inside the courtroom. The rocking horse was then placed up on the high shelf and knocked over. It came crashing down to the floor and the point was made.

Just as charts and graphs must accurately reflect underlying data, care must be taken to make sure the model is built to exact scale and precisely mirrors the original item it re-creates.

PhotoModeler Photogrammetry

PhotoModeler® is a Windows-based program tool that is being used extensively by accident reconstructionists to assist in the analysis of motor vehicle collisions. It is used to accurately map the damage that occurred to a vehicle in a collision by extracting measurements from photographs, a technique known as **photogrammetry**. The vehicle, including the damaged area, is marked with data points, which are then digitally photographed. The photograph data is downloaded into the PhotoModeler® computer program that can be used to build either a two-dimensional or three-dimensional diagram of the damaged vehicle. See Exhibit 9-7.

After downloading the data for the damaged vehicle, an undamaged exemplar vehicle is also marked with data points, digitally photographed, and downloaded to build a diagram. The diagrams of the damaged and undamaged vehicles are then overlaid so that precise measurements of the damage on the wrecked vehicle can be made for analysis. See Exhibit 9-8.

The vehicle diagrams can be imported into a CAD (computer-aided design) or other graphics program map of the accident scene. The undamaged vehicle model can be placed on the scene map in various locations to represent its approach to the impact. The damaged vehicle diagram can be placed on the map at various locations showing its path of travel from the impact to the point of rest. See Exhibit 9-9.

■ **PHOTOGRAMMETRY**
The process of making maps, surveys, or scale drawings by referring to photographs, especially aerial photographs.

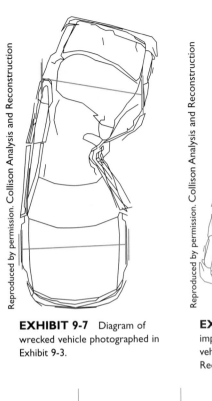

EXHIBIT 9-7 Diagram of wrecked vehicle photographed in Exhibit 9-3.

EXHIBIT 9-8 Diagram of super-imposed damaged and undamaged vehicles. "Collison Analysis and Reconstruction"

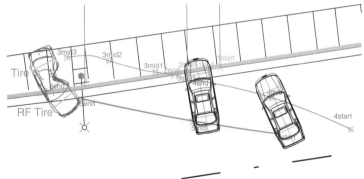

EXHIBIT 9-9 Photogrammetry map of accident site. "Collison Analysis and Reconstruction"

PhotoModeler® software is applicable to most areas of litigation where an exact diagram of physical objects is needed to give the jury a sense of an accident or murder scene. For example, a room where a trip and fall incident or an assault took place could be modeled and used to show the path of travel across the room of the persons involved.

Computer Animation

One of the more high-end types of demonstrative evidence is computer anima-tion. A vendor that specializes in this field must be hired to create the animation clip, and such an expensive endeavor will probably be used only in cases where a lot of money is at stake. Animation is used to re-create how a chain of events or actions occurred. Examples of this are how a 20-car pileup on an interstate freeway happened, where a fire started in a building and spread, how a surgical procedure was done, or how a person became dislodged from a safety restraint and was thrown from a carni-val ride. The new photomodeling technology described above can be imported into a computer animation program for this purpose.

Multimedia Presentations

VIDEO TEXT SYNCHRONIZATION
Technology that allows digitized videotaped dep-ositions to be linked with corresponding transcripts or deposition exhibits and shown on a monitor to the jury.

Multimedia software programs such as Trial Director® are now available and sim-ple enough to use that a computer-savvy trial team can use them to integrate docu-ments, graphics, and video clips to produce presentations that can be made to the jury during the trial. Technology called **video text synchronization** allows the attorney or paralegal to digitize videotaped depositions and link them to the corresponding elec-tronic or scanned versions of the transcripts or exhibits. The attorney can then open windows with a computer mouse and display a portion of the videotaped deposition next to the corresponding page of transcript or exhibit being discussed, allowing the jurors to read along while they watch the reactions of the witness. For example, take a look at Case Scenario No. 1 from Chapter 1, *Cellutronics v. Microcell*. Suppose you have a clip from the videotaped deposition of Jacob Richmond, swearing under oath that he never disclosed Omniphone technology to his new employer, Microcell Manufacturing. Using trial software programs and technology, the trial team can split the screen on the courtroom monitor and while displaying the video clip of Jacob on one side, display on the other side a copy of a memo subpoenaed from the CEO of Microcell congratulating and thanking Jacob for giving them a jump on the creation of the Pictophone through his design knowledge of the Omniphone. As stated at the beginning of this chapter, such a combination of verbal and nonverbal communication will cement itself in the jurors' minds and create a lasting impression.

It is important to remember that if the paralegal or attorney does not have the necessary computer expertise, outside vendors can be hired to create the presenta-tion and even accompany the trial team to the courtroom to set up and run the com-puter equipment.

PowerPoint® Presentations

Attorneys are more commonly making use of PowerPoint® and other similar presentation programs in their summations during closing argument. The purpose of the closing argument is to summarize for the judge and jury the major legal issues in the lawsuit, what evidence the party has presented to prove his case, and how the opposing party has failed to prove his case. By using a presentation program, the attorney can provide visual reinforcement during his closing argument with the use of summary slides outlining key points and displaying important exhibits. Paralegals are often asked to create the slides for their attorneys.

Other Types of Demonstrative Evidence

Paralegals should keep an open mind about the use of any prop or tool that can aid the trier of fact in understanding complicated or technical information. While the preceding types of demonstrative evidence are the most common, sometimes a particular case can benefit from a unique method. For example, suppose you are representing the plaintiff in a suit for product defect in an automobile engine design, which caused the engine to fail and the plaintiff's car to collide with another vehicle. Your expert witness, a design engineer, wants to demonstrate for the jury how the engine failed, but the subject vehicle was destroyed in the accident. One way to accomplish this is to locate substitute engines from the same vehicle model and year from junkyards. One can be cleaned and sandblasted to look new, one can be left as-is so that it can be partly disassembled by the expert witness at trial to show where the failures occurred. Another can be cut in cross-section to expose and illustrate the components in question.

PLANNING THE USE OF DEMONSTRATIVE EVIDENCE

The overriding test of any demonstrative evidence is whether it helps tell the client's story. Does it aid, educate, and instruct the judge and jury about the facts upon which the liability and damages are based? Or does it destroy the message by being distracting or poorly executed because of technological failures? When conceiving and preparing demonstrative evidence, the paralegal should remember several things.

- the cost involved and whether it is in the client's budget
- the skill of the paralegal or other in-house staff and whether an expert or

TIP

To stay current on new technologies and demonstrative evidence methods, the wise paralegal will read trade journals and attend seminars and continuing education in his field. At large continuing education events for paralegals and attorneys, there are often exhibitors present who can demonstrate their products and services for you.

vendor should be brought in to either create the demonstrative evidence or assist with its presentation at trial, or both the length of time it will take to create the evidence and complete it before the trial (the sooner you can start the process, the better)

- courtroom logistics, such as distances and the location of the jury box in relation to where the witness and judge will be sitting (discussed in more detail in Chapter 10)
- the availability of any special equipment in the courtroom and whether that equipment must be rented and brought in by the trial team

CONCLUSION

Demonstrative evidence is more important than ever in getting your client's message across to the jury in an easily understandable way. Paralegals are indispensable in assisting the trial team in creating and implementing a demonstrative evidence plan. Paralegals should network with other paralegals and attend conferences put on by local, state, or national paralegal associations or bar associations where they can meet vendors and keep on top of the latest technology available.

■ KEY TERMS

blowup   probative   video text synchronization

photogrammetry

■ REVIEW QUESTIONS

1. What is demonstrative evidence and why is it used during trial?
2. Why does demonstrative evidence have no probative value?
3. What is a blowup?
4. Give an example of how an aerial photograph could be used as demonstrative evidence.
5. Give a situation where a model would be useful in explaining events to a jury.
6. What is the overriding test of any type of demonstrative evidence?
7. When should the paralegal seek the help of a vendor or expert to create demonstrative evidence?
8. Who decides on the budget for demonstrative evidence?

■ APPLYING WHAT YOU HAVE LEARNED

1. Design a demonstrative evidence plan for the Olde v. CCI case scenario in Chapter 2.
2. Contact an accident reconstruction expert in your area and interview him about the steps he takes to analyze a motor vehicle collision.

3. Locate and summarize the rules in your state regarding the use of demonstrative evidence.

4. Design a demonstrative evidence plan for the Johnson v. Foxfire Boat Company case scenario in Chapter 5.

ILLUSTRATIVE CASE

Read the following case, excerpted from the U.S. Court of Appeals opinion, and answer the following questions:

1. Why do you think the court allows the jury to decide whether the summaries accurately reflect the evidence, rather than the court making a decision about whether or not to exclude the summaries?

2. What public purpose is satisfied by making summaries an exception to the hearsay rule?

EXCERPT FROM UNITED STATES OF AMERICA V. MICHAEL DEBOER, 966 F2D 1066

CERTIORARI TO THE UNITED STATES COURT OF APPEALS FOR THE SIXTH CIRCUIT, CASE NO. 91-2013 (1992)

KRUPANSY, Senior Circuit Judge, delivered the opinion of the Court.

Appellant, Michael DeBoer (defendant) appeals the district court's judgment finding him guilty of one count of conspiracy to distribute and aid and abet in the distribution of Tussend, a Schedule III controlled substance pursuant to 21 U.S.C. § 841(a)(1).

On October 25, 1990, the grand jury indicted the defendant on one count of conspiracy to distribute the cough syrup Tussend, a Schedule III controlled substance. The defendant worked at a drug store which was owned and operated by him and his parents. He functioned as both a manager and a pharmacy technician. His pharmaceutical duties included packaging the cough syrup, Tussend, into measured containers for sale to the public, as well as ordering drugs from wholesale suppliers. Occasionally, he filled prescriptions for customers when the pharmacists were either ill or late for work.

A jury trial commenced on June 17, 1991, in which the defendant was to be tried with three co-defendants. After the jury was selected, but before commencement of the trial, two of the co-defendants pleaded guilty and the charges against the third defendant were dismissed. Before the government commenced its presentation of evidence against the defendant on June 18, 1991, without defense objection, the court instructed the jury not to draw any inferences from the absence of the remaining co-defendants from the trial. The instruction was proper and legally correct.

At trial, employees, including a registered pharmacist, testified that Dr. Anthony Bergren (Bergren), a practicing medical doctor, prescribed eighty percent of the store's controlled substance prescriptions. They further testified that they were aware through customers that many pharmacists and pharmacies in the vicinity and elsewhere refused to honor Bergren's prescriptions. Furthermore, relief pharmacist, Floyd Rademacher (Rademacher), testified that the pharmacy's practices regarding Tussend prescriptions were outside the usual course of professional conduct. Specifically, he testified that Tussend was cough syrup rarely used by physicians because it was three times more powerful than codeine cough medicine. He stated that a normal pharmacy would fill three or four prescriptions for the drug per week during peak flu season as compared to the eleven or more Tussend prescriptions per day that were filled at defendant's pharmacy.

(continues)

ILLUSTRATIVE CASE *(continued)*

Further, the United States offered undisputed evidence that defendant's drug store received quantity shipments of Tussend from wholesalers from December, 1986 through November, 1988. The evidence disclosed that during this two year period, the said pharmacy received 3,902 sixteen ounce bottles of Tussend from three wholesalers, enough Tussend to fill 21 prescriptions every day for two years.

The United States also offered into evidence all the controlled substance prescriptions filled at the pharmacy during 1987, as well as summaries of that evidence. DEA agent, Karen Mysliewic (Mysliewic) testified over objection that from her calculations defendant's pharmacy filled an average of eleven Tussend prescriptions per day. The court overruled the objection and, as a cautionary measure, instructed the jury not to treat summaries as evidence and to disregard the summaries if they did not accurately reflect the facts and figures developed by the evidence. . . .

The defendant . . . asserted that the trial court erred when it admitted summaries of the business records without describing or proving the methodology applied in developing the summaries in controversy. He suggested that the authenticity and accuracy of the summaries was based on hearsay, and therefore inadmissible. However Fed.R.Evid. 1006, an exception to the hearsay rule, permits voluminous writings and records which cannot conveniently be examined in court to be condensed into summaries. *See United States v. Denton,* 556 F.2d 811, 816 (6ᵗʰ Cir.) *cert. denied,* 434 U.S. 892, 98 S.Ct. 269, 54 L.Ed.2d 178 (1977). Furthermore, notwithstanding Rule 1006, this Circuit has traditionally endorsed summary evidence so long as the appropriate limiting instruction informs the jury that "the chart is not itself evidence but is only an aid in evaluating the evidence." *United States v. Scales,* 54 F.2d 558, 563-64 (6ᵗʰ Cir.), *cert. denied,* 441 U.S. 946, 99 S.Ct. 2168, 60 L.Ed.2d 1049 (1979). Even though Mysliewic may not have had personal knowledge of the way bureau employees carried out her directive to select some days at random, she could testify that the summaries presented to the jury were summaries presented to her in response to her directions. Further, the district court properly instructed the jury that the summaries of these records were not evidence or proof of facts and could be disregarded if they did not correctly reflect the facts and figures shown by the evidence. Accordingly, this assignment of error is without merit.

For additional resources, visit our Web site at www.westlegalstudies.com

CHAPTER 10

The Use of
Evidence at
Settlement and Trial

■ OBJECTIVES

After studying this chapter you should be able to:

❑ understand and explain the various methods of resolving a lawsuit.

❑ prepare evidence for trial.

❑ serve trial subpoenas.

❑ assist the attorney at trial.

INTRODUCTION

Taking a thorough, detailed, and well-researched approach to a case from the beginning is crucial to a successful outcome because rarely do cases actually go to trial. The courts encourage negotiation, compromise, and alternative resolution throughout the process in an effort to save time and money for the clients and to reduce wear and tear on the judicial system.

In this chapter, we will discuss methods of resolving legal disputes short of trial as well as at trial.

ALTERNATIVE DISPUTE RESOLUTION

The long and painstaking process of gathering evidence through investigation, legal and nonlegal research, and pertinent discovery methods does not always culminate at a trial. Litigation has become so time-consuming and expensive that in an effort to provide the best representation, the legal team must always consider all possible methods of resolving disputes. These options may include **mediation**, **alternative dispute resolution**, binding or nonbinding **arbitration**, and **settlement** conferences. Methods of resolving disputes outside the state or federal judicial system are known as alternative dispute resolution (ADR).

Rule 16 of the Federal Rules of Civil Procedure states that the court may, at its discretion, direct the attorneys to appear before it for a conference or conferences for the purpose of, among other things, expediting the disposition of the action and facilitating the settlement of the case. State and local jurisdictions have their own rules governing alternative dispute resolution. Most states encourage the use of alternative dispute resolution in an effort to lighten the load on the court system as well as to save time and money for the parties. ADR has become a viable means to an end and has gained support within the legal community. Consumers of legal services are becoming better acquainted with ADR as well and are more aware of the options available to them to attain their desired goal of justice.

Mediation

Mediation is a nonbinding, informal procedure between the parties whose purpose is to promote resolution of a grievance through reconciliation, settlement, or compromise. Sometimes courts order a mediation or at least strongly suggest that the parties make every effort to resolve the dispute through mediation. Typically, one party will make an overture to the other regarding willingness to mediate the dispute. Many courts inquire if the parties are amenable to mediation. Other times, the court may order mediation believing it to be the best first attempt to resolve the issues. If the parties agree to mediate, they must agree on a **mediator**. A mediator is a neutral person, agreed to by the parties, whose job is to facilitate settlement negotiations and encourage compromise solutions among the parties. The mediator may be an outside attorney, a retired judge, an expert in some relevant field, or another judge. Mediators are usually specially trained individuals who are familiar with the court system and legal process. There are many local, regional, and national professional organizations and associations that are good resources for locating a mediator. These organizations maintain panels of experienced mediators. Many courts maintain a roster of court-certified mediators as well as guidelines for conducting mediation. If a case involves rather esoteric questions, it may be advisable to look for a mediator who is somewhat familiar with the issues at hand. Be sure to check your jurisdiction to see if there are particular rules regarding mediation.

The parties may file mediation briefs beforehand with the mediator. This document is similar to a trial brief in that it sets out a summary of the case and the issues

■ **MEDIATION**

An informal dispute resolution process using a neutral third party (the mediator) to help the disputing parties to reach an agreement.

■ **ALTERNATIVE DISPUTE RESOLUTION (ADR)**

Methods to resolve legal problems without a court decision.

■ **ARBITRATION**

Resolution of a dispute by a person other than the judge assigned to the case whose decision is binding. This person is called an arbitrator. Arbitration may be binding or nonbinding.

■ **SETTLEMENT**

An agreement between and among parties that resolves and concludes some or all of the disputed matters.

■ **MEDIATOR**

Someone who works to effect reconciliation, settlement, or compromise between parties in dispute or at variance.

and the particular party's stance. The parties are typically present at the mediation but, usually, witnesses are not called. However, exhibits may be used, although they are typically not formally introduced into evidence as they are at a trial. The mediator may review documents and other evidence. The parties are sometimes placed in separate rooms with their attorneys so that the mediator may go back and forth between them. The mediator will communicate issues, concerns, and desired outcomes from one party to the other. Using negotiation skills and after achieving an understanding of the case as well as the concerns of the parties, the mediator will suggest valuations and possible options for settlement. The mediator will attempt to help the parties come to a mutually acceptable agreement. All mediation discussions are confidential and may not be introduced as evidence in the event of trial or any other judicial proceeding. The mediator does not render an opinion or decision.

The parties may settle all, some, or none of the issues during mediation. If the parties are unable to agree to a settlement by way of mediation, the case remains in the judicial system.

Arbitration

Arbitration involves a neutral third party who renders a decision after both parties have presented their case. Arbitration can be binding or nonbinding. Arbitration is a contractual proceeding between parties who agree to present their case to the **arbitrator**, or sometimes to a panel of three arbitrators. The decision of the arbitrator is final and is enforceable in court. Arbitrators, like mediators, have been well trained and possess the experience and expertise to knowledgeably carry out their duties. Also, similar to mediators, there are professional organizations and associations of arbitrators.

Mediation and arbitration are both private processes that should be considered when looking into ADR. If the case involves trade secrets, sensitive employment or corporate information, strategic corporate planning, or other information the parties do not wish to be subject to public view and opinion, ADR may be a good choice. Information divulged during the course of mediation or arbitration will be held in strict confidence.

Arbitration does not normally include a right to appeal, except in the case of fraud, corruption, or the abuse of power during the arbitration process. Therefore, arbitration awards may be impossible to overturn. Awards are enforceable in state and federal courts. Title 9 of the United States Code is the Federal Arbitration Act, and state statutes will cover the laws governing arbitration in state courts. Reading these laws reveals that the grounds for court review of arbitration awards are very limited, unlike recourse available through the court system. It is therefore important that the client be made aware of the benefits and limitations of binding arbitration.

Arbitration that proceeds through the court system is known as judicial arbitration and is usually nonbinding. The American Arbitration Association (AAA) commonly handles private arbitrations. The AAA provides trained arbitrators with expertise in a variety of specific industries, including construction, automotive insurance claims, labor

■ **ARBITRATOR**
A person chosen to judge, settle, and/or decide a disputed matter.

CAREER TIP

Many paralegals have found great satisfaction by taking training and working as a mediator. If you enjoy a corporate environment, you could become a trained arbitrator. Not all courts require that mediators or arbitrators be attorneys.

and employment, sports, health care, Internet commerce, consumer finance, and mass claims. The AAA provides resumes of its arbitrators that detail training, education, areas of expertise and references.

The process for commencing an arbitration is similar to that of mediation: the parties agree to arbitrate and select an arbitrator. A hearing is set and preparation begins. Because of the finality of binding arbitration, the preparation is more detailed than for mediation. Evidence is gathered in more depth, exhibits prepared, witnesses may be subpoenaed to appear at the hearing, and the arbitration brief will cover the issues in detail. The attorney and paralegal should be very familiar with the statutes governing arbitration in the jurisdiction in which the arbitration occurs.

Settlement

Settlement may occur at any time during the pendancy of a lawsuit. Oftentimes, the parties attempt to settle a dispute before a complaint is filed but must file the initial pleadings in order to preserve their rights under the statute of limitations. A lawsuit may settle at any time from the filing of the complaint until after a verdict is rendered. It is not unusual for a case to proceed through trial and then settle during jury deliberations. The parties' interests are almost always better served by settlement than by trial, jury awards, and the appeal process. Judges encourage settlement at every step of the process by questioning the attorneys about what efforts they have made toward resolving the dispute. As discovery progresses and evidence is obtained and scrutinized, settlement may begin to seem appealing to one or the other of the parties.

Presentation of a settlement brochure by the plaintiff to the defendant is a strategy used to open the door to settlement negotiations. Such a document presents the plaintiff's case by logically yet dramatically setting out the factual and legal issues. For example, in the Olde case, a settlement brochure would present the facts of the case in an orderly and organized fashion from beginning to end. The chronology would start with a description of Mrs. Olde's health before she fell in her home and then proceed in detail through the events that led to her involvement with CCI. The chronology would be supported by evidence gathered up to that point, including photographs before and after the event, a personal and medical history of the plaintiff, medical records reflecting the time period covered by her complaint, and the extent of her physical, mental, and financial injuries. The settlement brochure would then set out the effects of her injuries, an evaluation of her claims, and a conclusion, including a detailed settlement demand. The settlement demand would set out the amount of damages, insurance coverage paid (if any) to offset medical and other bills, research regarding verdicts awarded in similar cases, and actuarial information about life span, earning ability, and expected income of someone of Mrs. Olde's age. If discovery has reached that point, the settlement brochure would also include any reports made by expert witnesses. The brochure would highlight the strengths of the plaintiff's case and point out the weaknesses and obstacles that would prevent a favorable outcome for the defendants. Many cases have an insurance carrier in the picture somewhere, either providing coverage for a named defendant or as an interested bystander, since it may have the case tendered to it at some point. Settlement brochures are especially effective when an insurance company will be responsible for paying some or all of the damages.

Settlement discussions may result in the resolution of all or any part of the claims of the parties. The litigation may conclude entirely or may proceed on fewer issues.

THE NECESSITY OF EVIDENCE IN ALTERNATIVE DISPUTE RESOLUTION

It should be noted that, in the case of resolution by mediation, arbitration, or settlement, evidence is still crucial. In fact, the decision to use any method of alternative dispute resolution often rests on the evidence gathered. Just because a case does not proceed all the way through trial does not lessen the importance of evidence gathering. Our courts are so overburdened, due in part to the increased complexity of lawsuits and decreasing budgets, that judges encourage the parties to make every effort to resolve disputes prior to trial. During the life of a lawsuit, the courts require that the parties advise the court of progress being made and efforts attempted to resolve the dispute short of trial.

No matter how a case is resolved, evidence will need to be gathered. Often, one party may discover a vital piece of evidence that can be used to steer a case directly to a speedy resolution. For example, in the case involving the stolen art, Henri's time cards from his place of employment direct the suspicion away from him as well as support his veracity and cooperation. Additionally, records of cell phone calls placed from Georgia's phone reveal that she had been calling various art dealers. By presenting these pieces of evidence to the prosecuting attorney, and barring any additional incriminating evidence the prosecutor may have, Henri's attorney may move to have charges against Henri dropped.

Perhaps, in the case of Mary Olde, as evidence gathered through the discovery process mounts against the convalescent hospital, the insurance company representing the hospital may wish to open informal settlement negotiations with the plaintiff in an effort to avoid the costs associated with preparing for and going to trial as well as the potential negative public relations that could result from losing at trial.

In each of these examples, the time, money, and effort expended to gather evidence will not be wasted by any means. Indeed, the success of gathering evidence paves the way for resolution prior to trial.

USE OF EVIDENCE AT TRIAL

The last few days before trial are often hectic and chaotic. Last minute settlement conversations may be taking place in an effort to resolve some or all of the triable issues. Motions are being prepared and heard regarding facts to be presented to the jury. Witness and exhibit lists are being exchanged. Subpoenas are being prepared and served on persons needed to testify at trial. Long work days for the legal team are the norm in the final days leading up to trial.

The presentation of evidence is the most important aspect of trying a case before a jury. The judge will instruct the jury at the beginning and end of the case that the opening statement and closing arguments of the lawyers are not evidence to be considered in the case. Evidence can come only from the witness stand. If the judge or jury does not understand the theory of the case or the testimony of the witnesses they will have a hard time ruling in your favor.

The evidence, witnesses, and proof are usually presented in chronological fashion so as not to confuse the jury. Remember, you are trying to tell a story and persuade the jury with the evidence and facts presented. However, the trial schedule and the availability of witnesses do not always come together in the order desired. If the facts or issues of a particular case dictate that an order other than chronological is necessary, that presentation should be simple and easy to understand.

Organizing the case is critical to a smooth and efficient presentation at trial. There is nothing more distracting and noticeable to a jury than an unorganized attorney. The factual and legal issues are challenging even when one is well prepared and organized. Successful organization during trial is a result of much preparation before trial. The pleadings and exhibits must be readily available at all times because you have no way of being certain how the opposing side will present its case. You must be prepared at all times to put your hands on evidence needed for cross-examination and rebuttal.

At this point you are well versed in the kinds of evidence available. There are myriad ways in which the evidence may be used at trial in order to facilitate the flow of factual information in a logical manner that best tells the story to the jurors or other triers of fact. Testimonial evidence may be supported by particular physical evidence. The attorney and paralegal must go over the strengths and weaknesses of the case with the witnesses and prepare them for the arguments that the opposing counsel will use against them. The witnesses must not waiver under cross-examination. The physical evidence may be explained by demonstrative evidence. Documentary evidence may be entered to tie it all together. In some instances, an attorney may decide that one kind of evidence, say, testimony from a strong, articulate witness, is so compelling that its impact may be most powerful standing alone. On the other hand, testimony given by an expert witness on a technical subject may need to be presented in conjunction with other forms of evidence in order to be interpreted by the jury.

THE USE OF EXHIBITS AT TRIAL

At trial, the proper use of the exhibits is critical. However, the effective use of the exhibits is not a last minute function. It is the culmination of planning that begins with an analysis of the evidence, the organization of the medical records, and finally, the effective use of the record as an exhibit. Blowups and illustrations and other demonstrative evidence go a long way in making difficult concepts easily understandable.

Every jurisdiction, in both state and federal courts, has its own local rules regarding trial. In fact, it is not uncommon for each judge to have rules governing how trial will be conducted in his or her courtroom. Usually, these rules will set out the practical issues involved in conducting a trial, such as how exhibits are to be marked, whether or not exhibits, files, reference materials, or other items may be kept in the courtroom overnight, when the courtroom is dark (closed), and other matters. Some courts have rules against chewing gum, rules governing attire, rules regarding who may sit at counsel table and more. The rules may appear to be mundane, but disobey them at your peril. The trial judge, clerk, **bailiff,** and other court personnel have determined how best to conduct the trial in a manner the judge prefers. It is important to contact the court several weeks before trial and obtain a copy of the local rules. For instance, it is best not to mark exhibits until learning the court's preference as to marking protocol.

■ **BAILIFF**
A sheriff's deputy or a court official who keeps the peace in court.

EXHIBIT CHECKLISTS

During trial, it is often the paralegal's job to keep track of exhibits introduced into evidence by all parties. This can be a daunting task, as you may not be familiar with exhibits introduced by other parties. Developing a checklist is quite useful. If you are developing a list on your own, be sure to include the information described in Exhibit 10-1.

It is not unusual for an attorney to refer to an exhibit before introducing it into evidence. It is important for purposes of appeal and a clear trial record that all exhibits be tracked in some manner. The checklist in Exhibit 10-1 may appear to be rather simplistic, but often a legal pad is all that is available to work with in the courtroom. The list can be entered into the computer later. The goal is to document and record the exhibits as they are used.

! TIP

The extent to which you develop and use explanatory exhibits will depend upon the nature, complexity, and value of the case. Bear in mind the costs involved in having exhibits made and always weigh the cost-benefit ratio. Sometimes simpler is better, and other times more elaborate exhibits aid the jury in understanding difficult concepts.

EXHIBIT 10-1   EXHIBIT CHECKLIST

EXHIBIT NO.	OFFERED INTO EVIDENCE BY	OBJECTIONS	ADMITTED	REFUSED	DESCRIPTION

MARKING EXHIBITS

As an example, the Superior Court of the State of California, County of Los Angeles, has specific rules covering such topics as the use of graphic devices in opening statements; documents produced through a nonparty; large, dangerous, and bulky exhibits; and the use of maps, plans, and diagrams. Further, the court gives clear direction regarding marking exhibits in the following rules.

8.60 Marking of Exhibits

All exhibits should be exchanged and prenumbered in accordance with LASCR, rule 7.9(d), except for those anticipated in good faith to be used for impeachment. All exhibits must be prenumbered before any reference thereto by counsel or a witness.

8.62 Uniform Method of Marking Exhibits

The most efficient method of marking exhibits is by the use of Arabic numerals. Each party shall be allocated a block of numbers, to be thereafter used sequentially. For instance, plaintiff may be allocated numbers 1 to 200, the first defendant numbers 201 to 400, and the second defendant numbers 401 to 600.

Wherever possible, documentary exhibits consisting of more than one page should be internally paginated in sequential numerical order to facilitate reference to the document during interrogation of witnesses.

The United States District Court for the District of Colorado has established its own rules regarding procedures at trial.

D.C.COLO.LCivR 43.1 – Hearing and Trial Procedures

Procedures pertaining to the hearing in or trial of a particular case will be established by the judicial officer trying the case. The procedures shall be in accordance with any written instructions of that judicial officer.

Some judges have actually created forms for exhibit lists that they require be used in their courtroom. In order to be able to focus on the case, judges set out procedures to streamline trial-related activities by the attorneys and other personnel who will be involved at trial. By creating guidelines and forms that meet the judge's specific needs, the parties will benefit by having their case heard by a judge who is not distracted and knows what to expect.

The Central District of California requires that three non-blue-backed copies each of exhibit list and witness list (in the order they are to be called) be delivered to the court clerk on the morning of the first day of trial. In addition, two exhibit notebooks (an original and the judge's copy) are required to be delivered to the court clerk on the morning of the first day of trial. No additional notebook is needed for witnesses. Counsel are to prepare their exhibits by placing them in three-hole notebooks, each containing an index listing the exhibits. The notebooks are to be tabbed down the right side with numeric tabs separating each exhibit. The exhibits are to be numbered in accordance with Local Rule 26.4 which states that each exhibit must have an exhibit tag stapled to the upper right-hand corner of its first page. The plaintiff's exhibits shall be tagged with yellow tags; and the defendant's exhibits shall be tagged with blue tags. The tags shall indicate the case number, case name, and exhibit number.

As you have surmised, it is very important to understand the rules not just of your jurisdiction but of the particular courtroom in which the matter will be tried. Always have several exhibit stickers or tags filled out, and don't lose track of the last number used. This way, if evidence brought out by the other side, through either witnesses or documents, creates a need for you to use additional or different exhibits, you will be prepared. Keep track of exhibits marked, offered, and admitted, and through which witness. Remind your attorney if exhibits were discussed but not offered into evidence so that the attorney may make the decision whether or not to formally have them admitted. It is not unusual for attorneys to refer to evidence that has not been admitted when examining or cross-examining a witness.

EXHIBIT STRATEGY

In addition to the rules established by the courts, it is important that the attorney establish guidelines for each case determining what evidence will be presented at trial and how it will be introduced and then used. As always, these guidelines may vary a bit case by case, or perhaps even during the course of a trial, as the opposing party reveals its strategy.

The attorney, with your help, will have planned in advance which exhibits will be offered and through which witness. The paralegal should be very familiar with every piece of evidence that will be used during trial. Each exhibit must be prepared in advance and marked according to the court's rules to be ready for the attorney when, and if, needed. The marked exhibits, in order, should be easily available for the attorney to introduce through the appropriate witness. However, no matter how well prepared you may be, there will often be a time during trial when you will be asked to find something on the spur of the moment. Perhaps a planned witness is running late, so the witness order is switched at the last minute. Perhaps, during testimony, it becomes clear that exhibits to be introduced through a particular witness would make more sense to the jury if they were introduced in a different order. You do not have to change the exhibit number; exhibits may be introduced out of chronological order. The important thing is to know where everything is. Have everything clearly labeled.

If you have prepared the exhibit list yourself, you know what is in the trial exhibits. If you did not prepare the list, make sure you are familiar with it.

The court reporter and the court clerk will be keeping a list of exhibits as well. It is a good idea to go over the admitted exhibits at the end of each day or at breaks with both of these people. Their lists can serve as a backup to your list, but do not rely upon the court reporter to do this task for you. The court clerk has final say about what has been admitted into evidence and what has not. Review not only the court clerk's list but also the actual exhibits. Keep them in numerical order if possible. Keep blank exhibit logs handy for those times exhibits not already listed are offered.

At the end of each day at trial, check your list of exhibits admitted that day by which party and the order in which they were admitted, together with objections raised. The next morning you should compare your list with that kept by the court reporter to make sure they match. If you have questions you can work with the court reporter and the paralegal for opposing counsel to make sure all lists are in agreement. As a result of this efficiency and thoroughness, you may find that the court reporter is coming to you to confirm his or her list.

TRIAL SUBPOENAS

We have discussed subpoenas at length previously as they relate to depositions and documents. A trial subpoena is similar in format but is used specifically to command an individual's appearance in court at a certain time and place to testify. Many jurisdictions use a form that works for trial or deposition by completing the appropriate section. See Exhibit 10-2.

EXHIBIT 10-2   TRIAL SUBPOENA

ISSUED BY THE

UNITED STATES DISTRICT COURT

_____ **DISTRICT OF** _____

_____ ,

    Plaintiff,

                                                        SUBPOENA IN A CIVIL CASE

v.

_____ ,

Defendant   **Case Number:**

TO: _____

YOU ARE COMMANDED to appear in the **United States District Court** at the place, date, and time specified below to testify in the above case.

(continues)

EXHIBIT 10-2   TRIAL SUBPOENA *(continued)*

PLACE OF TESTIMONY
COURTROOM
DATE AND TIME

YOU ARE COMMANDED to appear at the place, date, and time specified below to testify at the taking of a deposition in the above case.

PLACE OF DEPOSITION
DATE AND TIME

YOU ARE COMMANDED to produce and permit inspection and copying of the following documents or objects at the place, date, and time specified below (list documents or objects):

PLACE DATE AND TIME

YOU ARE COMMANDED to permit inspection of the following premises at the date and time specified below.

PREMISES
DATE AND TIME

Any organization not a party to this suit that is subpoenaed for the taking of a deposition shall designate one or more officers, directors, or managing agents, or other persons who consent to testify on its behalf, and may set forth, for each person designated, the matters on which the person will testify. Federal Rules of Civil Procedure, 30(b) (6).

ATTORNEY FOR PLAINTIFF OR DEFENDANT

DATE

ISSUING OFFICER'S NAME, ADDRESS, AND PHONE NUMBER

(*See* Rule **45,** Federal Rules of Civil Procedure, Parts C & D on Reverse) **If** action **is** pending **in** district other than district of issuance, state district under case number.

AO-88

Rule 45(a)(2) of the Federal Rules of Civil Procedure states that a subpoena commanding attendance at a trial or hearing shall issue from the court for the district in which the hearing or trial is to be held. Each jurisdiction has a form that must be used for a trial subpoena. The information on the form will include the name and address of the court, case name and number, witness name, required appearance date and time, and records to be brought (if applicable). In addition, the court attendance fee and mileage must be included when serving the subpoena. Be aware that there is a 100-mile limit that a witness is required to travel in order to comply with a federal subpoena. The rules regarding travel limitation vary in state courts.

It is important to try to serve the trial subpoena at least two to three weeks before trial. Failure to allow adequate time for compliance by the witness may result in the subpoena being quashed or modified.

Rule 45. Subpoena

(b) Service.

(2) Subject to the provisions of clause (ii) of subparagraph (c)(3)(A) of this rule, a subpoena may be served at any place within the district of the court by which it is issued, or at any place without the district that is within 100 miles of the place of the deposition, hearing, trial, production, or inspection specified in the subpoena or at any place within the state where a state statute or rule of court permits service of a subpoena issued by a state court of general jurisdiction sitting in the place of the deposition, hearing, trial, production, or inspection specified in the subpoena. When a statute of the United States provides therefore, the court upon proper application and cause shown may authorize the service of a subpoena at any other place. A subpoena directed to a witness in a foreign country who is a national or resident of the United States shall issue under the circumstances and in the manner and be served as provided in *Title 28, U.S.C. § 1783*.

IN THE COURTROOM

During trial, the paralegal will have close contact with the judge's secretary, the court reporter, and the bailiff, as well as courthouse security. It is a good idea to establish these relationships a few weeks prior to trial by becoming completely familiar with the rules of the judge hearing the case for the operation of his or her courtroom. These courtroom personnel have quite a bit of power in the day-to-day running of the courtroom. They know how the judge likes things to be done but will not necessarily share that information unless asked. Having a positive, professional, respectful, and egalitarian relationship will prove invaluable in the event that technical problems occur, a witness is running late, your attorney needs to attend a brief hearing in another courtroom, or any other emergency arises.

If possible, pay a visit to the courthouse a week or so before trial. Call the judge's secretary and tell him or her that you would like to introduce yourself and see the courtroom. It may not be possible to take a thorough look at the courtroom if another trial is under way, but it will help you and the attorney set up for trial if you know where the outlets are for any computer and overhead projector you use, whether or not there is cell phone reception in the hallway immediately outside the courtroom, how far you will have to carry boxes, where the elevators are, and so forth. These may seem like small things but the peace of mind that comes from knowing as much as possible in advance about the courtroom environment is invaluable.

You will want to know what the judge's policy is regarding keeping exhibits, computers, easels, screens, boxes, and other items and materials in the courtroom overnight. Some judges require that the courtroom be completely cleaned out every night. If you have established a good relationship with courtroom personnel, someone may be willing to help you find a place to keep things during the course of the trial. Learn what time the courthouse and the particular judge's courtroom open and close every day. You will most likely need to arrive as soon as the courtroom opens in order to set up and organize everything for the day. During trial, ask if there is anything you could do to make their lives easier. You may learn that by moving a projector screen slightly, the judge's secretary will have a better view. Do not gossip with them about the case, the jury, the judge, the witnesses, opposing counsel, or the attorney you are with. If they wish to offer their opinions and insights, listen carefully and then report it to your attorney later.

Courthouse security has been tightened up dramatically in recent years. Talk to the security guards at the courthouse and let them know you will be coming, how many days you expect to be there, and how many boxes you will be bringing in each day. Ask what you can do to make their job easier, such as using a different entrance, arriving at a time when the security lines are shortest, or packing boxes in a way that makes them easier for security to examine. Be sure to allot time in your daily schedule for you and everything you bring with you to go through security procedures, X-ray scanning, and whatever else is required by the courthouse. Advise security that you will have items such as scissors and box cutters that you will use in the courtroom. If you will be bringing in any exhibits that could be considered dangerous, such as a gun or chemicals, advise security and ask them what the best way will be for you to transport those items from the front door of the courthouse into the courtroom.

PRETRIAL RECONNAISSANCE

When you visit the courtroom prior to trial, take a look at the layout of the jury box, counsel tables, electrical plugs, lighting, and the best places to set easels, overhead projectors, TV/VCRs, your boxes, and so forth. Find out if the court has its own video equipment, easels, chalkboards, and dry erase boards and the procedures for using them. Sometimes they have to be reserved in advance. Find out the locations of the nearest copy machine, telephone, and fax machine. On the morning of trial, plan on arriving at the courthouse first so you can hold the counsel table of choice for your attorneys, if possible. The court may have rules regarding who sits where. Find out where you will sit. Some judges allow nonattorneys to sit at the counsel table, others do not.

With regard to large equipment such as projectors, screens, computers, large exhibits or models, easels, dry erase boards, and large flipchart paper, a vendor may need to be hired or someone brought from your office with expertise in using the particular equipment. That person should be completely reliable and knowledgeable and experienced, if possible, with setting up audiovisual equipment in the courthouse in which your trial is held. Make sure to have extra items such as extension cord, power strip, overhead projector, light bulbs for an overhead projector, and batteries on hand. Also, who will you call if there is a technical malfunction and you need another computer or other piece of equipment? All contingencies must be anticipated. Have telephone numbers available for technical support people you may need to contact for help or advice. If possible, let them know that you will be in trial and make sure their office does not close over the lunch hour or open late one day a week.

During trial you will need to have many supplies on hand and readily available. These items may be kept in a box that stays at your side. The contents will include extra exhibit stickers or tags, pens, stick-on notes, adhesive bandage strips, rubber bands, paper clips, binder clips, posting tape, markers, stapler, staples, staple remover, transparent tape, chalk, chalkboard eraser, legal pads, file folders, scissors, utility knives, and anything else that helps you and your attorney do your jobs. Your trial box is your portable office.

CONCLUSION

The paralegal will act as the technical director for the trial, solving each problem as it arises. Trial work will test your organizational and logistical skills to their utmost. The challenges are great but the rewards are well worth the effort.

■ KEY TERMS _____

alternative dispute resolution	bailiff	settlement
arbitration	mediation	
arbitrator	mediator	

■ REVIEW QUESTIONS _____

1. What are the benefits of alternative dispute resolution?
2. Briefly describe the advantages and disadvantages of mediation versus arbitration.
3. Who are the primary courtroom personnel and what is each one's function?
4. How does a paralegal obtain the rules regarding courtroom procedures for a particular jurisdiction and a particular courtroom?
5. Describe the role of the paralegal at trial.

■ APPLYING WHAT YOU HAVE LEARNED _____

1. What are the rules regarding marking exhibits for trial in your jurisdiction?
2. Draft a trial subpoena commanding the chief executive officer of Omniphone to appear at trial.
3. Prepare a table of contents for a settlement brochure to be used in the Olde case.

ILLUSTRATIVE CASE

Read the excerpts from the following case and answer the following questions:

1. How could this case have been settled short of trial?
2. Draft a chronology of events based upon the information contained in the opinion.
3. What rules would determine the use of testimony by Cruzan's housemate?
4. How do the Supreme Court and the State of Missouri apply the clear and convincing evidence rule?

U.S. SUPREME COURT

CRUZAN V. DIRECTOR, MDH, 497 U.S. 261 (1990)

497 U.S. 261

REHNQUIST, C.J., delivered the opinion of the Court, in which WHITE, O'CONNOR, SCALIA, and KENNEDY, J.J., joined. O'CONNOR, J., and SCALIA, J., filed concurring opinions. BRENNAN, J., filed a dissenting opinion, in which MARSHALL and BLACKMUN, J.J., joined. STEVENS, J., filed a dissenting opinion.

CRUZAN, BY HER PARENTS AND CO-GUARDIANS CRUZAN ET UX. v. DIRECTOR, MISSOURI DEPARTMENT OF HEALTH, ET AL. CERTIORARI TO THE SUPREME COURT OF MISSOURI No. 88-1503.
Argued December 6, 1989 Decided June 25, 1990

(continues)

ILLUSTRATIVE CASE *(continued)*

Petitioner Nancy Cruzan is incompetent, having sustained severe injuries in an automobile accident, and now lies in a Missouri state hospital in what is referred to as a persistent vegetative state: generally, a condition in which a person exhibits motor reflexes but evinces no indications of significant cognitive function. The State is bearing the cost of her care. Hospital employees refused, without court approval, to honor the request of Cruzan's parents, copetitioners her, to terminate her artificial nutrition and hydration, since that would result in death. A state trial court authorized the termination, finding that a person in Cruzan's condition has a fundamental right under the State and Federal Constitutions to direct or refuse the withdrawal of death-prolonging procedures, and that Cruzan's expression to a former housemate that she would not wish to continue her life if sick or injured unless she could live at least halfway normally suggested that she would not wish to continue on with her nutrition and hydration. The State Supreme Court reversed. While recognizing a right to refuse treatment embodied in the common-law doctrine of informed consent, the court questioned its applicability in this case. It also declined to read into the State Constitution a broad right to privacy that would support an unrestricted right to refuse treatment and expressed doubt that the Federal Constitution embodied such a right. The court then decided that the State Living Will statute embodied a state policy strongly favoring the preservation of life, and that Cruzan's statements to her housemate were unreliable for the purpose of determining her intent. It rejected the argument that her parents were entitled to order the termination of her medical treatment, concluding that no person can assume that choice for an incompetent in the absence of the formalities required by the Living Will statute or clear and convincing evidence of the patient's wishes.

Held:

1. The United States Constitution does not forbid Missouri to require that evidence of an incompetent's wishes as to the withdrawal of life-sustaining treatment be proved by clear and convincing evidence. Pp. 269–285. [497 U.S. 261, 262]

   (a) Most state courts have based a right to refuse treatment on the common law right to informed consent, or on both that right and a constitutional privacy right. In addition to relying on state constitutions and the common law, state courts have also turned to state statutes for guidance. However, these sources are not available to this Court, where the question is simply whether the Federal Constitution prohibits Missouri from choosing the rule of law which it did.

   (b) A competent person has a liberty interest under the Due Process Clause in refusing unwanted medical treatment. However, the question whether that constitutional right has been violated must be determined by balancing the liberty interest against relevant state interests. For purposes of this case, it is assumed that a competent person would have a constitutionally protected right to refuse lifesaving hydration and nutrition. This does not mean that an incompetent person should possess the same right, since such a person is unable to make an informed and voluntary choice to exercise that hypothetical right or any other right. While Missouri has in effect recognized that, under certain circumstances, a surrogate may act for the patient in electing to withdraw hydration and nutrition and thus cause death, it has established a procedural safeguard to assure that the surrogate's action conforms as best it may to the wishes expressed by the patient while competent.

(continues)

ILLUSTRATIVE CASE *(continued)*

(c) It is permissible for Missouri, in its proceedings, to apply a clear and convincing evidence standard, which is an appropriate standard when the individual interests at stake are both particularly important and more substantial than mere loss of money, Santosky v. Kramer, 455 U.S. 745, 756. Here, Missouri has a general interest in the protection and preservation of human life, as well as other, more particular interests, at stake. It may legitimately seek to safeguard the personal element of an individual's choice between life and death. The State is also entitled to guard against potential abuses by surrogates who may not act to protect the patient. Similarly, it is entitled to consider that a judicial proceeding regarding an incompetent's wishes may not be adversarial, with the added guarantee of accurate fact-finding that the adversary process brings with it. The State may also properly decline to make judgments about the "quality" of a particular individual's life, and simply assert an unqualified interest in the preservation of human life to be weighed against the constitutionally protected interests of the individual. It is self-evident that these interests are more substantial, both on an individual and societal level, than those involved in a common civil dispute. The clear and convincing evidence standard also serves as a societal judgment about how the risk of error should be distributed between the litigants. Missouri may permissibly place the increased risk of an erroneous decision on those seeking to terminate life-sustaining treatment. An erroneous decision not to terminate results in maintenance of the status quo, with at least the potential that a wrong decision will eventually be corrected or its impact mitigated by an event such as advancement in medical science or the patient's unexpected death. However, an erroneous decision to withdraw such treatment is not susceptible of correction. Although Missouri's proof requirement may have frustrated the effectuation of Cruzan's not-fully-expressed desires, the Constitution does not require general rules to work flawlessly.

2. The State Supreme Court did not commit constitutional error in concluding that the evidence adduced at trial did not amount to clear and convincing proof of Cruzan's desire to have hydration and nutrition withdrawn. The trial court had not adopted a clear and convincing evidence standard, and Cruzan's observations that she did not want to live life as a "vegetable" did not deal in terms with withdrawal of medical treatment or of hydration and nutrition.

3. The Due Process Clause does not require a State to accept the "substituted judgment" of close family members in the absence of substantial proof that their views reflect the patient's. This Court's decision upholding a State's favored treatment of traditional family relationships, Michael H. v. Gerald D., 491 U.S. 110, may not be turned into a constitutional requirement that a State must recognize the primacy of these relationships in a situation like this. Nor may a decision upholding a State's right to permit family decision-making, Parham v. J.R., 442 U.S. 584, be turned into a constitutional requirement that the State recognize such decision-making. Nancy Cruzan's parents would surely be qualified to exercise such a right of "substituted judgment" were it required by the Constitution. However, for the same reasons that Missouri may require clear and convincing evidence of a patient's wishes, it may also choose to defer only to those wishes, rather than confide the decision to close family members.

760 S.W.2d 408, affirmed.

For additional resources, visit our Web site at www.westlegalstudies.com

Evidence After Case Resolution and Additional Resources

After studying this chapter you should be able to:

❏ understand what happens to all evidence after trial or other resolution of a lawsuit.

❏ understand what happens to evidence pending post-trial matters.

❏ know what to do with evidence in your possession after any post-trial remedies have been exhausted.

❏ be aware of additional resources regarding evidence and the role of the paralegal.

INTRODUCTION

Throughout this book, various case scenarios have described the importance of evidence in developing, filing, pursuing, and trying a lawsuit either in court or through alternative dispute resolution or settlement. You have studied the development of a case from both the plaintiff's and defendant's perspective, from inception through the discovery process and on to trial. At this point, you should be well aware of how crucial the methodical, careful, and systematic approach to gathering evidence is to the success of your client's case.

The evidence referred to in the case scenarios comes in many forms: paper documents, witness testimony, and physical objects of various sizes. This chapter will discuss how to handle evidence after the initial phase of the lawsuit and then after post-trial remedies have been exhausted.

We will also provide additional resources for the paralegal's "toolbox" in the form of Web sites and professional development.

POST-TRIAL PROCEDURES

After the case has been tried at the trial court level and a decision rendered, a new time lines come into play. The Court will enter a judgment that will be provided to all counsel. For appellate purposes, the clock begins ticking on the date the judgment is entered. All evidence must be maintained during this period. In most situations, the documents and files used in the case are simply maintained and kept as they are in the usual course of business. Large pieces of evidence, such as the computer hardware or boat presented in the case scenarios, must continue to be stored in a secure location. Any exhibit stickers, tags or other markings made during the course of the trial should not be removed or altered in any way.

The losing party has a period of time in which to decide whether or not to request a new trial or appeal the decision against it. It is very important, once again, to be familiar with the jurisdiction's rules regarding post-trial motions. The unsuccessful party may file a motion for **trial de novo**, or motion for new trial, or motion to set aside the judgment. The unsuccessful party may also file an appeal with the appropriate court of appeal. It is also possible to appeal just a portion of a decision.

Either side may appeal a decision or part of a decision in a civil case. Only the defendant may appeal in a criminal matter. The government cannot appeal a case when a defendant is found not guilty; however, either side may appeal a sentence in a criminal case.

■ **TRIAL DE NOVO**
A trial in a higher court in which all issues of law and fact previously heard in a lower court are reconsidered as if the earlier trial had not occurred.

APPEALS

Appellate law is a specialized area, and some attorneys have created a specialty practice in this area. Appellate procedure includes the rules appellate courts use in reviewing trial court judgments. Some states have created the designation of certified appellate specialist for attorneys who have received training and met the qualifications in this practice area. The purpose of appellate court review of a case is to correct errors committed by the trial court, clarify issues of law, and promote the furtherance of justice. Appellate procedure determines what judgments are appealable and what is required for a reversal of a lower court's judgment, as well as the rules the parties must follow. Typically, a final judgment must have been entered before a case may be appealed, but there are exceptions to this rule.

Federal appellate courts are governed by the Federal Rules of Appellate Procedure. State courts have their own rules of appellate procedure. Almost all of the argument is made by briefs and there may be few, if any, appearances before the appellate court. Not all jurisdictions allow for oral argument as a usual procedure. When oral argument does take place, the purpose is to clarify legal issues raised in the briefs.

Appeals are not based on the facts of the case per se. Rather, they are based on how the trial court applied the law to the facts. Therefore, appeals require a great amount of legal research in order to determine how the law has been applied to similar facts in prior cases and how and why the law was rightly or wrongly applied to the facts of the case being appealed. The parties argue the law, not the facts. Arguments may arise as a result of how particular laws were applied to the facts or evidence in a case at the trial court level.

When a case has been appealed, the losing party may appeal that decision to the highest state appellate court or the U.S. Supreme Court. These further appeals are rare because they are very expensive. The U.S. Supreme Court, which operates under its own rules, does not have to accept every appeal. The Court usually hears cases only when they involve a very important legal principle or when two or more appellate courts have disagreed on the interpretation of the law.

Evidence must be kept while an appeal is pending because the appellate court may choose to **remand** the case to the trial court where the exhibits would be entered in the retrial. Such a decision would be based upon reversible error committed by the trial court, and the remedy for reversible error is to allow the case to be tried again. The evidence must be maintained until all legal remedies that the parties wish to pursue have been exhausted.

MAINTAINING EVIDENCE AFTER ALTERNATIVE DISPUTE RESOLUTION

In the case of alternative dispute resolution, evidence is also maintained until the parties or courts have determined that no further action will be taken. At that point a judgment or settlement agreement will have been executed by the parties and the court case will have been dismissed. The pertinent local, state, or federal rules must be closely followed in order to be certain that a case is truly finished.

MAINTAINING EVIDENCE AFTER FINAL RESOLUTION

In a small case, documentary evidence will be kept as part of the case file and stored with the file following established office procedures. If a case has been particularly "document heavy," documents may be stored off site at a secure location in accordance with established office procedures. The same is true for physical objects.

■ **REMAND**
To send back a case from one court to another, usually to a lower court or administrative agency. In criminal law, to send an accused back into custody, or to turn a prisoner over for continued detention.

The paralegal will have created a thorough and detailed list of all evidence gathered in the matter, whether or not the evidence was introduced or used at trial in any manner. At the end of trial, a party may wish to have some evidence returned. For example, in the criminal case scenario, the computer hardware and software that was removed from Henri's home may be returned to him.

Every office should have policies on the maintenance or return of all file materials. Any decisions regarding evidence after trial must be made by the attorney. If you return evidence to anyone outside of the office, clearly document in writing what evidence is being returned, by whom, to whom, and the date of the return. If you dispose of evidence in any other manner, such as by sale, keep clear records.

ETHICS AND THE PARALEGAL

Paralegals are held to a high standard of ethical behavior, with good reason. We often acquire the most personal information about our clients. We may gain access to the innermost workings of companies. We often learn the most intimate details of someone's life, whether that person is who we represent or an opposing party. Throughout this book we have stressed the importance of developing a trusting and respectful relationship with clients. This can be achieved only if the client has the utmost faith in the paralegal's respect for the attorney-client privilege.

Various entities have established ethical guidelines for paralegals to operate under. For examples refer to:

National Association of Legal Assistants Canons of Ethics and Model Standards and Guidelines for Utilization of Legal Assistants
National Federation of Paralegal Associations Model Code of Ethics and Professional Responsibility

Some areas of specialization have developed their own ethics regarding paralegals practicing in particular areas of the law. For example, the International Trademarks Association has issued a white paper regarding ethics for paralegals that practice in that area. State and local bar associations may have promulgated rules or guidelines regarding ethics and paralegals.

PROFESSIONAL DEVELOPMENT

It is incumbent upon all paralegals to remain current about changes in the laws, especially in the areas in which they practice. Periodicals such as *Legal Assistant Today* are geared toward keeping the paralegal abreast of trends and developments in the profession. State and local bar association publications often include information paralegals may find helpful.

The paralegal profession continues to grow and change over time. States are grappling with issues such as certification and educational requirements for paralegals. Courts and bar associations are working to develop definitions of legal services providers such as "paralegals," "legal assistants," and "legal documents preparers." Membership in professional organizations is helpful for learning about legislative actions affecting paralegals and the future of the profession. The two large national organizations are the National Association of Legal Assistants (NALA) and the National Federation of Paralegal Associations (NFPA). Although the organizations may differ somewhat philosophically, their goals remain to provide education and visibility to the profession. The national associations have regional groups that represent specific parts of the country. Local paralegal associations exist in nearly all parts of the country. Becoming involved in your local association provides rewarding opportunities to learn and share knowledge with others who have chosen to pursue this career.

CONTINUING EDUCATION

Keeping skills sharp and learning of new developments in one's profession are vital to maintaining interest and job satisfaction. Opportunities abound for paralegals to continue their growth in the field. Most state bar associations have a section for paralegals that offers seminars or courses in particular areas of the law or the paralegal profession. Private companies put on conferences and seminars for paralegals. Attending conferences or seminars or participating in courses not only increases knowledge but provides invaluable opportunities to network with colleagues and develop important professional relationships.

ADDITIONAL RESOURCES

We have stressed the importance of paralegals using resources wisely. The Internet is a rich source of information that helps the paralegal look for evidence in a case. Every state in the United States has a Web site devoted to its laws and courts. The state government Web sites also provide information on business filings, forms, and the departments and agencies within the state.

The following is a list of general legal Web sites that may be useful:

<*http://www.findlaw.com*> – A good starting point for legal research with links to state and federal laws and procedures
<*http://www.law.cornell.edu*> – Cornell University Law School's Legal Information Institute has state and federal laws as well as links to legal subjects
<*http://www.ilrg.com*>– Internet Legal Resource Group™ has a categorized index of Web sites including legal forms and downloadabl files
<*http://www.firstgov.gov*> – The U.S. government's official Web portal

All of these Web sites are good jumping-off points for legal information. They will link to agencies and departments as well as forms and documents.

Each practice area has several Web sites. Use a search engine such as <*http://www.google.com*> to help you locate these sites.

Web sites for professional development include the following:

> *<http://www.nala.org>* – National Association for Legal Assistants
> *<http://www.paralegals.org>* – National Federation of Paralegal Associations
> *<http://www.aafpe.org>* – American Association for Paralegal Education
> *<http://www.abanet.org>* – American Bar Association

State bar association Web sites often link to paralegal practice sections.

CONCLUSION

The paralegal profession continues to be one of the fastest-growing careers in the United States. As our society and its rules and laws become more complex, the need for legal service providers escalates. New areas of legal expertise are opening up as our population lives longer, technology develops at an increasingly rapid pace and the ever-present media makes the planet smaller. Paralegals are an important part of the legal team, and opportunities abound.

■ KEY TERMS _____

remand

trial de novo

For additional resources, visit our Web site at www.westlegalstudies.com

Federal Rules of Evidence

ARTICLE I. GENERAL PROVISIONS

Rule 101. Scope

These rules govern proceedings in the courts of the United States and before United States bankruptcy judges and United States magistrate judges, to the extent and with the exceptions stated in rule 1101.

Rule 102. Purpose and Construction

These rules shall be construed to secure fairness in administration, elimination of unjustifiable expense and delay, and promotion of growth and development of the law of evidence to the end that the truth may be ascertained and proceedings justly determined.

Rule 103. Rulings on Evidence

(a) **Effect of erroneous ruling.**—Error may not be predicated upon a ruling which admits or excludes evidence unless a substantial right of the party is affected, and

(1) **Objection.**—In case the ruling is one admitting evidence, a timely objection or motion to strike appears of record, stating the specific ground of objection, if the specific ground was not apparent from the context; or

(2) **Offer of proof.**—In case the ruling is one excluding evidence, the substance of the evidence was made known to the court by offer or was apparent from the context within which questions were asked.

Once the court makes a definitive ruling on the record admitting or excluding evidence, either at or before trial, a party need not renew an objection or offer of proof to preserve a claim of error for appeal.

(b) **Record of offer and ruling.**—The court may add any other or further statement which shows the character of the evidence, the form in which it was offered, the objection made, and the ruling thereon. It may direct the making of an offer in question and answer form.

(c) **Hearing of jury.**—In jury cases, proceedings shall be conducted, to the extent practicable, so as to prevent inadmissible evidence from being suggested to the jury by any means, such as making statements or offers of proof or asking questions in the hearing of the jury.

(d) **Plain error**—Nothing in this rule precludes taking notice of plain errors affecting substantial rights although they were not brought to the attention of the court.

Rule 104. Preliminary Questions

(a) **Questions of admissibility generally.**—Preliminary questions concerning the qualification of a person to be a witness, the existence of a privilege, or the admissibility of evidence shall be determined by the court, subject to the provisions of subdivision (b). In making its determination it is not bound by the rules of evidence except those with respect to privileges.

(b) **Relevancy conditioned on fact.**—When the relevancy of evidence depends upon the fulfillment of a condition of fact, the court shall admit it upon, or subject to, the introduction of evidence sufficient to support a finding of the fulfillment of the condition.

(c) **Hearing of jury.**—Hearings on the admissibility of confessions shall in all cases be conducted out of the hearing of the jury. Hearings on other preliminary matters shall be so conducted when the interests of justice require, or when an accused is a witness and so requests.

(d) **Testimony by accused.**—The accused does not, by testifying upon a preliminary matter, become subject to cross-examination as to other issues in the case.

(e) **Weight and credibility.**—This rule does not limit the right of a party to introduce before the jury evidence relevant to weight or credibility.

Rule 105. Limited Admissibility

When evidence which is admissible as to one party or for one purpose but not admissible as to another party or for another purpose is admitted, the court, upon request, shall restrict the evidence to its proper scope and instruct the jury accordingly.

Rule 106. Remainder of or Related Writings or Recorded Statements

When a writing or recorded statement or part thereof is introduced by a party, an adverse party may require the introduction at that time of any other part or any other writing or recorded statement which ought in fairness to be considered contemporaneously with it.

ARTICLE II. JUDICIAL NOTICE

Rule 201. Judicial Notice of Adjudicative Facts

(a) **Scope of rule.**—This rule governs only judicial notice of adjudicative facts.

(b) **Kinds of facts.**—A judicially noticed fact must be one not subject to reasonable dispute in that it is either (1) generally known within the territorial jurisdiction of the trial court or (2) capable of accurate and ready determination by resort to sources whose accuracy cannot reasonably be questioned.

(c) **When discretionary.**—A court may take judicial notice, whether requested or not.

(d) **When mandatory.**—A court shall take judicial notice if requested by a party and supplied with the necessary information.

(e) **Opportunity to be heard.**—A party is entitled upon timely request to an opportunity to be heard as to the propriety of taking judicial notice and the tenor of the matter noticed. In the absence of prior notification, the request may be made after judicial notice has been taken.

(f) **Time of taking notice.**—Judicial notice may be taken at any stage of the proceeding.

(g) **Instructing jury.**—In a civil action or proceeding, the court shall instruct the jury to accept as conclusive any fact judicially noticed. In a criminal case, the court shall instruct the jury that it may, but is not required to, accept as conclusive any fact judicially noticed.

ARTICLE III. PRESUMPTIONS IN CIVIL ACTIONS AND PROCEEDINGS

Rule 301. Presumptions in General Civil Actions and Proceedings

In all civil actions and proceedings not otherwise provided for by Act of Congress or by these rules, a presumption imposes on the party against whom it is directed the burden of going forward with evidence to rebut or meet the presumption, but does not shift to such party the burden of proof in the sense of the risk of nonpersuasion, which remains throughout the trial upon the party on whom it was originally cast.

Rule 302. Applicability of State Law in Civil Actions and Proceedings

In civil actions and proceedings, the effect of a presumption respecting a fact which is an element of a claim or defense as to which State law supplies the rule of decision is determined in accordance with State law.

ARTICLE IV. RELEVANCY AND ITS LIMITS

Rule 401. Definition of "Relevant Evidence"

"Relevant evidence" means evidence having any tendency to make the existence of any fact that is of consequence to the determination of the action more probable or less probable than it would be without the evidence.

Rule 402. Relevant Evidence Generally Admissible; Irrelevant Evidence Inadmissible

All relevant evidence is admissible, except as otherwise provided by the Constitution of the United States, by Act of Congress, by these rules, or by other rules prescribed by the Supreme Court pursuant to statutory authority. Evidence which is not relevant is not admissible.

Rule 403. Exclusion of Relevant Evidence on Grounds of Prejudice, Confusion, or Waste of Time

Although relevant, evidence may be excluded if its probative value is substantially outweighed by the danger of unfair prejudice, confusion of the issues, or misleading the jury, or by considerations of undue delay, waste of time, or needless presentation of cumulative evidence.

Rule 404. Character Evidence Not Admissible To Prove Conduct; Exceptions; Other Crimes

(a) **Character evidence generally.**—Evidence of a person's character or a trait of character is not admissible for the purpose of proving action in conformity therewith on a particular occasion, except:

(1) **Character of accused.**—Evidence of a pertinent trait of character offered by an accused, or by the prosecution to rebut the same, or if evidence of a trait of character of the alleged victim of the crime is offered by an accused and admitted under Rule 404 (a)(2), evidence of the same trait of character of the accused offered by the prosecution;

(2) **Character of alleged victim.**—Evidence of a pertinent trait of character of the alleged victim of the crime offered by an accused, or by the prosecution to rebut the same, or evidence of a character trait of peacefulness of the alleged victim offered by the prosecution in a homicide case to rebut evidence that the alleged victim was the first aggressor;

(3) **Character of witness.**—Evidence of the character of a witness, as provided in rules 607, 608, and 609.

(b) **Other crimes, wrongs, or acts.**—Evidence of other crimes, wrongs, or acts is not admissible to prove the character of a person in order to show action in conformity therewith. It may, however, be admissible for other purposes, such as proof of motive, opportunity, intent, preparation, plan, knowledge, identity, or absence of mistake or accident, provided that upon request by the accused, the prosecution in a criminal case shall provide reasonable notice in advance of trial, or during trial if the court excuses pretrial notice on good cause shown, of the general nature of any such evidence it intends to introduce at trial.

Rule 405. Methods of Proving Character

(a) **Reputation or opinion.**—In all cases in which evidence of character or a trait of character of a person is admissible, proof may be made by testimony as to reputation or by testimony in the form of an opinion. On cross-examination, inquiry is allowable into relevant specific instances of conduct.

(b) **Specific instances of conduct.**—In cases in which character or a trait of character of a person is an essential element of a charge, claim, or defense, proof may also be made of specific instances of that person's conduct.

Rule 406. Habit; Routine Practice

Evidence of the habit of a person or of the routine practice of an organization, whether corroborated or not and regardless of the presence of eyewitnesses, is relevant to prove that the conduct of the person or organization on a particular occasion was in conformity with the habit or routine practice.

Rule 407. Subsequent Remedial Measures

When, after an injury or harm allegedly caused by an event, measures are taken that, if taken previously, would have made the injury or harm less likely to occur, evidence of the subsequent measures is not admissible to prove negligence, culpable conduct, a defect in a product, a defect in a product's design, or a need for a warning or instruction. This rule does not require the exclusion of evidence of subsequent measures when offered for another purpose, such as proving ownership, control, or feasibility of precautionary measures, if controverted, or impeachment.

Rule 408. Compromise and Offers to Compromise

Evidence of (1) furnishing or offering or promising to furnish, or (2) accepting or offering or promising to accept, a valuable consideration in compromising or attempting to compromise a claim which was disputed as to either validity or amount, is not admissible to prove liability for or invalidity of the claim or its amount. Evidence of conduct or statements made in compromise negotiations is likewise not admissible. This rule does not require the exclusion of any evidence otherwise discoverable merely because it is presented in the course of compromise negotiations. This rule also does not require exclusion when the evidence is offered for another purpose, such as proving bias or prejudice of a witness, negating a contention of undue delay, or proving an effort to obstruct a criminal investigation or prosecution.

Rule 409. Payment of Medical and Similar Expenses

Evidence of furnishing or offering or promising to pay medical, hospital, or similar expenses occasioned by an injury is not admissible to prove liability for the injury.

Rule 410. Inadmissibility of Pleas, Plea Discussions, and Related Statements

Except as otherwise provided in this rule, evidence of the following is not, in any civil or criminal proceeding, admissible against the defendant who made the plea or was a participant in the plea discussions:

(1) a plea of guilty which was later withdrawn;

(2) a plea of nolo contendere;

(3) any statement made in the course of any proceedings under Rule 11 of the Federal Rules of Criminal Procedure or comparable state procedure regarding either of the foregoing pleas; or

(4) any statement made in the course of plea discussions with an attorney for the prosecuting authority which do not result in a plea of guilty or which result in a plea of guilty later withdrawn.

However, such a statement is admissible (i) in any proceeding wherein another statement made in the course of the same plea or plea discussions has been introduced and the statement ought in fairness be considered contemporaneously with it, or (ii) in a criminal proceeding for perjury or false statement if the statement was made by the defendant under oath, on the record and in the presence of counsel.

Rule 411. Liability Insurance

Evidence that a person was or was not insured against liability is not admissible upon the issue whether the person acted negligently or otherwise wrongfully. This rule does not require the exclusion of evidence of insurance against liability when offered for another purpose, such as proof of agency, ownership, or control, or bias or prejudice of a witness.

Rule 412. Sex Offense Cases; Relevance of Alleged Victim's Past Sexual Behavior or Alleged Sexual Predisposition

(a) **Evidence generally inadmissible.**—The following evidence is not admissible in any civil or criminal proceeding involving alleged sexual misconduct except as provided in subdivisions (b) and (c):

(1) Evidence offered to prove that any alleged victim engaged in other sexual behavior.

(2) Evidence offered to prove any alleged victim's sexual predisposition.

(b) **Exceptions.**

(1) In a criminal case, the following evidence is admissible, if otherwise admissible under these rules:

(A) evidence of specific instances of sexual behavior by the alleged victim offered to prove that a person other than the accused was the source of semen, injury, or other physical evidence;

(B) evidence of specific instances of sexual behavior by the alleged victim with respect to the person accused of the sexual misconduct offered by the accused to prove consent or by the prosecution; and

(C) evidence the exclusion of which would violate the constitutional rights of the defendant.

(2) In a civil case, evidence offered to prove the sexual behavior or sexual predisposition of any alleged victim is admissible if it is otherwise admissible under these rules and its probative value substantially outweighs the danger of harm to any victim and of unfair prejudice to any party. Evidence of an alleged victim's reputation is admissible only if it has been placed in controversy by the alleged victim.

(c) **Procedure to determine admissibility.**

(1) A party intending to offer evidence under subdivision (b) must —

(A) file a written motion at least 14 days before trial specifically describing the evidence and stating the purpose for which it is offered unless the court, for good cause requires a different time for filing or permits filing during trial; and

(B) serve the motion on all parties and notify the alleged victim or, when appropriate, the alleged victim's guardian or representative.

(2) Before admitting evidence under this rule the court must conduct a hearing in camera and afford the victim and parties a right to attend and be heard. The motion, related papers, and the record of the hearing must be sealed and remain under seal unless the court orders otherwise.

Rule 413. Evidence of Similar Crimes in Sexual Assault Cases

(a) In a criminal case in which the defendant is accused of an offense of sexual assault, evidence of the defendant's commission of another offense or offenses of sexual assault is admissible, and may be considered for its bearing on any matter to which it is relevant.

(b) In a case in which the Government intends to offer evidence under this rule, the attorney for the Government shall disclose the evidence to the defendant, including statements of witnesses or a summary of the substance of any testimony that is expected to be offered, at least fifteen days before the scheduled date of trial or at such later time as the court may allow for good cause.

(c) This rule shall not be construed to limit the admission or consideration of evidence under any other rule.

(d) For purposes of this rule and Rule 415, "offense of sexual assault" means a crime under Federal law or the law of a State (as defined in section 513 of title 18, United States Code) that involved—

(1) any conduct proscribed by chapter 109A of title 18, United States Code;

(2) contact, without consent, between any part of the defendant's body or an object and the genitals or anus of another person;

(3) contact, without consent, between the genitals or anus of the defendant and any part of another person's body;

(4) deriving sexual pleasure or gratification from the infliction of death, bodily injury, or physical pain on another person; or

(5) an attempt or conspiracy to engage in conduct described in paragraphs (1)-(4).

Rule 414. Evidence of Similar Crimes in Child Molestation Cases

(a) In a criminal case in which the defendant is accused of an offense of child molestation, evidence of the defendant's commission of another offense or offenses of child molestation is admissible, and may be considered for its bearing on any matter to which it is relevant.

(b) In a case in which the Government intends to offer evidence under this rule, the attorney for the Government shall disclose the evidence to the defendant, including statements of witnesses or a summary of the substance of any testimony that is expected to be offered, at least fifteen days before the scheduled date of trial or at such later time as the court may allow for good cause.

(c) This rule shall not be construed to limit the admission or consideration of evidence under any other rule.

(d) For purposes of this rule and Rule 415, "child" means a person below the age of fourteen, and "offense of child molestation" means a crime under Federal law or the law of a State (as defined in section 513 of title 18, United States Code) that involved—

(1) any conduct proscribed by chapter 109A of title 18, United States Code, that was committed in relation to a child;

(2) any conduct proscribed by chapter 110 of title 18, United States Code;

(3) contact between any part of the defendant's body or an object and the genitals or anus of a child;

(4) contact between the genitals or anus of the defendant and any part of the body of a child;

(5) deriving sexual pleasure or gratification from the infliction of death, bodily injury, or physical pain on a child; or

(6) an attempt or conspiracy to engage in conduct described in paragraphs (1)-(5).

Rule 415. Evidence of Similar Acts in Civil Cases Concerning Sexual Assault or Child Molestation

(a) In a civil case in which a claim for damages or other relief is predicated on a party's alleged commission of conduct constituting an offense of sexual assault or child molestation, evidence of that party's commission of another offense or offenses of sexual assault or child molestation is admissible and may be considered as provided in Rule 413 and Rule 414 of these rules.

(b) A party who intends to offer evidence under this Rule shall disclose the evidence to the party against whom it will be offered, including statements of witnesses or a summary of the substance of any testimony that is expected to be offered, at least fifteen days before the scheduled date of trial or at such later time as the court may allow for good cause.

(c) This rule shall not be construed to limit the admission or consideration of evidence under any other rule.

ARTICLE V. PRIVILEGES

Rule 501. General Rule

Except as otherwise required by the Constitution of the United States or provided by Act of Congress or in rules prescribed by the Supreme Court pursuant to statutory authority, the privilege of a witness, person, government, State, or political subdivision thereof shall be governed by the principles of the common law as they may be interpreted by the courts of the United States in the light of reason and experience. However, in civil actions and proceedings, with respect to an element of a claim or defense as to which State law supplies the rule of decision, the privilege of a witness, person, government, State, or political subdivision thereof shall be determined in accordance with State law.

ARTICLE VI. WITNESSES

Rule 601. General Rule of Competency

Every person is competent to be a witness except as otherwise provided in these rules. However, in civil actions and proceedings, with respect to an element of a claim or defense as to which State law supplies the rule of decision, the competency of a witness shall be determined in accordance with State law.

Rule 602. Lack of Personal Knowledge

A witness may not testify to a matter unless evidence is introduced sufficient to support a finding that the witness has personal knowledge of the matter. Evidence to prove personal knowledge may, but need not, consist of the witness' own testimony. This rule is subject to the provisions of rule 703, relating to opinion testimony by expert witnesses.

Rule 603. Oath or Affirmation

Before testifying, every witness shall be required to declare that the witness will testify truthfully, by oath or affirmation administered in a form calculated to awaken the witness' conscience and impress the witness' mind with the duty to do so.

Rule 604. Interpreters

An interpreter is subject to the provisions of these rules relating to qualification as an expert and the administration of an oath or affirmation to make a true translation.

Rule 605. Competency of Judge as Witness

The judge presiding at the trial may not testify in that trial as a witness. No objection need be made in order to preserve the point.

Rule 606. Competency of Juror as Witness

(a) **At the trial.**—A member of the jury may not testify as a witness before that jury in the trial of the case in which the juror is sitting. If the juror is called so to testify, the opposing party shall be afforded an opportunity to object out of the presence of the jury.

(b) **Inquiry into validity of verdict or indictment.**—Upon an inquiry into the validity of a verdict or indictment, a juror may not testify as to any matter or statement occurring during the course of the jury's deliberations or to the effect of anything upon that or any other juror's mind or emotions as influencing the juror to assent to or dissent from the verdict or indictment or concerning the juror's mental processes in connection therewith, except that a juror may testify on the question whether extraneous prejudicial information was improperly brought to the jury's attention or whether any outside influence was improperly brought to bear upon any juror. Nor may a juror's affidavit or evidence of any statement by the juror concerning a matter about which the juror would be precluded from testifying be received for these purposes.

Rule 607. Who May Impeach

The credibility of a witness may be attacked by any party, including the party calling the witness.

Rule 608. Evidence of Character and Conduct of Witness

(a) **Opinion and reputation evidence of character.**—The credibility of a witness may be attacked or supported by evidence in the form of opinion or reputation, but subject to these limitations: (1) the evidence may refer only to character for truthfulness or untruthfulness, and (2) evidence of truthful character is admissible only after the character of the witness for truthfulness has been attacked by opinion or reputation evidence or otherwise.

(b) **Specific instances of conduct.**—Specific instances of the conduct of a witness, for the purpose of attacking or supporting the witness' character for truthfulness, other than conviction of crime as provided in rule 609, may not be proved by extrinsic evidence. They may, however, in the discretion of the court, if probative of truthfulness or untruthfulness, be inquired into on cross-examination of the witness (1) concerning the witness' character for truthfulness or untruthfulness, or (2) concerning the character for truthfulness or untruthfulness of another witness as to which character the witness being cross-examined has testified.

The giving of testimony, whether by an accused or by any other witness, does not operate as a waiver of the accused's or the witness's privilege against self-incrimination when examined with respect to matters that relate only to character for truthfulness.

Rule 609. Impeachment by Evidence of Conviction of Crime

(a) **General rule.**—For the purpose of attacking the credibility of a witness,

(1) evidence that a witness other than an accused has been convicted of a crime shall be admitted, subject to Rule 403, if the crime was punishable by death or imprisonment in excess of one year under the law under which the witness was convicted, and evidence that an accused has been convicted of such a crime shall be admitted if the court determines that the probative value of admitting this evidence outweighs its prejudicial effect to the accused; and

(2) evidence that any witness has been convicted of a crime shall be admitted if it involved dishonesty or false statement, regardless of the punishment.

(b) **Time limit.**—Evidence of a conviction under this rule is not admissible if a period of more than ten years has elapsed since the date of the conviction or of the release of the witness from the confinement imposed for that conviction, whichever is the later date, unless the court determines, in the interests of justice, that the probative value of the conviction supported by specific facts and circumstances substantially outweighs its prejudicial effect. However, evidence of a conviction more than 10 years old as calculated herein, is not admissible unless the proponent gives to the adverse party sufficient advance written notice of intent to use such evidence to provide the adverse party with a fair opportunity to contest the use of such evidence.

(c) **Effect of pardon, annulment, or certificate of rehabilitation.**—Evidence of a conviction is not admissible under this rule if (1) the conviction has been the subject of a pardon, annulment, certificate of rehabilitation, or other equivalent procedure based on a finding of the rehabilitation of the person convicted, and that person has not been convicted of a subsequent crime which was punishable by death or imprisonment in excess of one year, or (2) the conviction has been the subject of a pardon, annulment, or other equivalent procedure based on a finding of innocence.

(d) **Juvenile adjudications.**—Evidence of juvenile adjudications is generally not admissible under this rule. The court may, however, in a criminal case allow evidence of a juvenile adjudication of a witness other than the accused if conviction of the offense would be admissible to attack the credibility of an adult and the court is satisfied that admission in evidence is necessary for a fair determination of the issue of guilt or innocence.

(e) **Pendency of appeal.**—The pendency of an appeal therefrom does not render evidence of a conviction inadmissible. Evidence of the pendency of an appeal is admissible.

Rule 610. Religious Beliefs or Opinions

Evidence of the beliefs or opinions of a witness on matters of religion is not admissible for the purpose of showing that by reason of their nature the witness' credibility is impaired or enhanced.

Rule 611. Mode and Order of Interrogation and Presentation

(a) **Control by court.**—The court shall exercise reasonable control over the mode and order of interrogating witnesses and presenting evidence so as to (1) make the interrogation and presentation effective for the ascertainment of the truth, (2) avoid needless consumption of time, and (3) protect witnesses from harassment or undue embarrassment.

(b) **Scope of cross-examination.**—Cross-examination should be limited to the subject matter of the direct examination and matters affecting the credibility of the witness. The court may, in the exercise of discretion, permit inquiry into additional matters as if on direct examination.

(c) **Leading questions.**—Leading questions should not be used on the direct examination of a witness except as may be necessary to develop the witness' testimony. Ordinarily leading questions should be permitted on cross-examination. When a party calls a hostile witness, an adverse party, or a witness identified with an adverse party, interrogation may be by leading questions.

Rule 612. Writing Used to Refresh Memory

Except as otherwise provided in criminal proceedings by section 3500 of title 18, United States Code, if a witness uses a writing to refresh memory for the purpose of testifying, either—

(1) while testifying, or

(2) before testifying, if the court in its discretion determines it is necessary in the interests of justice, an adverse party is entitled to have the writing produced at the hearing, to inspect it, to cross-examine the witness thereon, and to introduce in evidence those portions which relate to the testimony of the witness. If it is claimed that the writing contains matters not related to the subject matter of the testimony the court shall examine the writing in camera, excise any portions not so related, and order delivery of the remainder to the party entitled thereto. Any portion withheld over objections shall be preserved and made available to the appellate court in the event of an appeal. If a writing is not produced or delivered pursuant to order under this rule, the court shall make any order justice requires, except that in criminal cases when the prosecution elects not to comply, the order shall be one striking the testimony or, if the court in its discretion determines that the interests of justice so require, declaring a mistrial.

Rule 613. Prior Statements of Witnesses

(a) **Examining witness concerning prior statement.**—In examining a witness concerning a prior statement made by the witness, whether written or not, the statement need not be shown nor its contents disclosed to the witness at that time, but on request the same shall be shown or disclosed to opposing counsel.

(b) **Extrinsic evidence of prior inconsistent statement of witness.**—Extrinsic evidence of a prior inconsistent statement by a witness is not admissible unless the witness is afforded an opportunity to explain or deny the same and the opposite party is afforded an opportunity to interrogate the witness thereon, or the interests of justice otherwise require.

This provision does not apply to admissions of a party-opponent as defined in rule 801(d)(2).

Rule 614. Calling and Interrogation of Witnesses by Court

(a) **Calling by court.**—The court may, on its own motion or at the suggestion of a party, call witnesses, and all parties are entitled to cross-examine witnesses thus called.

(b) **Interrogation by court.**—The court may interrogate witnesses, whether called by itself or by a party.

(c) **Objections.**—Objections to the calling of witnesses by the court or to interrogation by it may be made at the time or at the next available opportunity when the jury is not present.

Rule 615. Exclusion of Witnesses

At the request of a party the court shall order witnesses excluded so that they cannot hear the testimony of other witnesses, and it may make the order of its own motion. This rule does not authorize exclusion of (1) a party who is a natural person, or (2) an officer or employee of a party which is not a natural person designated as its representative by its attorney, or (3) a person whose presence is shown by a party to be essential to the presentation of the party's cause, or (4) a person authorized by statute to be present.

ARTICLE VII. OPINIONS AND EXPERT TESTIMONY

Rule 701. Opinion Testimony by Lay Witnesses

If the witness is not testifying as an expert, the witness' testimony in the form of opinions or inferences is limited to those opinions or inferences which are (a) rationally based on the perception of the witness, and (b) helpful to a clear understanding of the witness' testimony or the determination of a fact in issue, and (c) not based on scientific, technical, or other specialized knowledge within the scope of Rule 702.

Rule 702. Testimony by Experts

If scientific, technical, or other specialized knowledge will assist the trier of fact to understand the evidence or to determine a fact in issue, a witness qualified as an expert by knowledge, skill, experience, training, or education, may testify thereto in the form of an opinion or otherwise, if (1) the testimony is based upon sufficient facts or data, (2) the testimony is the product of reliable principles and methods, and (3) the witness has applied the principles and methods reliably to the facts of the case.

Rule 703. Bases of Opinion Testimony by Experts

The facts or data in the particular case upon which an expert bases an opinion or inference may be those perceived by or made known to the expert at or before the hearing. If of a type reasonably relied upon by experts in the particular field in forming opinions or inferences upon the subject, the facts or data need not be admissible in evidence in order for the opinion or inference to be admitted. Facts or data that are otherwise inadmissible shall not be disclosed to the jury by the proponent of the opinion or inference unless the court determines that their probative value in assisting the jury to evaluate the expert's opinion substantially outweighs their prejudicial effect.

Rule 704. Opinion on Ultimate Issue

(a) Except as provided in subdivision (b), testimony in the form of an opinion or inference otherwise admissible is not objectionable because it embraces an ultimate issue to be decided by the trier of fact.

(b) No expert witness testifying with respect to the mental state or condition of a defendant in a criminal case may state an opinion or inference as to whether the defendant did or did not have the mental state or condition constituting an element of the crime charged or of a defense thereto. Such ultimate issues are matters for the trier of fact alone.

Rule 705. Disclosure of Facts or Data Underlying Expert Opinion

The expert may testify in terms of opinion or inference and give reasons therefore without first testifying to the underlying facts or data, unless the court requires otherwise. The expert may in any event be required to disclose the underlying facts or data on cross-examination.

Rule 706. Court Appointed Experts

(a) **Appointment.**—The court may on its own motion or on the motion of any party enter an order to show cause why expert witnesses should not be appointed, and may request the parties to submit nominations. The court may appoint any expert witnesses agreed upon by the parties, and may appoint expert witnesses of its own selection. An expert witness shall not be appointed by the court unless the witness consents to act. A witness so appointed shall be informed of the witness' duties by the court in writing, a copy of which shall be filed with the clerk, or at a conference in which the parties shall have opportunity to participate. A witness so appointed shall advise the parties of the witness' findings, if any; the witness' deposition may be taken by any party; and the witness may be called to testify by the court or any party. The witness shall be subject to cross-examination by each party, including a party calling the witness.

(b) **Compensation.**—Expert witnesses so appointed are entitled to reasonable compensation in whatever sum the court may allow. The compensation thus fixed is payable from funds which may be provided by law in criminal cases and civil actions and proceedings involving just compensation under the fifth amendment. In other civil actions and proceedings the compensation shall be paid by the parties in such proportion and at such time as the court directs, and thereafter charged in like manner as other costs.

(c) **Disclosure of appointment.**—In the exercise of its discretion, the court may authorize disclosure to the jury of the fact that the court appointed the expert witness.

(d) **Parties' experts of own selection.**—Nothing in this rule limits the parties in calling expert witnesses of their own selection.

ARTICLE VIII. HEARSAY

Rule 801. Definitions

The following definitions apply under this article:

(a) 214**Statement.**—A "statement" is (1) an oral or written assertion or (2) nonverbal conduct of a person, if it is intended by the person as an assertion.

(b) **Declarant.**—A "declarant" is a person who makes a statement.

(c) **Hearsay.**—"Hearsay" is a statement, other than one made by the declarant while testifying at the trial or hearing, offered in evidence to prove the truth of the matter asserted.

(d) **Statements which are not hearsay.**—A statement is not hearsay if—

(1) *Prior statement by witness.* The declarant testifies at the trial or hearing and is subject to cross-examination concerning the statement, and the statement is (A) inconsistent with the declarant's testimony, and was given under oath subject to the penalty of perjury at a trial, hearing, or other proceeding, or in a deposition, or (B) consistent with the declarant's testimony and is offered to rebut an express or implied charge against the declarant of recent fabrication or improper influence or motive, or (C) one of identification of a person made after perceiving the person; or

(2) *Admission by party-opponent.* The statement is offered against a party and is

(A) the party's own statement, in either an individual or a representative capacity or

(B) a statement of which the party has manifested an adoption or belief in its truth, or

(C) a statement by a person authorized by the party to make a statement concerning the subject, or

(D) a statement by the party's agent or servant concerning a matter within the scope of the agency or employment, made during the existence of the relationship, or

(E) a statement by a coconspirator of a party during the course and in furtherance of the conspiracy.

The contents of the statement shall be considered but are not alone sufficient to establish the declarant's authority under subdivision (C), the agency or employment relationship and scope thereof under subdivision (D), or the existence of the conspiracy and the participation therein of the declarant and the party against whom the statement is offered under subdivision (E).

Rule 802. Hearsay Rule

Hearsay is not admissible except as provided by these rules or by other rules prescribed by the Supreme Court pursuant to statutory authority or by Act of Congress.

Rule 803. Hearsay Exceptions; Availability of Declarant Immaterial

The following are not excluded by the hearsay rule, even though the declarant is available as a witness:

(1) **Present sense impression**. A statement describing or explaining an event or condition made while the declarant was perceiving the event or condition, or immediately thereafter.

(2) **Excited utterance**. A statement relating to a startling event or condition made while the declarant was under the stress of excitement caused by the event or condition.

(3) **Then existing mental, emotional, or physical condition**. A statement of the declarant's then existing state of mind, emotion, sensation, or physical condition (such as intent, plan, motive, design, mental feeling, pain, and bodily health), but not including a statement of memory or belief to prove the fact remembered or believed unless it relates to the execution, revocation, identification, or terms of declarant's will.

(4) **Statements for purposes of medical diagnosis or treatment**. Statements made for purposes of medical diagnosis or treatment and describing medical history, or past or present symptoms, pain, or sensations, or the inception or general

character of the cause or external source thereof insofar as reasonably pertinent to diagnosis or treatment.

(5) **Recorded recollection**. A memorandum or record concerning a matter about which a witness once had knowledge but now has insufficient recollection to enable the witness to testify fully and accurately, shown to have been made or adopted by the witness when the matter was fresh in the witness' memory and to reflect that knowledge correctly. If admitted, the memorandum or record may be read into evidence but may not itself be received as an exhibit unless offered by an adverse party.

(6) **Records of regularly conducted activity**. A memorandum, report, record, or data compilation, in any form, of acts, events, conditions, opinions, or diagnoses, made at or near the time by, or from information transmitted by, a person with knowledge, if kept in the course of a regularly conducted business activity, and if it was the regular practice of that business activity to make the memorandum, report, record or data compilation, all as shown by the testimony of the custodian or other qualified witness, or by certification that complies with Rule 902(11), Rule 902(12), or a statute permitting certification, unless the source of information or the method or circumstances of preparation indicate lack of trustworthiness. The term "business" as used in this paragraph includes business, institution, association, profession, occupation, and calling of every kind, whether or not conducted for profit.

(7) **Absence of entry in records kept in accordance with the provisions of paragraph (6)**. Evidence that a matter is not included in the memoranda reports, records, or data compilations, in any form, kept in accordance with the provisions of paragraph (6), to prove the nonoccurrence or nonexistence of the matter, if the matter was of a kind of which a memorandum, report, record, or data compilation was regularly made and preserved, unless the sources of information or other circumstances indicate lack of trustworthiness.

(8) **Public records and reports**. Records, reports, statements, or data compilations, in any form, of public offices or agencies, setting forth (A) the activities of the office or agency, or (B) matters observed pursuant to duty imposed by law as to which matters there was a duty to report, excluding, however, in criminal cases matters observed by police officers and other law enforcement personnel, or (C) in civil actions and proceedings and against the Government in criminal cases, factual findings resulting from an investigation made pursuant to authority granted by law, unless the sources of information or other circumstances indicate lack of trustworthiness.

(9) **Records of vital statistics**. Records or data compilations, in any form, of births, fetal deaths, deaths, or marriages, if the report thereof was made to a public office pursuant to requirements of law.

(10) **Absence of public record or entry**. To prove the absence of a record, report, statement, or data compilation, in any form, or the nonoccurrence or nonexistence of a matter of which a record, report, statement, or data compilation, in any form, was regularly made and preserved by a public office or agency, evidence in the form of a certification in accordance with rule 902, or testimony, that diligent search failed to disclose the record, report, statement, or data compilation, or entry.

(11) **Records of religious organizations**. Statements of births, marriages, divorces, deaths, legitimacy, ancestry, relationship by blood or marriage, or other similar facts of personal or family history, contained in a regularly kept record of a religious organization.

(12) **Marriage, baptismal, and similar certificates**. Statements of fact contained in a certificate that the maker performed a marriage or other ceremony or administered a sacrament, made by a clergyman, public official, or other person authorized by the rules or practices of a religious organization or by law to perform the act certified, and purporting to have been issued at the time of the act or within a reasonable time thereafter.

(13) **Family records**. Statements of fact concerning personal or family history contained in family Bibles, genealogies, charts, engravings on rings, inscriptions on family portraits, engravings on urns, crypts, or tombstones, or the like.

(14) **Records of documents affecting an interest in property**. The record of a document

purporting to establish or affect an interest in property, as proof of the content of the original recorded document and its execution and delivery by each person by whom it purports to have been executed, if the record is a record of a public office and an applicable statute authorizes the recording of documents of that kind in that office.

(15) **Statements in documents affecting an interest in property**. A statement contained in a document purporting to establish or affect an interest in property if the matter stated was relevant to the purpose of the document, unless dealings with the property since the document was made have been inconsistent with the truth of the statement or the purport of the document.

(16) **Statements in ancient documents**. Statements in a document in existence twenty years or more the authenticity of which is established.

(17) **Market reports, commercial publications**. Market quotations, tabulations, lists, directories, or other published compilations, generally used and relied upon by the public or by persons in particular occupations.

(18) **Learned treatises**. To the extent called to the attention of an expert witness upon cross-examination or relied upon by the expert witness in direct examination, statements contained in published treatises, periodicals, or pamphlets on a subject of history, medicine, or other science or art, established as a reliable authority by the testimony or admission of the witness or by other expert testimony or by judicial notice. If admitted, the statements may be read into evidence but may not be received as exhibits.

(19) **Reputation concerning personal or family history**. Reputation among members of a person's family by blood, adoption, or marriage, or among a person's associates, or in the community, concerning a person's birth, adoption, marriage, divorce, death, legitimacy, relationship by blood, adoption, or marriage, ancestry, or other similar fact of personal or family history.

(20) **Reputation concerning boundaries or general history**. Reputation in a community, arising before the controversy, as to boundaries of or customs affecting lands in the community, and reputation as to events of general history important to the community or State or nation in which located.

(21) **Reputation as to character**. Reputation of a person's character among associates or in the community.

(22) **Judgment of previous conviction**. Evidence of a final judgment, entered after a trial or upon a plea of guilty (but not upon a plea of nolo contendere), adjudging a person guilty of a crime punishable by death or imprisonment in excess of one year, to prove any fact essential to sustain the judgment, but not including, when offered by the Government in a criminal prosecution for purposes other than impeachment, judgments against persons other than the accused. The pendency of an appeal may be shown but does not affect admissibility.

(23) **Judgment as to personal, family or general history, or boundaries**. Judgments as proof of matters of personal, family or general history, or boundaries, essential to the judgment, if the same would be provable by evidence of reputation.

(24) [**Other exceptions**.][Transferred to Rule 807]

Rule 804. Hearsay Exceptions; Declarant Unavailable

(a) **Definition of unavailability.**—"Unavailability as a witness" includes situations in which the declarant—

(1) is exempted by ruling of the court on the ground of privilege from testifying concerning the subject matter of the declarant's statement; or

(2) persists in refusing to testify concerning the subject matter of the declarant's statement despite an order of the court to do so; or

(3) testifies to a lack of memory of the subject matter of the declarant's statement; or

(4) is unable to be present or to testify at the hearing because of death or then existing physical or mental illness or infirmity; or

(5) is absent from the hearing and the proponent of a statement has been unable to procure the declarant's attendance (or in the case of a hearsay exception under subdivision (b)(2), (3), or (4), the

declarant's attendance or testimony) by process or other reasonable means.

A declarant is not unavailable as a witness if exemption, refusal, claim of lack of memory, inability, or absence is due to the procurement or wrongdoing of the proponent of a statement for the purpose of preventing the witness from attending or testifying.

(b) **Hearsay exceptions.**—The following are not excluded by the hearsay rule if the declarant is unavailable as a witness:

(1) *Former testimony.* Testimony given as a witness at another hearing of the same or a different proceeding, or in a deposition taken in compliance with law in the course of the same or another proceeding, if the party against whom the testimony is now offered, or, in a civil action or proceeding, a predecessor in interest, had an opportunity and similar motive to develop the testimony by direct, cross, or redirect examination.

(2) *Statement under belief of impending death.* In a prosecution for homicide or in a civil action or proceeding, a statement made by a declarant while believing that the declarant's death was imminent, concerning the cause or circumstances of what the declarant believed to be impending death.

(3) *Statement against interest.* A statement which was at the time of its making so far contrary to the declarant's pecuniary or proprietary interest, or so far tended to subject the declarant to civil or criminal liability, or to render invalid a claim by the declarant against another, that a reasonable person in the declarant's position would not have made the statement unless believing it to be true. A statement tending to expose the declarant to criminal liability and offered to exculpate the accused is not admissible unless corroborating circumstances clearly indicate the trustworthiness of the statement.

(4) *Statement of personal or family history.* (A) A statement concerning the declarant's own birth, adoption, marriage, divorce, legitimacy, relationship by blood, adoption, or marriage, ancestry, or other similar fact of personal or family history, even though declarant had no means of acquiring personal knowledge of the matter stated; or (B) a statement concerning the foregoing matters, and death also, of another person, if the declarant was related to the other by blood, adoption, or marriage or was so intimately associated with the other's family as to be likely to have accurate information concerning the matter declared.

(5) [**Other exceptions.**][Transferred to Rule 807]

(6) *Forfeiture by wrongdoing.* A statement offered against a party that has engaged or acquiesced in wrongdoing that was intended to, and did, procure the unavailability of the declarant as a witness.

Rule 805. Hearsay Within Hearsay

Hearsay included within hearsay is not excluded under the hearsay rule if each part of the combined statements conforms with an exception to the hearsay rule provided in these rules.

Rule 806. Attacking and Supporting Credibility of Declarant

When a hearsay statement, or a statement defined in Rule 801(d)(2)(C), (D), or (E), has been admitted in evidence, the credibility of the declarant may be attacked, and if attacked may be supported, by any evidence which would be admissible for those purposes if declarant had testified as a witness. Evidence of a statement or conduct by the declarant at any time, inconsistent with the declarant's hearsay statement, is not subject to any requirement that the declarant may have been afforded an opportunity to deny or explain. If the party against whom a hearsay statement has been admitted calls the declarant as a witness, the party is entitled to examine the declarant on the statement as if under cross-examination.

Rule 807. Residual Exception

A statement not specifically covered by Rule 803 or 804 but having equivalent circumstantial guarantees of trustworthiness, is not excluded by the hearsay rule, if the court determines that (A) the statement is offered as evidence of a material fact; (B) the statement is more probative on the point for which it is offered than any other evidence which the proponent can procure through reasonable efforts; and (C) the general purposes of these rules and the interests of justice will best be served by admission of the statement into evidence. However, a statement may not be admitted under this exception unless the proponent of it makes known to the adverse party sufficiently in advance of the trial or hearing to provide the adverse party with a fair opportunity to prepare to meet it, the proponent's intention to offer the statement and the particulars of it, including the name and address of the declarant.

ARTICLE IX. AUTHENTICATION AND IDENTIFICATION

Rule 901. Requirement of Authentication or Identification

(a) **General provision.**—The requirement of authentication or identification as a condition precedent to admissibility is satisfied by evidence sufficient to support a finding that the matter in question is what its proponent claims.

(b) **Illustrations.**—By way of illustration only, and not by way of limitation, the following are examples of authentication or identification conforming with the requirements of this rule:

(1) *Testimony of witness with knowledge.* Testimony that a matter is what it is claimed to be.

(2) *Nonexpert opinion on handwriting.* Nonexpert opinion as to the genuineness of handwriting, based upon familiarity not acquired for purposes of the litigation.

(3) *Comparison by trier or expert witness.* Comparison by the trier of fact or by expert witnesses with specimens which have been authenticated.

(4) *Distinctive characteristics and the like.* Appearance, contents, substance, internal patterns, or other distinctive characteristics, taken in conjunction with circumstances.

(5) *Voice identification.* Identification of a voice, whether heard firsthand or through mechanical or electronic transmission or recording, by opinion based upon hearing the voice at any time under circumstances connecting it with the alleged speaker.

(6) *Telephone conversations.* Telephone conversations, by evidence that a call was made to the number assigned at the time by the telephone company to a particular person or business, if (A) in the case of a person, circumstances, including self-identification, show the person answering to be the one called, or (B) in the case of a business, the call was made to a place of business and the conversation related to business reasonably transacted over the telephone.

(7) *Public records or reports.* Evidence that a writing authorized by law to be recorded or filed and in fact recorded or filed in a public office, or a purported public record, report, statement, or data compilation, in any form, is from the public office where items of this nature are kept.

(8) *Ancient documents or data compilation.* Evidence that a document or data compilation, in any form, (A) is in such condition as to create no suspicion concerning its authenticity, (B) was in a place where it, if authentic, would likely be, and (C) has been in existence 20 years or more at the time it is offered.

(9) *Process or system.* Evidence describing a process or system used to produce a result and showing that the process or system produces an accurate result.

(10) *Methods provided by statute or rule.* Any method of authentication or identification provided by Act of Congress or by other rules prescribed by the Supreme Court pursuant to statutory authority.

Rule 902. Self-authentication

Extrinsic evidence of authenticity as a condition precedent to admissibility is not required with respect to the following:

(1) **Domestic public documents under seal.** A document bearing a seal purporting to be that of the United States, or of any State, district, Commonwealth, territory, or insular possession thereof, or the Panama Canal Zone, or the Trust Territory of the Pacific Islands, or of a political subdivision, department, officer, or agency thereof, and a signature purporting to be an attestation or execution.

(2) **Domestic public documents not under seal.** A document purporting to bear the signature in the official capacity of an officer or employee of any entity included in paragraph (1) hereof, having no seal, if a public officer having a seal and having official duties in the district or political subdivision of the officer or employee certifies under seal that the signer has the official capacity and that the signature is genuine.

(3) **Foreign public documents.** A document purporting to be executed or attested in an official capacity by a person authorized by the laws of a foreign country to make the execution or attestation, and accompanied by a final certification as to the genuineness of the signature and official position (A) of the executing or attesting person, or (B) of any foreign official whose certificate of genuineness of signature and official position relates to the execution or attestation or is in a chain of certificates of genuineness of signature and official position relating to the execution or attestation. A final certification may be made by a secretary of an embassy or legation, consul general, consul, vice consul, or consular agent of the United States, or a diplomatic or consular official of the foreign country assigned or accredited to the United States. If reasonable opportunity has been given to all parties to investigate the authenticity and accuracy of official documents, the court may, for good cause shown, order that they be treated as presumptively authentic without final certification or permit them to be evidenced by an attested summary with or without final certification.

(4) **Certified copies of public records.** A copy of an official record or report or entry therein, or of a document authorized by law to be recorded or filed and actually recorded or filed in a public office, including data compilations in any form, certified as correct by the custodian or other person authorized to make the certification, by certificate complying with paragraph (1), (2), or (3) of this rule or complying with any Act of Congress or rule prescribed by the Supreme Court pursuant to statutory authority.

(5) **Official publications.** Books, pamphlets, or other publications purporting to be issued by public authority.

(6) **Newspapers and periodicals.** Printed materials purporting to be newspapers or periodicals.

(7) **Trade inscriptions and the like.** Inscriptions, signs, tags, or labels purporting to have been affixed in the course of business and indicating ownership, control, or origin.

(8) **Acknowledged documents.** Documents accompanied by a certificate of acknowledgment executed in the manner provided by law by a notary public or other officer authorized by law to take acknowledgments.

(9) **Commercial paper and related documents.** Commercial paper, signatures thereon, and documents relating thereto to the extent provided by general commercial law.

(10) **Presumptions under Acts of Congress.** Any signature, document, or other matter declared by Act of Congress to be presumptively or prima facie genuine or authentic.

(11) **Certified domestic records of regularly conducted activity.** The original or a duplicate of a domestic record of regularly conducted activity that would be admissible under Rule 803(6) if accompanied by a written declaration of its custodian or other qualified person, in a manner complying with any Act of Congress or rule prescribed by the Supreme Court pursuant to statutory authority, certifying that the record:

(A) was made at or near the time of the occurrence of the matters set forth by, or from information transmitted by, a person with knowledge of those matters;

(B) was kept in the course of the regularly conducted activity; and

(C) was made by the regularly conducted activity as a regular practice.

A party intending to offer a record into evidence under this paragraph must provide written notice of that intention to all adverse parties, and must make the record and declaration available for inspection sufficiently in advance of their offer into evidence to provide an adverse party with a fair opportunity to challenge them.

(12) **Certified foreign records of regularly conducted activity.** In a civil case, the original or a duplicate of a foreign record of regularly conducted activity that would be admissible under Rule 803(6) if accompanied by a written declaration by its custodian or other qualified person certifying that the record:

(A) was made at or near the time of the occurrence of the matters set forth by, or from information transmitted by, a person with knowledge of those matters;

(B) was kept in the course of the regularly conducted activity; and

(C) was made by the regularly conducted activity as a regular practice.

The declaration must be signed in a manner that, if falsely made, would subject the maker to criminal penalty under the laws of the country where the declaration is signed. A party intending to offer a record into evidence under this paragraph must provide written notice of that intention to all adverse parties, and must make the record and declaration available for inspection sufficiently in advance of their offer into evidence to provide an adverse party with a fair opportunity to challenge them.

Rule 903. Subscribing Witness' Testimony Unnecessary

The testimony of a subscribing witness is not necessary to authenticate a writing unless required by the laws of the jurisdiction whose laws govern the validity of the writing.

ARTICLE X. CONTENTS OF WRITINGS, RECORDINGS, AND PHOTOGRAPHS

Rule 1001. Definitions

For purposes of this article the following definitions are applicable:

(1) **Writings and recordings.** "Writings" and "recordings" consist of letters, words, or numbers, or their equivalent, set down by handwriting, typewriting, printing, photostating, photographing, magnetic impulse, mechanical or electronic recording, or other form of data compilation.

(2) **Photographs.** "Photographs" include still photographs, X-ray films, video tapes, and motion pictures.

(3) **Original.** An "original" of a writing or recording is the writing or recording itself or any counterpart intended to have the same effect by a person executing or issuing it. An "original" of a photograph includes the negative or any print therefrom. If data are stored in a computer or similar device, any printout or other output readable by sight, shown to reflect the data accurately, is an "original."

(4) **Duplicate.** A "duplicate" is a counterpart produced by the same impression as the original, or from the same matrix, or by means of photography, including enlargements and miniatures, or by mechanical or electronic re-recording, or by chemical reproduction, or by other equivalent techniques which accurately reproduces the original.

Rule 1002. Requirement of Original

To prove the content of a writing, recording, or photograph, the original writing, recording, or photograph is required, except as otherwise provided in these rules or by Act of Congress.

Rule 1003. Admissibility of Duplicates

A duplicate is admissible to the same extent as an original unless (1) a genuine question is raised as to the authenticity of the original or (2) in the circumstances it would be unfair to admit the duplicate in lieu of the original.

Rule 1004. Admissibility of Other Evidence of Contents

The original is not required, and other evidence of the contents of a writing, recording, or photograph is admissible if—

(1) **Originals lost or destroyed.** All originals are lost or have been destroyed, unless the proponent lost or destroyed them in bad faith; or

(2) **Original not obtainable.** No original can be obtained by any available judicial process or procedure; or

(3) **Original in possession of opponent.** At a time when an original was under the control of the party against whom offered, that party was put on notice, by the pleadings or otherwise, that the contents would be a subject of proof at the hearing, and that party does not produce the original at the hearing; or

(4) **Collateral matters.** The writing, recording, or photograph is not closely related to a controlling issue.

Rule 1005. Public Records

The contents of an official record, or of a document authorized to be recorded or filed and actually recorded or filed, including data compilations in any form, if otherwise admissible, may be proved by copy, certified as correct in accordance with rule 902 or testified to be correct by a witness who has compared it with the original. If a copy which complies with the foregoing cannot be obtained by the exercise of reasonable diligence, then other evidence of the contents may be given.

Rule 1006. Summaries

The contents of voluminous writings, recordings, or photographs which cannot conveniently be examined in court may be presented in the form of a chart, summary, or calculation. The originals, or duplicates, shall be made available for examination or copying, or both, by other parties at reasonable time and place. The court may order that they be produced in court.

Rule 1007. Testimony or Written Admission of Party

Contents of writings, recordings, or photographs may be proved by the testimony or deposition of the party against whom offered or by that party's written admission, without accounting for the nonproduction of the original.

Rule 1008. Functions of Court and Jury

When the admissibility of other evidence of contents of writings, recordings, or photographs under these rules depends upon the fulfillment of a condition of fact, the question whether the condition has been fulfilled is ordinarily for the court to determine in accordance with the provisions of rule 104. However, when an issue is raised (a) whether the asserted writing ever existed, or (b) whether another writing, recording, or photograph produced at the trial is the original, or (c) whether other evidence of contents correctly reflects the contents, the issue is for the trier of fact to determine as in the case of other issues of fact.

ARTICLE XI: MISCELLANEOUS RULES

Rule 1101. Applicability of Rules

(a) **Courts and judges.**—These rules apply to the United States district courts, the District Court of Guam, the District Court of the Virgin Islands, the District Court for the Northern Mariana Islands, the United States courts of appeals, the United States Claims Court, and to the United States bankruptcy judges and United States magistrate judges, in the actions, cases, and proceedings and to the extent hereinafter set forth. The terms "judge" and "court" in these rules include United States bankruptcy judges and United States magistrate judges.

(b) **Proceedings generally.**—These rules apply generally to civil actions and proceedings, including admiralty and maritime cases, to criminal cases and proceedings, to contempt proceedings except those in which the court may act summarily, and to proceedings and cases under title 11, United States Code.

(c) **Rule of privilege.**—The rule with respect to privileges applies at all stages of all actions, cases, and proceedings.

(d) **Rules inapplicable.**—The rules (other than with respect to privileges) do not apply in the following situations:

(1) *Preliminary questions of fact.* The determination of questions of fact preliminary to admissibility of evidence when the issue is to be determined by the court under rule 104.

(2) *Grand jury.* Proceedings before grand juries.

(3) *Miscellaneous proceedings.* Proceedings for extradition or rendition; preliminary examinations in criminal cases; sentencing, or granting or revoking probation; issuance of warrants for arrest,

criminal summonses, and search warrants; and proceedings with respect to release on bail or otherwise.

(e) **Rules applicable in part.**—In the following proceedings these rules apply to the extent that matters of evidence are not provided for in the statutes which govern procedure therein or in other rules prescribed by the Supreme Court pursuant to statutory authority: the trial of misdemeanors and other petty offenses before United States magistrate judge; review of agency actions when the facts are subject to trail de novo under section 706(2)(F) of title 5, United States Code; review of orders of the Secretary of Agriculture under section 2 of the Act entitled "An Act to authorize association of producers of agricultural products" approved February 18, 1922 (7 U.S.C. 292), and under section 6 and 7(c) of the Perishable Agricultural Commodities Act, 1930 (7 U.S.C. 499f, 499g(c)); naturalization and revocation of naturalization under sections 310 - 318 of the Immigration and Nationality Act (8 U.S.C. 1421 - 1429); prize proceedings in admiralty under sections 7651 - 7681 of title 10, United States Code; review of orders of the Secretary of the Interior under section 2 of the Act entitled "An Act authorizing associations of producers of aquatic products" approved June 25, 1934 (15 U.S.C. 522); review of orders of petroleum control boards under section 5 of the Act entitled "An act to regulate interstate and foreign commerce in petroleum and its products by prohibiting the shipment in such commerce of petroleum and its products produced in violation of State law, and for other purposes", approved February 22, 1935 (15 U.S.C. 715d);

actions for fines, penalties, or forfeitures under part V of title IV of the Tariff Act of 1930 (19 U.S.C. 1581 - 1624), or under the Anti-Smuggling Act (19 U.S.C. 1701 - 1711); criminal libel for condemnation, exclusion of imports, or other proceedings under the Federal Food, Drug, and Cosmetic Act (21 U.S.C. 301 - 392); disputes between seamen under sections 4079, 4080, and 4081 of the Revised Statutes (22 U.S.C. 256 - 258); habeas corpus under sections 2241 - 2254 of title 28, United States Code; motions to vacate, set aside or correct sentence under section 2255 of title 28, United States Code; actions for penalties for refusal to transport destitute seamen under section 4578 of the Revised Statutes (46 U.S.C. 679); actions against the United States under the Act entitled "An Act authorizing suits against the United States in admiralty for damage caused by and salvage service rendered to public vessels belonging to the United States, and for other purposes", approved March 3, 1925 (46 U.S.C. 781 - 790), as implemented by section 7730 of title 10, United States Code.

Rule 1102. Amendments

Amendments to the Federal Rules of Evidence may be made as provided in section 2072 of title 28 of the United States Code.

Rule 1103. Title

These rules may be known and cited as the Federal Rules of Evidence.

Pertinent Excerpts from the Federal Rules of Civil Procedure

Rule 26. General Provisions Governing Discovery; Duty of Disclosure

(a) **Required Disclosures; Methods to Discover Additional Matter.**

(1) Initial Disclosures.—Except in categories of proceedings specified in Rule 26(a)(1)(E), or to the extent otherwise stipulated or directed by order, a party must, without awaiting a discovery request, provide to other parties:

(A) the name and, if known, the address and telephone number of each individual likely to have discoverable information that the disclosing party may use to support its claims or defenses, unless solely for impeachment, identifying the subjects of the information;

(B) a copy of, or a description by category and location of, all documents, data compilations, and tangible things that are in the possession, custody, or control of the party and that the disclosing party may use to support

its claims or defenses, unless solely for impeachment;

(C) a computation of any category of damages claimed by the disclosing party, making available for inspection and copying as under Rule 34 the documents or other evidentiary material, not privileged or protected from disclosure, on which such computation is based, including materials bearing on the nature and extent of injuries suffered; and

(D) for inspection and copying as under Rule 34 any insurance agreement under which any person carrying on an insurance business may be liable to satisfy part or all of a judgment which may be entered in the action or to indemnify or reimburse for payments made to satisfy the judgment.

(E) The following categories of proceedings are exempt from initial disclosure under Rule 26(a)(1):

(i) an action for review on an administrative record;

(ii) a petition for habeas corpus or other proceeding to challenge a criminal conviction or sentence;

(iii) an action brought without counsel by a person in custody of the United States, a state, or a state subdivision;

(iv) an action to enforce or quash an administrative summons or subpoena;

(v) an action by the United States to recover benefit payments;

(vi) an action by the United States to collect on a student loan guaranteed by the United States;

(vii) a proceeding ancillary to proceedings in other courts; and

(viii) an action to enforce an arbitration award.

These disclosures must be made at or within 14 days after the Rule 26(f) conference unless a different time is set by stipulation or court order, or unless a party objects during the conference that initial disclosures are not appropriate in the circumstances of the action and states the objection in the Rule 26(f) discovery plan. In ruling on the objection, the court must determine what disclosures—if any—are to be made, and set the time for disclosure. Any party first served or otherwise joined after the Rule 26(f) conference must make these disclosures within 30 days after being served or joined unless a different time is set by stipulation or court order. A party must make its initial disclosures based on the information then reasonably available to it and is not excused from making its disclosures because it has not fully completed its investigation of the case or because it challenges the sufficiency of another party's disclosures or because another party has not made its disclosures.

(2) *Disclosure of Expert Testimony.*

(A) In addition to the disclosures required by paragraph (1), a party shall disclose to other parties the identity of any person who may be used at trial to present evidence under Rules 702, 703, or 705 of the Federal Rules of Evidence.

(B) Except as otherwise stipulated or directed by the court, this disclosure shall, with respect to a witness who is retained or specially employed to provide expert testimony in the case or whose duties as an employee of the party regularly involve giving expert testimony, be accompanied by a written report prepared and signed by the witness. The report shall contain a complete statement of all opinions to be expressed and the basis and reasons therefor; the data or other information considered by the witness in forming the opinions; any exhibits to be used as a summary of or support for the opinions; the qualifications of the witness, including a list of all publications authored by the witness within the preceding ten years; the compensation to be paid for the study and testimony; and a listing of any other cases in which the witness has testified as an expert at trial or by deposition within the preceding four years.

(C) These disclosures shall be made at the times and in the sequence directed by the court. In the absence of other directions from the court or stipulation by the parties, the disclosures shall be made at least 90 days before the trial date or the date the case is to be ready for trial or, if the evidence is intended solely to contradict or rebut evidence on the same subject matter identified by another party under paragraph (2)(B), within 30 days after the disclosure made by the other party. The parties shall supplement these disclosures when required under subdivision (e)(1).

(3) *Pretrial Disclosures.*—In addition to the disclosures required by Rule 26(a)(1) and (2), a party must provide to other parties and promptly file with the court the following information regarding the evidence that it may present at trial other than solely for impeachment:

(A) the name and, if not previously provided, the address and telephone number of each witness, separately identifying those whom the party expects to present and those whom the party may call if the need arises;

(B) the designation of those witnesses whose testimony is expected to be presented by means of a deposition and, if not taken stenographically, a transcript of the pertinent portions of the deposition testimony; and

(C) an appropriate identification of each document or other exhibit, including summaries of other evidence, separately identifying those which the party expects to offer and those which the party may offer if the need arises.

Unless otherwise directed by the court, these disclosures must be made at least 30 days before trial. Within 14 days thereafter, unless a different time is specified by the court, a party may serve and promptly file a list disclosing (i) any objections to the use under Rule 32(a) of a deposition designated by another party under Rule 26(a)(3)(B), and (ii) any objection, together with the grounds therefor, that may be made to the admissibility of materials identified under Rule 26(a)(3)(C). Objections not so disclosed, other than objections under Rules 402 and 403 of the Federal Rules of Evidence, are waived unless excused by the court for good cause.

(4) *Form of Disclosures; Filing.*—Unless the court orders otherwise, all disclosures under Rules 26(a)(1) through (3) must be made in writing, signed, and served.

(5) *Methods to Discover Additional Matter.*—Parties may obtain discovery by one or more of the following methods: depositions upon oral examination or written questions; written interrogatories; production of documents or things or permission to enter upon land or other property under Rule 34 or 45(a)(1)(C), for inspection and other purposes; physical and mental examinations; and requests for admission.

(b) **Discovery Scope and Limits.**—Unless otherwise limited by order of the court in accordance with these rules, the scope of discovery is as follows:

(1) *In General.*—Parties may obtain discovery regarding any matter, not privileged, that is relevant to the claim or defense of any party, including the existence, description, nature, custody, condition, and location of any books, documents, or other tangible things and the identity and location of persons having knowledge of any discoverable matter. For good cause, the court may order discovery of any matter relevant to the subject matter involved in the action. Relevant information need not be admissible at the trial if the discovery appears reasonably calculated to lead to the discovery of admissible evidence.

All discovery is subject to the limitations imposed by Rule 26(b)(2)(i), (ii), and (iii).

(2) *Limitations.*—By order, the court may alter the limits in these rules on the number of depositions and interrogatories or the length of depositions under Rule 30. By order or local rule, the court may also limit the number of requests under Rule 36. The frequency or extent of use of the discovery methods otherwise permitted under these rules and by any local rule shall be limited by the court if it determines that: (i) the discovery sought is unreasonably cumulative or duplicative, or is obtainable from some other source that is more convenient, less burdensome, or less expensive; (ii) the party seeking discovery has had ample opportunity by discovery in the action to obtain the information sought; or (iii) the burden or expense of the proposed discovery outweighs its likely benefit, taking into account the needs of the case, the amount in controversy, the parties' resources, the importance of the issues at stake in the litigation, and the importance of the proposed discovery in resolving the issues. The court may act upon its own initiative after reasonable notice or pursuant to a motion under Rule 26(c).

(3) *Trial Preparation: Materials.*—Subject to the provisions of subdivision (b)(4) of this rule, a party may obtain discovery of documents and tangible things otherwise discoverable under subdivision (b)(1) of this rule and prepared in anticipation of litigation or for trial by or for another party or by or for that other party's representative (including the other party's attorney, consultant, surety, indemnitor, insurer, or agent) only upon a showing that the party seeking discovery has substantial need of the materials in the preparation of the party's case and that the party is unable without undue hardship to obtain the substantial equivalent of the materials by other means. In ordering discovery of such materials when the required showing has been made, the court shall protect against disclosure of the mental impressions, conclusions, opinions, or legal theories of an attorney or other representative of a party concerning the litigation.

A party may obtain without the required showing a statement concerning the action or its subject matter previously made by that party. Upon request, a person not a party may obtain without the required showing a statement concerning the action or its subject matter previously made by that person. If the request is refused, the person may move for a court order. The provisions of Rule 37(a)(4) apply to the award of expenses incurred in relation to the motion. For purposes of this paragraph, a statement previously made is (A) a written statement signed or otherwise adopted or approved by the person making it, or (B) a stenographic, mechanical, electrical, or other recording, or a transcription thereof, which is a substantially verbatim recital of an oral statement by the person making it and contemporaneously recorded.

(4) Trial Preparation: Experts.

(A) A party may depose any person who has been identified as an expert whose opinions may be presented at trial. If a report from the expert is required under subdivision (a)(2)(B), the deposition shall not be conducted until after the report is provided.

(B) A party may, through interrogatories or by deposition, discover facts known or opinions held by an expert who has been retained or specially employed by another party in anticipation of litigation or preparation for trial and who is not expected to be called as a witness at trial, only as provided in Rule 35(b) or upon a showing of exceptional circumstances under which it is impracticable for the party seeking discovery to obtain facts or opinions on the same subject by other means.

(C) Unless manifest injustice would result, (i) the court shall require that the party seeking discovery pay the expert a reasonable fee for time spent in responding to discovery under this subdivision; and (ii) with respect to discovery obtained under subdivision (b)(4)(B) of this rule the court shall require the party seeking discovery to pay the other party a fair portion of the fees and expenses reasonably incurred by the latter party in obtaining facts and opinions from the expert.

(5) Claims of Privilege or Protection of Trial Preparation Materials.—When a party withholds information otherwise discoverable under these rules by claiming that it is privileged or subject to protection as trial preparation material, the party shall make the claim expressly and shall describe the nature of the documents, communications, or things not produced or disclosed in a manner that, without revealing information itself privileged or protected, will enable other parties to assess the applicability of the privilege or protection.

(c) **Protective Orders.**—Upon motion by a party or by the person from whom discovery is sought, accompanied by a certification that the movant has in good faith conferred or attempted to confer with other affected parties in an effort to resolve the dispute without court action, and for good cause shown, the court in which the action is pending or alternatively, on matters relating to a deposition, the court in the district where the deposition is to be taken may make any order which justice requires to protect a party or person from annoyance, embarrassment, oppression, or undue burden or expense, including one or more of the following:

(1) that the disclosure or discovery not be had;

(2) that the disclosure or discovery may be had only on specified terms and conditions, including a designation of the time or place;

(3) that the discovery may be had only by a method of discovery other than that selected by the party seeking discovery;

(4) that certain matters not be inquired into, or that the scope of the disclosure or discovery be limited to certain matters;

(5) that the discovery be conducted with no one present except persons designated by the court;

(6) that a deposition, after being sealed, be opened only by order of the court;

(7) that a trade secret or other confidential research, development, or commercial information not be revealed or be revealed only in a designated way; and

(8) that the parties simultaneously file specified documents or information enclosed in sealed envelopes to be opened as directed by the court.

If the motion for a protective order is denied in whole or in part, the court may, on such terms and conditions as are just, order that any party or other person provide or permit discovery. The provisions of Rule 37(a)(4) apply to the award of expenses incurred in relation to the motion.

(d) **Timing and Sequence of Discovery.**— Except in categories of proceedings exempted from initial disclosure under Rule 26(a)(1)(E), or when authorized under these rules or by order or agreement of the parties, a party may not seek discovery from any source before the parties have conferred as required by Rule 26(f). Unless the court upon motion, for the convenience of parties and witnesses and in the interests of justice, orders otherwise, methods of discovery may be used in any sequence, and the fact that a party is conducting discovery, whether by deposition or otherwise, does not operate to delay any other party's discovery.

(e) **Supplementation of Disclosures and Responses.**—A party who has made a disclosure under subdivision (a) or responded to a request for discovery with a disclosure or response is under a duty to supplement or correct the disclosure or response to include information thereafter acquired if ordered by the court or in the following circumstances:

(1) A party is under a duty to supplement at appropriate intervals its disclosures under subdivision (a) if the party learns that in some material respect the information disclosed is incomplete or incorrect and if the additional or corrective information has not otherwise been made known to the other parties during the discovery process or in writing. With respect to testimony of an expert from whom a report is required under subdivision (a)(2)(B) the duty extends both to information contained in the report and to information provided through a deposition of the expert, and any additions or other changes to this information shall be disclosed by the time the party's disclosures under Rule 26(a)(3) are due.

(2) A party is under a duty seasonably to amend a prior response to an interrogatory, request for production, or request for admission if the party learns that the response is in some material respect incomplete or incorrect and if the additional or corrective information has not otherwise been made known to the other parties during the discovery process or in writing.

(f) **Meeting of Parties; Planning for Discovery.**—Except in categories of proceedings exempted from initial disclosure under Rule 26(a)(1)(E) or when otherwise ordered, the parties must, as soon as practicable and in any event at least 21 days before a scheduling conference is held or a scheduling order is due under Rule 16(b), confer to consider the nature and basis of their claims and defenses and the possibilities for a prompt settlement or resolution of the case, to make or arrange for the disclosures required by Rule 26(a)(1), and to develop a proposed discovery plan that indicates the parties' views and proposals concerning:

(1) what changes should be made in the timing, form, or requirement for disclosures under Rule 26(a), including a statement as to when disclosures under Rule 26(a)(1) were made or will be made;

(2) the subjects on which discovery may be needed, when discovery should be completed, and whether discovery should be conducted in phases or be limited to or focused upon particular issues;

(3) what changes should be made in the limitations on discovery imposed under these rules or by local rule, and what other limitations should be imposed; and

(4) any other orders that should be entered by the court under Rule 26(c) or under Rule 16(b) and (c).

The attorneys of record and all unrepresented parties that have appeared in the case are jointly responsible for arranging the conference, for attempting in good faith to agree on the proposed discovery plan, and for submitting to the court within 14 days after the conference a written report outlining the plan. A court may order that the parties or attorneys attend the conference in person. If necessary to comply with its expedited schedule for Rule 16(b) conferences, a court may by local rule (i) require that the conference between the parties occur fewer than 21 days before the scheduling conference is held or a scheduling order is due under Rule 16(b), and (ii) require that the written report outlining the discovery plan be filed fewer than 14 days after the conference between the parties, or excuse the parties from submitting a written report and permit them to report orally on their discovery plan at the Rule 16(b) conference.

(g) **Signing of Disclosures, Discovery Requests, Responses, and Objections.**

(1) Every disclosure made pursuant to subdivision (a)(1) or subdivision (a)(3) shall be signed by at least one attorney of record in the attorney's individual name, whose address shall be stated. An unrepresented party shall sign the disclosure and state the party's address. The signature of the attorney or party constitutes a certification that to the best of the signer's knowledge, information, and belief, formed after a reasonable inquiry, the disclosure is complete and correct as of the time it is made.

(2) Every discovery request, response, or objection made by a party represented by an attorney shall be signed by at least one attorney of record in the attorney's individual name, whose address shall be stated. An unrepresented party shall sign the request, response, or objection and state the party's address. The signature of the attorney or party constitutes a certification that to the best of the signer's knowledge, information, and belief, formed after a reasonable inquiry, the request, response, or objection is:

(A) consistent with these rules and warranted by existing law or a good faith argument for the extension, modification, or reversal of existing law;

(B) not interposed for any improper purpose, such as to harass or to cause unnecessary delay or needless increase in the cost of litigation; and

(C) not unreasonable or unduly burdensome or expensive, given the needs of the case, the discovery already had in the case, the amount in controversy, and the importance of the issues at stake in the litigation.

If a request, response, or objection is not signed, it shall be stricken unless it is signed promptly after the omission is called to the attention of the party making the request, response, or objection, and a party shall not be obligated to take any action with respect to it until it is signed.

(3) If without substantial justification a certification is made in violation of the rule, the court, upon motion or upon its own initiative, shall impose upon the person who made the certification, the party on whose behalf the disclosure, request, response, or objection is made, or both, an appropriate sanction, which may include an order to pay the amount of the reasonable expenses incurred because of the violation, including a reasonable attorney's fee.

Rule 27. Depositions Before Action or Pending Appeal

(a) **Before Action.**

(1) Petition.—A person who desires to perpetuate testimony regarding any matter that may be cognizable in any court of the United States may file a verified petition in the United States district court in the district of the residence of any expected adverse party. The petition shall be entitled in the name of the petitioner and shall show: 1, that the petitioner expects to be a party to an action cognizable in a court of the United States but is presently unable to bring it or cause it to be brought; 2, the subject matter of the expected action and the petitioner's interest therein; 3, the facts which the petitioner desires to establish by the proposed testimony and the reasons for desiring to perpetuate it; 4, the names or a description of the persons the petitioner expects will be adverse parties and their addresses so far as known; and 5, the names and addresses of the persons to be examined and the substance of the testimony which the petitioner expects to elicit from each, and shall ask for an order authorizing the petitioner to take

the depositions of the persons to be examined named in the petition, for the purpose of perpetuating their testimony.

(2) Notice and Service.—The petitioner shall thereafter serve a notice upon each person named in the petition as an expected adverse party, together with a copy of the petition, stating that the petitioner will apply to the court, at a time and place named therein, for the order described in the petition. At least 20 days before the date of hearing the notice shall be served either within or without the district or state in the manner provided in Rule 4(d) for service of summons; but if such service cannot with due diligence be made upon any expected adverse party named in the petition, the court may make such order as is just for service by publication or otherwise, and shall appoint, for persons not served in the manner provided in Rule 4(d), an attorney who shall represent them, and, in case they are not otherwise represented, shall cross-examine the deponent. If any expected adverse party is a minor or incompetent the provisions of Rule 17(c) apply.

(3) Order and Examination.—If the court is satisfied that the perpetuation of the testimony may prevent a failure or delay of justice, it shall make an order designating or describing the persons whose depositions may be taken and specifying the subject matter of the examination and whether the depositions shall be taken upon oral examination or written interrogatories. The depositions may then be taken in accordance with these rules; and the court may make orders of the character provided for by Rules 34 and 35. For the purpose of applying these rules to depositions for perpetuating testimony, each reference therein to the court in which the action is pending shall be deemed to refer to the court in which the petition for such deposition was filed.

(4) Use of Deposition.—If a deposition to perpetuate testimony is taken under these rules or if, although not so taken, it would be admissible in evidence in the courts of the state in which it is taken, it may be used in any action involving the same subject matter subsequently brought in a United States district court, in accordance with the provisions of Rule 32(a).

(b) **Pending Appeal.**—If an appeal has been taken from a judgment of a district court or before the taking of an appeal if the time therefor has not expired, the district court in which the judgment was rendered may allow the taking of the depositions of witnesses to perpetuate their testimony for use in the event of further proceedings in the district court. In such case the party who desires to perpetuate the testimony may make a motion in the district court for leave to take the depositions, upon the same notice and service thereof as if the action was pending in the district court. The motion shall show: (1) the names and addresses of persons to be examined and the substance of the testimony which the party expects to elicit from each; (2) the reasons for perpetuating their testimony. If the court finds that the perpetuation of the testimony is proper to avoid a failure or delay of justice, it may make an order allowing the depositions to be taken and may make orders of the character provided for by Rules 34 and 35, and thereupon the depositions may be taken and used in the same manner and under the same conditions as are prescribed in these rules for depositions taken in actions pending in the district court.

(c) **Perpetuation by Action.**—This rule does not limit the power of a court to entertain an action to perpetuate testimony.

Rule 28. Persons Before Whom Depositions May Be Taken

(a) **Within the United States.**—Within the United States or within a territory or insular possession subject to the jurisdiction of the United States, depositions shall be taken before an officer authorized to administer oaths by the laws of the United States or of the place where the examination is held, or before a person appointed by the court in which the action is pending. A person so appointed has power to administer oaths and take testimony. The term officer as used in Rules 30, 31, and 32 includes a person appointed by the court or designated by the parties under Rule 29.

(b) **In Foreign Countries.**—Depositions may be taken in a foreign country (1) pursuant to any applicable treaty or convention, or (2) pursuant to a letter of request (whether or not captioned a letter rogatory), or (3) on notice before a person authorized to administer oaths in the place where the examination is held, either by the law thereof or by the law of the United States, or (4) before a person commissioned by the court, and a person so commissioned shall have the power by virtue of the commission to administer any necessary oath and take testimony. A commission or a letter of request shall be issued on application and notice and on terms that are just and appropriate. It is not requisite to the issuance of a commission or a letter of request that the taking of the deposition in any other manner is impracticable or inconvenient; and both a commission and a letter of request may be issued in proper cases. A notice or commission may designate the person before whom the deposition is to be taken either by name or descriptive title. A letter of request may be addressed "To the Appropriate Authority in [here name the country]." When a letter of request or any other device is used pursuant to any applicable treaty or convention, it shall be captioned in the form prescribed by that treaty or convention. Evidence obtained in response to a letter of request need not be excluded merely because it is not a verbatim transcript, because the testimony was not taken under oath, or because of any similar departure from the requirements for depositions taken within the United States under these rules.

(c) **Disqualification for Interest.**—No deposition shall be taken before a person who is a relative or employee or attorney or counsel of any of the parties, or is a relative or employee of such attorney or counsel, or is financially interested in the action.

Rule 29. Stipulations Regarding Discovery Procedure

Unless otherwise directed by the court, the parties may by written stipulation (1) provide that depositions may be taken before any person, at any time or place, upon any notice, and in any manner and when so taken may be used like other depositions, and (2) modify other procedures governing or limitations placed upon discovery, except that stipulations extending the time provided in Rules 33, 34, and 36 for responses to discovery may, if they would interfere with any time set for completion of discovery, for hearing of a motion, or for trial, be made only with the approval of the court.

Rule 30. Deposition Upon Oral Examination

(a) **When Depositions May Be Taken; When Leave Required.**

(1) A party may take the testimony of any person, including a party, by deposition upon oral examination without leave of court except as provided in paragraph (2). The attendance of witnesses may be compelled by subpoena as provided in Rule 45.

(2) A party must obtain leave of court, which shall be granted to the extent consistent with the principles stated in Rule 26(b)(2), if the person to be examined is confined in prison or if, without the written stipulation of the parties:

(A) a proposed deposition would result in more than ten depositions being taken under this rule or Rule 31 by the plaintiffs, or by the defendants, or by third-party defendants;

(B) the person to be examined already has been deposed in the case; or

(C) a party seeks to take a deposition before the time specified in Rule 26(d) unless the notice contains a certification, with supporting facts, that the person to be examined is expected to leave the United States and be unavailable for examination in this country unless deposed before that time.

(b) **Notice of Examination: General Requirements; Method of Recording; Production of Documents and Things; Deposition of Organization; Deposition by Telephone.**

(1) A party desiring to take the deposition of any person upon oral examination shall give reasonable notice in writing to every other party to the action.

The notice shall state the time and place for taking the deposition and the name and address of each person to be examined, if known, and, if the name is not known, a general description sufficient to identify the person or the particular class or group to which the person belongs. If a subpoena duces tecum is to be served on the person to be examined, the designation of the materials to be produced as set forth in the subpoena shall be attached to, or included in, the notice.

(2) The party taking the deposition shall state in the notice the method by which the testimony shall be recorded. Unless the court orders otherwise, it may be recorded by sound, sound-and-visual, or stenographic means, and the party taking the deposition shall bear the cost of the recording. Any party may arrange for a transcription to be made from the recording of a deposition taken by non-stenographic means.

(3) With prior notice to the deponent and other parties, any party may designate another method to record the deponent's testimony in addition to the method specified by the person taking the deposition. The additional record or transcript shall be made at that party's expense unless the court otherwise orders.

(4) Unless otherwise agreed by the parties, a deposition shall be conducted before an officer appointed or designated under Rule 28 and shall begin with a statement on the record by the officer that includes (A) the officer's name and business address; (B) the date, time and place of the deposition; (C) the name of the deponent; (D) the administration of the oath or affirmation to the deponent; and (E) an identification of all persons present. If the deposition is recorded other than stenographically, the officer shall repeat items (A) through (C) at the beginning of each unit of recorded tape or other recording medium. The appearance or demeanor of deponents or attorneys shall not be distorted through camera or sound-recording techniques. At the end of the deposition, the officer shall state on the record that the deposition is complete and shall set forth any stipulations made by

counsel concerning the custody of the transcript or recording and the exhibits, or concerning other pertinent matters.

(5) The notice to a party deponent may be accompanied by a request made in compliance with Rule 34 for the production of documents and tangible things at the taking of the deposition. The procedure of Rule 34 shall apply to the request.

(6) A party may in the party's notice and in a subpoena name as the deponent a public or private corporation or a partnership or association or governmental agency and describe with reasonable particularity the matters on which examination is requested. In that event, the organization so named shall designate one or more officers, directors, or managing agents, or other persons who consent to testify on its behalf, and may set forth, for each person designated, the matters on which the person will testify. A subpoena shall advise a non-party organization of its duty to make such a designation. The persons so designated shall testify as to matters known or reasonably available to the organization. This subdivision (b)(6) does not preclude taking a deposition by any other procedure authorized in these rules.

(7) The parties may stipulate in writing or the court may upon motion order that a deposition be taken by telephone or other remote electronic means. For the purposes of this rule and Rules 28(a), 37(a)(1), and 37(b)(1), a deposition taken by such means is taken in the district and at the place where the deponent is to answer questions.

(c) **Examination and Cross-Examination; Record of Examination; Oath; Objections.**— Examination and cross-examination of witnesses may proceed as permitted at the trial under the provisions of the Federal Rules of Evidence except Rules 103 and 615. The officer before whom the deposition is to be taken shall put the witness on oath or affirmation and shall personally, or by someone acting under the officer's direction and in the officer's presence, record the testimony of the witness. The testimony shall be taken stenographically or recorded by any other method authorized by subdivision (b)(2) of this rule. All objections made at the time of the examination to the qualifications of the officer taking the deposition, to the manner of taking it, to the evidence presented, to the conduct of any party, or to any other aspect of the proceedings shall be noted by the officer upon the record of the deposition; but the examination shall proceed, with the testimony being taken subject to the objections. In lieu of participating in the oral examination, parties may serve written questions in a sealed envelope on the party taking the deposition and the party taking the deposition shall transmit them to the officer, who shall propound them to the witness and record the answers verbatim.

(d) **Schedule and Duration; Motion to Terminate or Limit Examination.**

(1) Any objection during a deposition must be stated concisely and in a non-argumentative and non-suggestive manner. A person may instruct a deponent not to answer only when necessary to preserve a privilege, to enforce a limitation directed by the court, or to present a motion under Rule 30(d)(4).

(2) Unless otherwise authorized by the court or stipulated by the parties, a deposition is limited to one day of seven hours. The court must allow additional time consistent with Rule 26(b)(2) if needed for a fair examination of the deponent or if the deponent or another person, or other circumstance, impedes or delays the examination.

(3) If the court finds that any impediment, delay, or other conduct has frustrated the fair examination of the deponent, it may impose upon the persons responsible an appropriate sanction, including the reasonable costs and attorney's fees incurred by any parties as a result thereof.

(4) At any time during a deposition, on motion of a party or of the deponent and upon a showing that the examination is being conducted in bad faith or in such manner as unreasonably to annoy, embarrass, or oppress the deponent or party, the court in which the action is pending or the court in the district where the deposition is being taken may order the officer conducting the examination to cease forthwith from taking the deposition, or may limit the scope and manner of the taking of the deposition as provided in Rule 26(c). If the order made terminates the examination, it may be resumed thereafter only upon the order of the court in which the action is pending. Upon demand of the objecting party or deponent, the taking of the deposition must be suspended for the time necessary to make a motion for an order. The provisions of Rule 37(a)(4) apply to the award of expenses incurred in relation to the motion.

(e) **Review by Witness; Changes; Signing.**—If requested by the deponent or a party before completion of the deposition, the deponent shall have 30 days after being notified by the officer that the transcript or recording is available in which to review the transcript or recording and, if there are changes in form or substance, to sign a statement reciting such changes and the reasons given by the deponent for making them. The officer shall indicate in the certificate prescribed by subdivision (f)(1) whether any review was requested and, if so, shall append any changes made by the deponent during the period allowed.

(f) **Certification and Filing by Officer; Exhibits; Copies; Notices of Filing.**

(1) The officer must certify that the witness was duly sworn by the officer and that the deposition is a true record of the testimony given by the witness. This certificate must be in writing and accompany the record of the deposition. Unless otherwise ordered by the court, the officer must securely seal the deposition in an envelope or package indorsed with the title of the action and marked "Deposition of [here insert name of witness]" and must promptly send it to the attorney who arranged for the transcript or recording, who must store it under conditions that will protect it against loss, destruction, tampering, or deterioration. Documents and things produced for inspection during the examination of the witness must, upon the request of a party, be marked for identification and annexed to the deposition and may be inspected and copied by any party, except that if the person producing the materials desires to retain them the person may (A) offer copies to be marked for identification and annexed to the deposition and to serve thereafter as

originals if the person affords to all parties fair opportunity to verify the copies by comparison with the originals, or (B) offer the originals to be marked for identification, after giving to each party an opportunity to inspect and copy them, in which event the materials may then be used in the same manner as if annexed to the deposition. Any party may move for an order that the original be annexed to and returned with the deposition to the court, pending final disposition of the case.

(2) Unless otherwise ordered by the court or agreed by the parties, the officer shall retain stenographic notes of any deposition taken stenographically or a copy of the recording of any deposition taken by another method. Upon payment of reasonable charges therefor, the officer shall furnish a copy of the transcript or other recording of the deposition to any party or to the deponent.

(3) The party taking the deposition shall give prompt notice of its filing to all other parties.

(g) **Failure to Attend or to Serve Subpoena; Expenses.**

(1) If the party giving the notice of the taking of a deposition fails to attend and proceed therewith and another party attends in person or by attorney pursuant to the notice, the court may order the party giving the notice to pay to such other party the reasonable expenses incurred by that party and that party's attorney in attending, including reasonable attorney's fees.

(2) If the party giving the notice of the taking of a deposition of a witness fails to serve a subpoena upon the witness and the witness because of such failure does not attend, and if another party attends in person or by attorney because that party expects the deposition of that witness to be taken, the court may order the party giving the notice to pay to such other party the reasonable expenses incurred by that party and that party's attorney in attending, including reasonable attorney's fees.

Rule 31. Depositions Upon Written Questions

(a) **Serving Questions; Notice.**

(1) A party may take the testimony of any person, including a party, by deposition upon written questions without leave of court except as provided in paragraph (2). The attendance of witnesses may be compelled by the use of subpoena as provided in Rule 45.

(2) A party must obtain leave of court, which shall be granted to the extent consistent with the principles stated in Rule 26(b)(2), if the person to be examined is confined in prison or if, without the written stipulation of the parties:

(A) a proposed deposition would result in more than ten depositions being taken under this rule or Rule 30 by the plaintiffs, or by the defendants, or by third-party defendants;

(B) the person to be examined has already been deposed in the case; or

(C) a party seeks to take a deposition before the time specified in Rule 26(d).

(3) A party desiring to take a deposition upon written questions shall serve them upon every other party with a notice stating (1) the name and address of the person who is to answer them, if known, and if the name is not known, a general description sufficient to identify the person or the particular class or group to which the person belongs, and (2) the name or descriptive title and address of the officer before whom the deposition is to be taken. A deposition upon written questions may be taken of a public or private corporation or a partnership or association or governmental agency in accordance with the provisions of Rule 30(b)(6).

(4) Within 14 days after the notice and written questions are served, a party may serve cross questions upon all other parties. Within 7 days after being served with cross questions, a party may serve redirect questions upon all other parties. Within 7 days after being served with redirect questions, a party may serve recross questions upon all other parties. The court may for cause shown enlarge or shorten the time.

(b) **Officer to Take Responses and Prepare Record.**—A copy of the notice and copies of all questions served shall be delivered by the party taking the deposition to the officer designated in the notice, who shall proceed promptly, in the manner provided by Rule 30(c), (e), and (f), to take the testimony of the witness in response to the questions and to prepare, certify, and file or mail the deposition, attaching thereto the copy of the notice and the questions received by the officer.

(c) **Notice of Filing.**—When the deposition is filed the party taking it shall promptly give notice thereof to all other parties.

Rule 32. Use of Depositions in Court Proceedings

(a) **Use of Depositions.**—At the trial or upon the hearing of a motion or an interlocutory proceeding, any part or all of a deposition, so far as admissible under the rules of evidence applied as though the witness were then present and testifying, may be used against any party who was present or represented at the taking of the deposition or who had reasonable notice thereof, in accordance with any of the following provisions:

(1) Any deposition may be used by any party for the purpose of contradicting or impeaching the testimony of deponent as a witness, or for any other purpose permitted by the Federal Rules of Evidence.

(2) The deposition of a party or of anyone who at the time of taking the deposition was an officer, director, or managing agent, or a person designated under Rule 30(b)(6) or 31(a) to testify on behalf of a public or private corporation, partnership or association or governmental agency which is a party may be used by an adverse party for any purpose.

(3) The deposition of a witness, whether or not a party, may be used by any party for any purpose if the court finds:

(A) that the witness is dead; or

(B) that the witness is at a greater distance than 100 miles from the place of trial or hearing, or is out of the United States, unless it appears that the absence of the witness was procured by the party offering the deposition; or

(C) that the witness is unable to attend or testify because of age, illness, infirmity, or imprisonment; or

(D) that the party offering the deposition has been unable to procure the attendance of the witness by subpoena; or

(E) upon application and notice, that such exceptional circumstances exist as to make it desirable, in the interest of justice and with due regard to the importance of presenting the testimony of witnesses orally in open court, to allow the deposition to be used.

A deposition taken without leave of court pursuant to a notice under Rule 30(a)(2)(C) shall not be used against a party who demonstrates that, when served with the notice, it was unable through the exercise of diligence to obtain counsel to represent it at the taking of the deposition; nor shall a deposition be used against a party who, having received less than 11 days notice of a deposition, has promptly upon receiving such notice filed a motion for a protective order under Rule 26(c)(2) requesting that the deposition not be held or be held at a different time or place and such motion is pending at the time the deposition is held.

(4) If only part of a deposition is offered in evidence by a party, an adverse party may require the offeror to introduce any other part which ought in fairness to be considered with the part introduced, and any party may introduce any other parts.

Substitution of parties pursuant to Rule 25 does not affect the right to use depositions previously taken; and, when an action has been brought in any court of the United States or of any State and another action involving the same subject matter is afterward brought between the same parties or their representatives or successors in interest, all depositions lawfully taken and duly filed in the former action may be used in the latter as if originally taken therefor. A deposition previously taken may also be used as permitted by the Federal Rules of Evidence.

(b) **Objections to Admissibility.**—Subject to the provisions of Rule 28(b) and subdivision (d)(3) of this rule, objection may be made at the trial or hearing to receiving in evidence any deposition or part thereof for any reason which would require the exclusion of the evidence if the witness were then present and testifying.

(c) **Form of presentation.**—Except as otherwise directed by the court, a party offering deposition testimony pursuant to this rule may offer it in stenographic or nonstenographic form, but, if in nonstenographic form, the party shall also provide the court with a transcript of the portions so offered. On request of any party in a case tried before a jury, deposition testimony offered other than for impeachment purposes shall be presented in nonstenographic form, if available, unless the court for good cause orders otherwise.

(d) **Effect of Errors and Irregularities in Depositions.**

(1) As to Notice.—All errors and irregularities in the notice for taking a deposition are waived unless written objection is promptly served upon the party giving the notice.

(2) As to Disqualification of Officer.—Objection to taking a deposition because of disqualification of the officer before whom it is to be taken is waived unless made before the taking of the deposition begins or as soon thereafter as the disqualification becomes known or could be discovered with reasonable diligence.

(3) As to Taking of Deposition.

(A) Objections to the competency of a witness or to the competency, relevancy, or materiality of testimony are not waived by failure to make them before or during the taking of the deposition, unless the ground of the objection is one which might have been obviated or removed if presented at that time.

(B) Errors and irregularities occurring at the oral examination in the manner of taking the deposition, in the form of the questions or answers, in the oath or affirmation, or in the conduct of parties, and errors of any kind which might be obviated, removed, or cured if promptly presented, are waived unless seasonable objection thereto is made at the taking of the deposition.

(C) Objections to the form of written questions submitted under Rule 31 are waived unless served in writing upon the party propounding them within the time allowed for serving the succeeding cross or other questions and within 5 days after service of the last questions authorized.

(4) As to Completion and Return of Deposition.—Errors and irregularities in the manner in which the testimony is transcribed or the deposition is prepared, signed, certified, sealed, indorsed, transmitted, filed, or otherwise dealt with by the officer under Rules 30 and 31 are waived unless a motion to suppress the deposition or some part thereof is made with reasonable promptness after such defect is, or with due diligence might have been, ascertained.

Rule 33. Interrogatories to Parties

(a) **Availability.**—Without leave of court or written stipulation, any party may serve upon any other party written interrogatories, not exceeding 25 in number including all discrete subparts, to be answered by the party served or, if the party served is a public or private corporation or a partnership or association or governmental agency, by any officer or agent, who shall furnish such information as is available to the party. Leave to serve additional interrogatories shall be granted to the extent consistent with the principles of Rule 26(b)(2). Without leave of court or written stipulation, interrogatories may not be served before the time specified in Rule 26(d).

(b) **Answers and Objections.**

(1) Each interrogatory shall be answered separately and fully in writing under oath, unless it is objected to, in which event the objecting party shall state the reasons for objection and shall answer to the extent the interrogatory is not objectionable.

(2) The answers are to be signed by the person making them, and the objections signed by the attorney making them.

(3) The party upon whom the interrogatories have been served shall serve a copy of the answers, and objections if any, within 30 days after the service of the interrogatories. A shorter or longer time may be directed by the court or, in the absence of such an order, agreed to in writing by the parties subject to Rule 29.

(4) All grounds for an objection to an interrogatory shall be stated with specificity. Any ground not stated in a timely objection is waived unless the party's failure to object is excused by the court for good cause shown.

(5) The party submitting the interrogatories may move for an order under Rule 37(a) with respect to any objection to or other failure to answer an interrogatory.

(c) **Scope; Use at Trial.**—Interrogatories may relate to any matters which can be inquired into under Rule 26(b)(1), and the answers may be used to the extent permitted by the rules of evidence.

An interrogatory otherwise proper is not necessarily objectionable merely because an answer to the interrogatory involves an opinion or contention that relates to fact or the application of law to fact, but the court may order that such an interrogatory need not be answered until after designated discovery has been completed or until a pre-trial conference or other later time.

(d) **Option to Produce Business Records.**— Where the answer to an interrogatory may be derived or ascertained from the business records of the party upon whom the interrogatory has been served or from an examination, audit or inspection of such business records, including a compilation, abstract or summary thereof, and the burden of deriving or ascertaining the answer is substantially the same for the party serving the interrogatory as for the party served, it is a sufficient answer to such interrogatory to specify the records from which the answer may be derived or ascertained and to afford to the party serving the interrogatory reasonable opportunity to examine, audit or inspect such records and to make copies, compilations, abstracts or summaries. A specification shall be in sufficient detail to permit the interrogating party to locate and to identify, as readily as can the party served, the records from which the answer may be ascertained.

Rule 34. Production of Documents and Things and Entry Upon Land for Inspection and Other Purposes

(a) **Scope.**—Any party may serve on any other party a request (1) to produce and permit the party making the request, or someone acting on the requestor's behalf, to inspect and copy, any designated documents (including writings, drawings, graphs, charts, photographs, phonorecords, and other data compilations from which information can be obtained, translated, if necessary, by the respondent through detection devices into reasonably usable form), or to inspect and copy, test, or sample any tangible things which constitute or contain matters within the scope of Rule 26(b) and which are in the possession, custody or control of the party upon whom the request is served; or (2) to permit entry upon designated land or other property in the possession or control of the party upon whom the request is served for the purpose of inspection and measuring, surveying, photographing, testing, or sampling the property or any designated object or operation thereon, within the scope of Rule 26(b).

(b) **Procedure.**—The request shall set forth, either by individual item or by category, the items to be inspected, and describe each with reasonable particularity. The request shall specify a reasonable time, place, and manner of making the inspection and performing the related acts. Without leave of court or written stipulation, a request may not be served before the time specified in Rule 26(d).

The party upon whom the request is served shall serve a written response within 30 days after the service of the request. A shorter or longer time may be directed by the court or, in the absence of such an order, agreed to in writing by the parties, subject to Rule 29. The response shall state, with respect to each item or category, that inspection and related activities will be permitted as requested, unless the request is objected to, in which event the reasons for the objection shall be stated. If objection is made to part of an item or category, the part shall be specified and inspection permitted of the remaining parts. The party submitting the request may move for an order under Rule 37(a) with respect to any objection to or other failure to respond to the request or any part thereof, or any failure to permit inspection as requested.

A party who produces documents for inspection shall produce them as they are kept in the usual course of business or shall organize and label them to correspond with the categories in the request.

(c) **Persons Not Parties.**—A person not a party to the action may be compelled to produce documents and things or to submit to an inspection as provided in Rule 45.

Rule 35. Physical and Mental Examination of Persons

(a) **Order for Examination.**—When the mental or physical condition (including the blood group) of a party or of a person in the custody or under the legal control of a party, is in controversy, the court in which the action is pending may order the party to submit to a physical or mental examination by a suitably licensed or certified examiner or to produce for examination the person in the party's custody or legal control. The order may be made only on motion for good cause shown and upon notice to the person to be examined and to all parties and shall specify the time, place, manner, conditions, and scope of the examination and the person or persons by whom it is to be made.

(b) **Report of Examiner.**

(1) If requested by the party against whom an order is made under Rule 35(a) or the person examined, the party causing the examination to be made shall deliver to the requesting party a copy of the detailed written report of the examiner setting out the examiner's findings, including results of all tests made, diagnoses and conclusions, together with like reports of all earlier examinations of the same condition. After delivery the party causing the examination shall be entitled upon request to receive from the party against whom the order is made a like report of any examination, previously or thereafter made, of the same condition, unless, in the case of a report of examination of a person not a party, the party shows that the party is unable to obtain it. The court on motion may make an order against a party requiring delivery of a report on such terms as are just, and if an examiner fails or refuses to make a report the court may exclude the examiner's testimony if offered at trial.

(2) By requesting and obtaining a report of the examination so ordered or by taking the deposition of the examiner, the party examined waives any

privilege the party may have in that action or any other involving the same controversy, regarding the testimony of every other person who has examined or may thereafter examine the party in respect of the same mental or physical condition.

(3) This subdivision applies to examinations made by agreement of the parties, unless the agreement expressly provides otherwise. This subdivision does not preclude discovery of a report of an examiner or the taking of a deposition of the examiner in accordance with the provisions of any other rule.

(c) **Definitions.**—For the purpose of this rule, a psychologist is a psychologist licensed or certified by a State or the District of Columbia.

Rule 36. Requests for Admission

(a) **Request for Admission.**—A party may serve upon any other party a written request for the admission, for purposes of the pending action only, of the truth of any matters within the scope of Rule 26(b)(1) set forth in the request that relate to statements or opinions of fact or of the application of law to fact, including the genuineness of any documents described in the request. Copies of documents shall be served with the request unless they have been or are otherwise furnished or made available for inspection and copying. Without leave of court or written stipulation, requests for admission may not be served before the time specified in Rule 26(d).

Each matter of which an admission is requested shall be separately set forth. The matter is admitted unless, within 30 days after service of the request, or within such shorter or longer time as the court may allow or as the parties may agree to in writing, subject to Rule 29, the party to whom the request is directed serves upon the party requesting the admission a written answer or objection addressed to the matter, signed by the party or by the party's attorney. If objection is made, the reasons therefor shall be stated. The answer shall specifically deny the matter or set forth in detail the reasons why the answering party cannot truthfully admit or deny the matter. A denial shall fairly meet the substance of the requested admission, and when good faith requires that a party qualify an answer or deny only a part of the matter of which an admission is requested, the party shall specify so much of it as is true and qualify or deny the remainder. An answering party may not give lack of information or knowledge as a reason for failure to admit or deny unless the party states that the party has made reasonable inquiry and that the information known or readily obtainable by the party is insufficient to enable the party to admit or deny. A party who considers that a matter of which an admission has been requested presents a genuine issue for trial may not, on that ground alone, object to the request; the party may, subject to the provisions of Rule 37(c), deny the matter or set forth reasons why the party cannot admit or deny it.

The party who has requested the admissions may move to determine the sufficiency of the answers or objections. Unless the court determines that an objection is justified, it shall order that an answer be served. If the court determines that an answer does not comply with the requirements of this rule, it may order either that the matter is admitted or that an amended answer be served. The court may, in lieu of these orders, determine that final disposition of the request be made at a pre-trial conference or at a designated time prior to trial. The provisions of Rule 37(a)(4) apply to the award of expenses incurred in relation to the motion.

(b) **Effect of Admission.**—Any matter admitted under this rule is conclusively established unless the court on motion permits withdrawal or amendment of the admission. Subject to the provision of Rule 16 governing amendment of a pre-trial order, the court may permit withdrawal or amendment when the presentation of the merits of the action will be subserved thereby and the party who obtained the admission fails to satisfy the court that withdrawal or amendment will prejudice that party in maintaining the action or defense on the merits. Any admission made by a party under this rule is for the purpose of the pending action only and is not an admission for any other purpose nor may it be used against the party in any other proceeding.

Rule 37. Failure to Make or Cooperate in Discovery; Sanctions

(a) **Motion for Order Compelling Disclosure or Discovery.**—A party, upon reasonable notice to other parties and all persons affected thereby, may apply for an order compelling disclosure or discovery as follows:

(1) *Appropriate Court.*—An application for an order to a party shall be made to the court in which the action is pending. An application for an order to a person who is not a party shall be made to the court in the district where the discovery is being, or is to be, taken.

(2) *Motion.*

(A) If a party fails to make a disclosure required by Rule 26(a), any other party may move to compel disclosure and for appropriate sanctions. The motion must include a certification that the movant has in good faith conferred or attempted to confer with the party not making the disclosure in an effort to secure the disclosure without court action.

(B) If a deponent fails to answer a question propounded or submitted under Rules 30 or 31, or a corporation or other entity fails to make a designation under Rule 30(b)(6) or 31(a), or a party fails to answer an interrogatory submitted under Rule 33, or if a party, in response to a request for inspection submitted under Rule 34, fails to respond that inspection will be permitted as requested or fails to permit inspection as requested, the discovering party may move for an order compelling answer, or a designation, or an order compelling inspection in accordance with the request. The motion must include a certification that the movant has in good faith conferred or attempted to confer with the person or party failing to make the discovery in an effort to secure the information or material without court action. When taking a deposition on oral examination, the proponent of the question may complete or adjourn the examination before applying for an order.

(3) Evasive or Incomplete Disclosure, Answer, or Response.—For purposes of this subdivision an evasive or incomplete disclosure, answer, or response is to be treated as a failure to disclose, answer, or respond.

(4) Expenses and Sanctions.

(A) If the motion is granted or if the disclosure or requested discovery is provided after the motion was filed, the court shall, after affording an opportunity to be heard, require the party or deponent whose conduct necessitated the motion or the party or attorney advising such conduct or both of them to pay to the moving party the reasonable expenses incurred in making the motion, including attorney's fees, unless the court finds that the motion was filed without the movant's first making a good faith effort to obtain the disclosure or discovery without court action, or that the opposing party's nondisclosure, response, or objection was substantially justified, or that other circumstances make an award of expenses unjust.

(B) If the motion is denied, the court may enter any protective order authorized under Rule 26(c) and shall, after affording an opportunity to be heard, require the moving party or the attorney filing the motion or both of them to pay to the party or deponent who opposed the motion the reasonable expenses incurred in opposing the motion, including attorney's fees, unless the court finds that the making of the motion was substantially justified or that other circumstances make an award of expenses unjust.

(C) If the motion is granted in part and denied in part, the court may enter any protective order authorized under Rule 26(c) and may, after affording an opportunity to be heard, apportion the reasonable expenses incurred in relation to the motion among the parties and persons in a just manner.

(b) **Failure to comply with order.**

(1) Sanctions by Court in District Where Deposition is Taken.—If a deponent fails to be sworn or to answer a question after being directed to do so by the court in the district in which the deposition is being taken, the failure may be considered a contempt of that court.

(2) Sanctions by Court in Which Action Is Pending.—If a party or an officer, director, or managing agent of a party or a person designated under Rule 30(b)(6) or 31(a) to testify on behalf of a party fails to obey an order to provide or permit discovery, including an order made under subdivision (a) of this rule or Rule 35, or if a party fails to obey an order entered under Rule 26(f), the court in which the action is pending may make such orders in regard to the failure as are just, and among others the following:

(A) An order that the matters regarding which the order was made or any other designated facts shall be taken to be established for the purposes of the action in accordance with the claim of the party obtaining the order;

(B) An order refusing to allow the disobedient party to support or oppose designated claims or defenses, or prohibiting that party from introducing designated matters in evidence;

(C) An order striking out pleadings or parts thereof, or staying further proceedings until the order is obeyed, or dismissing the action or proceeding or any part thereof, or rendering a judgment by default against the disobedient party;

(D) In lieu of any of the foregoing orders or in addition thereto, an order treating as a contempt of court the failure to obey any orders except an order to submit to a physical or mental examination;

(E) Where a party has failed to comply with an order under Rule 35(a) requiring that party to produce another for examination, such orders as are listed in paragraphs (A), (B), and (C) of this subdivision, unless the party failing to comply shows that that party is unable to produce such person for examination.

In lieu of any of the foregoing orders or in addition thereto, the court shall require the party failing to obey the order or the attorney advising that party or both to pay the reasonable expenses, including attorney's fees, caused by the failure, unless the court finds that the failure was substantially justified or that other circumstances make an award of expenses unjust.

(c) **Failure to Disclose; False or Misleading Disclosure; Refusal to Admit.**

(1) A party that without substantial justification fails to disclose information required by Rule 26(a) or 26(e)(1), or to amend a prior response to discovery as required by Rule 26(e)(2), is not, unless such failure is harmless, permitted to use as evidence at a trial, at a hearing, or on a motion any witness or information not so disclosed. In addition to or in lieu of this sanction, the court, on motion and after affording an opportunity to be heard, may impose other appropriate sanctions. In addition to requiring payment of reasonable expenses, including attorney's fees, caused by the failure, these sanctions may include any of the actions authorized under Rule 37(b)(2)(A), (B), and (C) and may include informing the jury of the failure to make the disclosure.

(2) If a party fails to admit the genuineness of any document or the truth of any matter as requested under Rule 36, and if the party requesting the admissions thereafter proves the genuineness of the document or the truth of the matter, the requesting party may apply to the court for an order requiring the other party to pay the reasonable expenses incurred in making that proof, including reasonable attorney's fees. The court shall make the order unless it finds that (A) the request was held objectionable pursuant to Rule 36(a), or (B) the admission sought was of no substantial importance, or (C) the party failing to admit had reasonable ground to believe that the party might prevail on the matter, or (D) there was other good reason for the failure to admit.

(d) **Failure of Party to Attend at Own Deposition or Serve Answers to Interrogatories or Respond to Request for Inspection.**—If a party or an officer, director, or managing agent of a party or a person designated under Rule 30(b)(6) or 31(a) to testify on behalf of a party fails (1) to appear before the officer who is to take the deposition, after being served with a proper notice, or (2) to serve answers or objections to interrogatories submitted under Rule 33, after proper service of the interrogatories, or (3) to serve a written response to a request for inspection submitted under Rule 34, after proper service of the request, the court in which the action is pending on motion may make such orders in regard to the failure as are just, and among others it may take any action authorized under subparagraphs (A), (B), and (C) of subdivision (b)(2) of this rule. Any motion specifying a failure under clause (2) or (3) of this subdivision shall include a certification that the movant has in good faith conferred or attempted to confer with the party failing to answer or respond in an effort to obtain such answer or response without court action. In lieu of any order or in addition thereto, the court shall require the party failing to act or the attorney advising that party or both to pay the reasonable expenses, including attorney's fees, caused by the failure unless the court finds that the failure was substantially justified or that other circumstances make an award of expenses unjust.

The failure to act described in this subdivision may not be excused on the ground that the discovery sought is objectionable unless the party failing to act has a pending motion for a protective order as provided by Rule 26(c).

(e) **[Abrogated]**

(f) **[Repealed]**

(g) **Failure to Participate in the Framing of a Discovery Plan.**—If a party or a party's attorney fails to participate in the development and submission of a proposed discovery plan as required by Rule 26(f), the court may, after opportunity for hearing, require such party or attorney to pay to any other party the reasonable expenses, including attorney's fees, caused by the failure.

Pertinent Excerpts from the Federal Rules of Criminal Procedure Regarding Discovery

Rule 15. Depositions

(a) **When Taken.**

(1) In General.—A party may move that a prospective witness be deposed in order to preserve testimony for trial. The court may grant the motion because of exceptional circumstances and in the interest of justice. If the court orders the deposition to be taken, it may also require the deponent to produce at the deposition any designated material that is not privileged, including any book, paper, document, record, recording, or data.

(2) Detained Material Witness.—A witness who is detained under 18 U.S.C. § 3144 may request to be deposed by filing a written motion and giving notice to the parties. The court may then order that the deposition be taken and may discharge the witness after the witness has signed under oath the deposition transcript.

(b) **Notice.**

(1) In General.—A party seeking to take a deposition must give every other party reasonable written notice of the deposition's date and location. The notice must state the name and address of each deponent. If requested by a party receiving the notice, the court may, for good cause, change the deposition's date or location.

(2) To the Custodial Officer.—A party seeking to take the deposition must also notify the officer who has custody of the defendant of the scheduled date and location.

(c) **Defendant's Presence.**

(1) Defendant in Custody.—The officer who has custody of the defendant must produce the defendant

at the deposition and keep the defendant in the witness's presence during the examination, unless the defendant:

(A) waives in writing the right to be present; or

(B) persists in disruptive conduct justifying exclusion after being warned by the court that disruptive conduct will result in the defendant's exclusion.

(2) *Defendant Not in Custody.*—A defendant who is not in custody has the right upon request to be present at the deposition, subject to any conditions imposed by the court. If the government tenders the defendant's expenses as provided in Rule 15(d) but the defendant still fails to appear, the defendant—absent good cause—waives both the right to appear and any objection to the taking and use of the deposition based on that right.

(d) **Expenses.**—If the deposition was requested by the government, the court may—or if the defendant is unable to bear the deposition expenses, the court must—order the government to pay:

(1) any reasonable travel and subsistence expenses of the defendant and the defendant's attorney to attend the deposition; and

(2) the costs of the deposition transcript.

(e) **Manner of Taking.**—Unless these rules or a court order provides otherwise, a deposition must be taken and filed in the same manner as a deposition in a civil action, except that:

(1) A defendant may not be deposed without that defendant's consent.

(2) The scope and manner of the deposition examination and cross-examination must be the same as would be allowed during trial.

(3) The government must provide to the defendant or the defendant's attorney, for use at the deposition, any statement of the deponent in the government's possession to which the defendant would be entitled at trial.

(f) **Use as Evidence.**—A party may use all or part of a deposition as provided by the Federal Rules of Evidence.

(g) **Objections.**—A party objecting to deposition testimony or evidence must state the grounds for the objection during the deposition.

(h) **Depositions by Agreement Permitted.**—The parties may by agreement take and use a deposition with the court's consent.

Rule 16. Discovery and Inspection

(a) **Government's Disclosure.**

(1) *Information Subject to Disclosure.*

(A) *Defendant's Oral Statement.*—Upon a defendant's request, the government must disclose to the defendant the substance of any relevant oral statement made by the defendant, before or after arrest, in response to interrogation by a person the defendant knew was a government agent if the government intends to use the statement at trial.

(B) *Defendant's Written or Recorded Statement.*—Upon a defendant's request, the government must disclose to the defendant, and make available for inspection, copying, or photographing, all of the following:

(i) any relevant written or recorded statement by the defendant if:

the statement is within the government's possession, custody, or control; and

the attorney for the government knows—or through due diligence could know—that the statement exists;

(ii) the portion of any written record containing the substance of any relevant oral statement made before or after arrest if the defendant made the statement in response to interrogation by a person the defendant knew was a government agent; and

(iii) the defendant's recorded testimony before a grand jury relating to the charged offense.

(C) *Organizational Defendant.*—Upon a defendant's request, if the defendant is an organization, the government must disclose to the defendant any statement described in Rule 16(a)(1)(A) and (B) if the government contends that the person making the statement:

(i) was legally able to bind the defendant regarding the subject of the statement because of that person's position as the defendant's director, officer, employee, or agent; or

(ii) was personally involved in the alleged conduct constituting the offense and was legally able to bind the defendant regarding that conduct because of that person's position as the defendant's director, officer, employee, or agent.

(D) Defendant's Prior Record.—Upon a defendant's request, the government must furnish the defendant with a copy of the defendant's prior criminal record that is within the government's possession, custody, or control if the attorney for the government knows—or through due diligence could know—that the record exists.

(E) Documents and Objects.—Upon a defendant's request, the government must permit the defendant to inspect and to copy or photograph books, papers, documents, data, photographs, tangible objects, buildings or places, or copies or portions of any of these items, if the item is within the government's possession, custody, or control and:

(i) the item is material

Rule 17. Subpoena

(a) **Content.**—A subpoena must state the court's name and the title of the proceeding, include the seal of the court, and command the witness to attend and testify at the time and place the subpoena specifies. The clerk must issue a blank subpoena—signed and sealed—to the party requesting it, and that party must fill in the blanks before the subpoena is served.

(b) **Defendant Unable to Pay.**—Upon a defendant's ex parte application, the court must order that a subpoena be issued for a named witness if the defendant shows an inability to pay the witness's fees and the necessity of the witness's presence for an adequate defense. If the court orders a subpoena to be issued, the process costs and witness fees will be paid in the same manner as those paid for witnesses the government subpoenas.

(c) **Producing Documents and Objects.**

(1) In General.—A subpoena may order the witness to produce any books, papers, documents, data, or other objects the subpoena designates. The court may direct the witness to produce the designated items in court before trial or before they are to be offered in evidence. When the items arrive, the court may permit the parties and their attorneys to inspect all or part of them.

(2) Quashing or Modifying the Subpoena.—On motion made promptly, the court may quash or modify the subpoena if compliance would be unreasonable or oppressive.

(d) **Service.**—A marshal, a deputy marshal, or any nonparty who is at least 18 years old may serve a subpoena. The server must deliver a copy of the subpoena to the witness and must tender to the witness one day's witness-attendance fee and the legal mileage allowance. The server need not tender the attendance fee or mileage allowance when the United States, a federal officer, or a federal agency has requested the subpoena.

(e) **Place of Service.**

(1) In the United States.—A subpoena requiring a witness to attend a hearing or trial may be served at any place within the United States.

(2) In a Foreign Country.—If the witness is in a foreign country, 28 U.S.C. § 1783 governs the subpoena's service.

(f) **Issuing a Deposition Subpoena.**

(1) Issuance.—A court order to take a deposition authorizes the clerk in the district where the deposition is to be taken to issue a subpoena for any witness named or described in the order.

(2) Place.—After considering the convenience of the witness and the parties, the court may order—and the subpoena may require—the witness to appear anywhere the court designates.

(g) **Contempt.**—The court (other than a magistrate judge) may hold in contempt a witness who, without adequate excuse, disobeys a subpoena issued by a federal court in that district. A magistrate judge may hold in contempt a witness who, without adequate excuse, disobeys a subpoena issued by that magistrate judge as provided in 28 U.S.C. § 636(e).

(h) **Information Not Subject to a Subpoena.**—No party may subpoena a statement of a witness or of a prospective witness under this rule. Rule 26.2 governs the production of the statement.

National Federation of Paralegal Associations, Inc.

MODEL CODE OF ETHICS AND PROFESSIONAL RESPONSIBILITY AND GUIDELINES FOR ENFORCEMENT

PREAMBLE

The National Federation of Paralegal Associations, Inc. (NFPA) is a professional organization comprised of paralegal associations and individual paralegals throughout the United States and Canada. Members of NFPA have varying backgrounds, experiences, education and job responsibilities that reflect the diversity of the paralegal profession. NFPA promotes the growth, development and recognition of the paralegal profession as an integral partner in the delivery of legal services.

In May 1993 NFPA adopted its Model Code of Ethics and Professional Responsibility ("Model Code") to delineate the principles for ethics and conduct to which every paralegal should aspire.

Many paralegal associations throughout the United States have endorsed the concept and content of NFPA's Model Code through the adoption of their own ethical codes. In doing so, paralegals have confirmed the profession's commitment to increase the quality and efficiency of legal services, as well as recognized its responsibilities to the public, the legal community, and colleagues.

Paralegals have recognized, and will continue to recognize, that the profession must continue to evolve to enhance their roles in the delivery of legal services. With increased levels of responsibility comes the need to define and enforce mandatory rules of professional conduct. Enforcement of codes of paralegal conduct is a logical and necessary step to enhance and ensure the confidence of the legal community and the public in the integrity and professional responsibility of paralegals.

In April 1997 NFPA adopted the Model Disciplinary Rules ("Model Rules") to make possible the enforcement of the Canons and Ethical Considerations contained in the NFPA Model Code. A concurrent determination was made that the Model Code of Ethics and Professional Responsibility, formerly aspirational in nature, should be recognized as setting forth the enforceable obligations of all paralegals.

The Model Code and Model Rules offer a framework for professional discipline, either voluntarily or through formal regulatory programs.

DEFINITIONS

"Appellate Body" means a body established to adjudicate an appeal to any decision made by a Tribunal or other decision-making body with respect to formally heard Charges of Misconduct.

"Charge of Misconduct" means a written submission by any individual or entity to an ethics committee, paralegal association, bar association, law enforcement agency, judicial body, government agency, or other appropriate body or entity, that sets forth non-confidential information regarding any instance of alleged misconduct by an individual paralegal or paralegal entity.

"Charging Party" means any individual or entity who submits a Charge of Misconduct against an individual paralegal or paralegal entity.

"Competency" means the demonstration of: diligence, education, skill, and mental, emotional, and physical fitness reasonably necessary for the performance of paralegal services.

"Confidential Information" means information relating to a client, whatever its source, that is not public knowledge nor available to the public. ("Non-Confidential Information" would generally include the name of the client and the identity of the matter for which the paralegal provided services.)

"Disciplinary Hearing" means the confidential proceeding conducted by a committee or other designated body or entity concerning any instance of alleged misconduct by an individual paralegal or paralegal entity.

"Disciplinary Committee" means any committee that has been established by an entity such as a paralegal association, bar association, judicial body, or government agency to: (a) identify, define and investigate general ethical considerations and concerns with respect to paralegal practice; (b) administer and enforce the Model Code and Model Rules and; (c) discipline any individual paralegal or paralegal entity found to be in violation of same.

"Disclose" means communication of information reasonably sufficient to permit identification of the significance of the matter in question.

"Ethical Wall" means the screening method implemented in order to protect a client from a conflict of interest. An Ethical Wall generally includes, but is not limited to, the following elements: (1) prohibit the paralegal from having any connection with the matter; (2) ban discussions with or the transfer of documents to or from the paralegal; (3) restrict access to files; and (4) educate all members of the firm, corporation, or entity as to the separation of the paralegal (both organizationally and physically) from the pending matter. For more information regarding the Ethical Wall, see the NFPA publication entitled "The Ethical Wall - Its Application to Paralegals."

"Ex parte" means actions or communications conducted at the instance and for the benefit of one party only, and without notice to, or contestation by, any person adversely interested.

"Investigation" means the investigation of any charge(s) of misconduct filed against an individual paralegal or paralegal entity by a Committee.

"Letter of Reprimand" means a written notice of formal censure or severe reproof administered to an individual paralegal or paralegal entity for unethical or improper conduct.

"Misconduct" means the knowing or unknowing commission of an act that is in direct violation of those Canons and Ethical Considerations of any and all applicable codes and/or rules of conduct.

"Paralegal" is synonymous with "Legal Assistant" and is defined as a person qualified through education, training, or work experience to perform substantive legal work that requires knowledge of legal concepts and is customarily, but not exclusively performed by a lawyer. This person may be retained or employed by a lawyer, law office, governmental agency, or other entity or may be authorized by administrative, statutory, or court authority to perform this work.

"Pro Bono Publico" means providing or assisting to provide quality legal services in order to enhance access to justice for persons of limited means; charitable, religious, civic, community, governmental and educational organizations in matters that are designed primarily to address the legal needs of persons with limited means; or individuals, groups or organizations seeking to secure or protect civil rights, civil liberties or public rights.

"Proper Authority" means the local paralegal association, the local or state bar association, Committee(s) of the local paralegal or bar association(s), local prosecutor, administrative agency, or other tribunal empowered to investigate or act upon an instance of alleged misconduct.

"Responding Party" means an individual paralegal or paralegal entity against whom a Charge of Misconduct has been submitted.

"Revocation" means the recision of the license, certificate or other authority to practice of an individual paralegal or paralegal entity found in violation of those Canons and Ethical Considerations of any and all applicable codes and/or rules of conduct.

"Suspension" means the suspension of the license, certificate or other authority to practice of an individual paralegal or paralegal entity found in violation of those Canons and Ethical Considerations of any and all applicable codes and/or rules of conduct.

"Tribunal" means the body designated to adjudicate allegations of misconduct.

Reprinted by permission from The National Federation of Paralegal Associations, Inc., http://www.paralegals.org.

NALA Code of Ethics and Professional Responsibility

Each NALA member agrees to follow the canons of the NALA Code of Ethics and Professional Responsibility. Violations of the Code may result in cancellation of membership. First adopted by the NALA membership in May of 1975, the Code of Ethics and Professional Responsibility is the foundation of ethical practices of paralegals in the legal community.

A legal assistant must adhere strictly to the accepted standards of legal ethics and to the general principles of proper conduct. The performance of the duties of the legal assistant shall be governed by specific canons as defined herein so that justice will be served and goals of the profession attained. (See Model Standards and Guidelines for Utilization of Legal Assistants, Section II.)

The canons of ethics set forth hereafter are adopted by the National Association of Legal Assistants, Inc., as a general guide intended to aid legal assistants and attorneys. The enumeration of these rules does not mean there are not others of equal importance although not specifically mentioned. Court rules, agency rules and statutes must be taken into consideration when interpreting the canons.

Definition: Legal assistants, also known as paralegals, are a distinguishable group of persons who assist attorneys in the delivery of legal services. Through formal education, training and experience, legal assistants have knowledge and expertise regarding the legal system and substantive and procedural law which qualify them to do work of a legal nature under the supervision of an attorney.

In **2001**, NALA members also adopted the ABA definition of a legal assistant/paralegal, as follows:

A legal assistant or paralegal is a person qualified by education, training or work experience who is employed or retained by a lawyer, law office, corporation, governmental agency or other entity who performs specifically delegated substantive legal work for which a lawyer is responsible. (Adopted by the ABA in 1997)

Canon 1.

A legal assistant must not perform any of the duties that attorneys only may perform nor take any actions that attorneys may not take.

Canon 2.

A legal assistant may perform any task which is properly delegated and supervised by an attorney, as long as the attorney is ultimately responsible to the client, maintains a direct relationship with the client, and assumes professional responsibility for the work product.

Canon 3.

A legal assistant must not: (a) engage in, encourage, or contribute to any act which could constitute the unauthorized practice of law; and (b) establish attorney-client relationships, set fees, give legal opinions or advice or represent a client before a court or agency unless so authorized by that court or agency; and (c) engage in conduct or take any action which would assist or involve the attorney in a violation of professional ethics or give the appearance of professional impropriety.

Canon 4.

A legal assistant must use discretion and professional judgment commensurate with knowledge and experience but must not render independent legal judgment in place of an attorney. The services of an attorney are essential in the public interest whenever such legal judgment is required.

Canon 5.

A legal assistant must disclose his or her status as a legal assistant at the outset of any professional relationship with a client, attorney, a court or administrative agency or personnel thereof, or a member of the general public. A legal assistant must act prudently in determining the extent to which a client may be assisted without the presence of an attorney.

Canon 6.

A legal assistant must strive to maintain integrity and a high degree of competency through education and training with respect to professional responsibility, local rules and practice, and through continuing education in substantive areas of law to better assist the legal profession in fulfilling its duty to provide legal service.

Canon 7.

A legal assistant must protect the confidences of a client and must not violate any rule or statute now in effect or hereafter enacted controlling the doctrine of privileged communications between a client and an attorney.

Canon 8.

A legal assistant must do all other things incidental, necessary, or expedient for the attainment of the ethics and responsibilities as defined by statute or rule of court.

Canon 9.

A legal assistant's conduct is guided by bar associations' codes of professional responsibility and rules of professional conduct.

Copyright 1975; revised 1979, 1988, 1995. Reprinted with permission of the National Association of Legal Assistants, www.nala.org, 1516 S. Boston, #200, Tulsa, OK 74119.

Glossary

A

active data Information on computer hard drives that is readily accessible and visible to the operating system and/or application software used to create it. It is readily accessible to users without deletion, modification, or reconstruction.

arbitration Resolution of a dispute by a person other than the judge assigned to the case whose decision is binding. This person is called an arbitrator. Arbitration may be binding or nonbinding. In binding arbitration, the dispute is presented to a neutral individual (arbitrator) or panel (arbitration panel) for issuance of a non-appealable decision. In nonbinding arbitration, the dispute is presented to a neutral individual (arbitrator) for issuance of an award or decision. Either party can reject the award by filing the appropriate documentation (e.g. a complaint with the trial court) within the appropriate time after the arbitrator's decision. If neither party rejects the award or decision within the allotted time period, the arbitrator's decision may be made binding.

arbitrator A person chosen to judge, settle, and/or decide a disputed matter.

archival data Information that an organization maintains for long-term storage and record keeping. The information is usually not subject to change, such as medical records or completed reports. Archival data may be written to electronic storage devices such as

CDs, backup tapes, or other electronic media. It may also be maintained on hard drives, usually in a compressed format.

admissible Proper to be used in reaching a decision; describes evidence that should be "let in" or introduced in court, or evidence that the jury may use.

allegation A statement in a pleading that sets out a fact that the side filing the pleading expects to prove.

alternative dispute resolution (ADR) Methods to resolve legal problems without a court decision.

attest Swear to; act as a witness to; certify formally, usually in writing.

attorney-client privilege The right of a client, and the duty of that client's lawyer, to keep confidential the contents of almost all communication between them.

attorney work-product privilege An attorney's right to withhold from discovery all documents or things gathered and prepared in preparation for or during the course of litigation, including any notes or memos that reflect the attorney's impressions or conclusions about the lawsuit.

authentic Evidence that is proven to be what it seems to be.

authentication 1. A formal act certifying that a public document (a law, a record of deeds, etc.) is official and correct, often so that it may be admitted as evidence. 2. Any evidence that proves that a document actually is what it seems to be. 3. An "authentic act" may be something sworn to before a notary public.

B

backup data Information not presently used and stored separately in order to free up data space on the hard drive and permit recovery.

bailiff A sheriff's deputy or a court official who keeps the peace in court.

best evidence rule A rule of evidence law that often requires that the most reliable available proof of a fact must be produced. For example, if a painting (best primary evidence) is available as evidence, a photograph of the painting (secondary evidence) may not do.

BlackBerry A handheld wireless device providing e-mail, telephone, text messaging, and Web browsing services.

black box Equipment that records information about the performance of an aircraft or automobile during operation.

blowup An enlargement of a document, photograph, or piece of demonstrative evidence for use at trial or pretrial; used as a method to draw attention to key information.

C

cause of action 1. Facts sufficient to support a valid lawsuit. 2. The legal theory upon which a lawsuit ("action") is based.

chain of custody The chronological list of those in continuous possession of a specific physical object. A person who presents physical evidence at a trial (such as a gun used in a crime) must account for its possession from the time of receipt to the time of trial in order for the evidence to be "admitted" by the judge. It must thus be shown that the chain of custody was unbroken.

class action A lawsuit brought for yourself and other persons in the same situation. To bring a class action you must convince the court that there are too many persons in the class (group) to make them all individually a part of the lawsuit and that your interests are the same as theirs, so that you can adequately represent their needs.

commercial paper A negotiable instrument related to business.

compel To use the authority of law to force someone to do something.

computer chip (*Electronics*) A circuit fabricated in one piece on a small, thin substrate.

computer forensics The science of recovering deleted, erased, or hidden information. For purposes of computer forensics, the computer or other technology is considered to be a "crime scene" and the forensics expert gathers information regarding computer-related conduct and actions.

condition precedent An event that must happen before a right or obligation is created.

confidential relation Any relationship where one person has a right to expect a higher than usual level of care and faithfulness from another person.

contention A point or assertion put forward as part of an argument.

contract An agreement between two or more parties that creates in each party a duty to do or not do something and a right to performance of the other's duty or a remedy for the breach of the other's duty. Also, a document embodying such an agreement.

court reporter A stenographer who records and transcribes a verbatim transcription of proceedings in a court or other legal proceeding.

D

damages 1. Money that a court orders paid to a person who has suffered damage (a loss or harm) by the person who caused the injury (the violation of the person's rights). 2. A plaintiff's claim in a legal pleading for the money defined above. Damages may be actual and compensatory (directly related to the amount of the loss) or they may be, in addition, exemplary and punitive (extra money given to punish the defendant and to help keep a particularly bad act from happening again). Also, merely nominal damages may be given (a tiny sum when the loss suffered is either very small or of unproved amount).

declarant A person who makes a statement or declaration, whether formal or informal.

declaration 1. An unsworn statement made out of court. 2. A formal statement.

defendant The person against whom a legal action is brought. This legal action may be civil or criminal.

defense 1. The sum of the facts, law, and arguments presented by the side against whom legal action is brought. 2. Any counterargument or counterforce.

demonstrative evidence Visual aids that have been created specifically to illustrate or demonstrate a key point or issue during a trial, such as charts or graphs.

demonstrative video Video made for the purpose of creating demonstrative evidence, specifically to show a judge or jury during a trial or for settlement purposes. Types of video recordings that fall into this category are videotaped depositions, sub-rosa videos, and day-in-the-life videos.

denial 1. Any part of a pleading that contradicts claims made in an opponent's previous pleading. 2. A refusal or rejection; for example, a denial of welfare benefits to a family that makes too much money to qualify. 3. A deprivation or withholding; for example, a denial of a constitutional right.

deponent Person who gives sworn testimony out of court.

deposition 1. The process of taking a witness's sworn out-of-court testimony. The questioning is usually done by a lawyer, with the lawyer from the other side given a chance to attend and participate. 2. The written record of no. 1.

deposition notice A document used to require an individual to appear at a specific date, time, and place for the purpose of being deposed.

destructive testing Examination and testing, usually by an expert witness, of physical evidence in a case that will result in the permanent or temporary destruction of that evidence. Examples of temporary destructive testing are disassembling a motor or

knocking out the wall of a house to look for mold infestation. Permanent destructive testing includes the analysis of blood samples or chemical testing of defective fire retardant.

discovery The formal and informal exchange of information between sides in a lawsuit.

dispositive Clearly settling a legal issue or dispute.

document Something with a message on it; for example, a **contract**, a map, a photograph of a message on wood, etc. An *ancient document* is an old document, produced from proper custody (safekeeping), which is presumed to be genuine if it is over a certain age. A *public document* is a document that is, or should be, open for public inspection.

documentary evidence Evidence supplied by writings and all other documents.

duty 1. An obligation to obey a law. 2. A legal obligation to another person who has a corresponding right. 3. Any obligation, whether legal, moral, or ethical.

E

electronic evidence Data and information with investigative value stored on or transmitted by any electronic device.

evidence 1. All types of information (observations, recollections, documents, concrete objects, etc.) presented at a trial or other hearing. 2. Any information that might be used for a future trial.

examination 1. A questioning; for example, the questioning of a witness under oath or the questioning in a hearing of a bankrupt about his or her financial situation. 3. The order of questioning a witness is usually "direct examination" (by the side that called the witness), "cross-examination" (by the other side), "redirect," "re-cross," etc.

exculpatory Tending to or serving to excuse or clear from alleged fault or guilt.

exhibit 1. Any object or document offered and marked as evidence in a trial, hearing, deposition, etc. 2. Any document attached to a pleading, affidavit, or other formal paper.

expert witness A person possessing special knowledge or experience who is allowed to testify at trial not only about facts (like an ordinary witness) but also about the professional conclusions he or she draws from these facts.

F

fact 1. An act; a thing that took place; an event. 2. Something that exists and is real as opposed to what should exist. For example, a "question of fact" is about what is or what happened, while a "question of law" is about how the law affects what happened and what should have happened according to law. 3. Something that exists and is real as opposed to opinion or supposition.

Federal Rules The Federal Rules of Civil Procedure, Criminal Procedure, Appellate Procedure, and Evidence. These rules also serve as models for many state rules. Specialized rules also cover bankruptcy, admiralty, and other proceedings, as well as proceedings before U.S. magistrates.

forensic technologist A person trained to use scientifically proven methods to gather, process, interpret, and use digital evidence to provide a conclusive description of activities.

fraud Any kind of trickery used to cheat another of money or property.

Freedom of Information Act (5 U.S.C. § 552) A 1966 federal law that makes all records held by the federal government, except for certain specific types of records (such as certain military secrets), available to the public. Procedures are set up to get these records and to appeal decisions to withhold them.

G

ghost image An exact replica of the contents of a storage device such as a hard disk drive or CD-ROM that is stored on a second storage device.

H

hard drive A nonremovable disk in a computer that stores and reads data. It is the primary storage device on a computer.

hearsay A statement about what someone else said (or wrote or otherwise communicated). Hearsay evidence is evidence concerning what someone said outside of a court proceeding and is offered in the proceeding to prove the truth of what was said. The hearsay rule bars the admission of hearsay as evidence to prove the hearsay's truth unless allowed by a hearsay exception.

I

impeach To show that a witness is untruthful, either by evidence of past conduct or by showing directly that the witness is not telling the truth.

incident report A report usually prepared by a law enforcement agency to describe a collision, accident, assault, or other incident. The report contains such information as the date and time of the incident, the weather, the names of persons who were involved in the incident or witnessed it, a description of what happened, and measurements taken at the scene.

instant Present or current. The "instant case" means the current lawsuit.

interrogatories Written questions sent from one side in a lawsuit to another, attempting to get written answers to factual questions or seeking an explanation of the other side's legal contentions. These are a part of the formal discovery process in a lawsuit and usually take place before the trial.

introduction of evidence Admission of evidence. Sometimes used to mean the offer or submission of something for admission.

IPS (**I**ntrusion **P**revention **S**ystem) Software that prevents an attack on a network or computer system. An IPS resides in-line like a firewall, intercepting and forwarding packets. It can thus block attacks in real time.

J

jurisdiction 1. The geographical area within which a court or a public official has the right and power to operate. 2. The persons about whom and the subject matters about which a court has the right and power to make decisions that are legally binding.

jury A group of persons selected by law and sworn in to consider certain facts and determine the truth.

L

LAN Local area network for communication between computers within one or more offices within one location.

litigation A lawsuit or series of lawsuits.

M

material A document or person determined to be useful for or made the object of consideration or study.

mediation An informal dispute resolution process using a neutral third party (the mediator) to help the disputing parties to reach an agreement.

mediator Someone who works to effect reconciliation, settlement, or compromise between parties in dispute or at variance.

meet and confer A requirement of courts that before certain types of motions and/or petitions will be heard by the judge, the lawyers (and sometimes their clients) must "meet and confer" to try to resolve the matter or determine the points of conflict. The benefit is that it may resolve many matters, reducing the time for arguments and making the lawyers and clients face up to the realities of their positions.

metadata Data that describes data.

multimedia Software programs used to integrate documents, graphics, and video clips to produce presentations that can be made to the jury during a trial.

N

negligence The failure to exercise a reasonable amount of care in a situation that causes harm to someone or something.

O

object 1. Purpose. 2. To claim that an action by your adversary in a lawsuit (such as the use of a particular piece of evidence) is improper, unfair, or illegal, and ask the judge for a ruling on the point. 3. To formally state a disagreement with a judge's ruling, usually to preserve the right to appeal based on that ruling.

obligation A broad word that can mean any duty, and legal duty, a duty imposed by a contract, a formal written promise to pay money (such as a government bond), a duty to the government, a tax owed, etc.

opinion evidence Evidence of what a witness thinks, believes, or concludes about facts, rather than what the witness saw, heard, etc. Opinion evidence is usually accepted only from an expert witness.

order A written command or direction given by a judge.

ordinary course of business In the context of document preparation, it means that a document was prepared to memorialize a routine business event, as opposed to a document that was prepared in anticipation of litigation.

P

parol Oral, not in writing. Parol evidence is oral evidence (the evidence a witness gives). It usually refers to evidence about an agreement's meaning that is not clear from the written contract.

parol evidence rule The principle that the meaning of a written agreement, in which the parties have expressly stated that it is their complete and final agreement, cannot be contradicted or changed by using prior oral or written statements or agreements as evidence. Exceptions to the rule include situations in which there was duress, fraud, or mistake.

party 1. A person concerned with or taking part in any contract, matter, affair, or proceeding. 2. A person who is either a plaintiff or a defendant in a lawsuit.

patent A grant of a right given by the federal government to a person to exclusively control, for a limited number of years, the manufacture and sale of something that person has discovered or invented.

PDA Personal digital assistant. PalmPilot was the name given to several early models of PDAs. More recent models of PDA manufactured by Palm are not named Pilots due to name infringement lawsuits, but "PalmPilot" has entered the vernacular as a synonym for PDA, regardless of brand.

PDF (Portable Document Format) The native file format for Adobe Systems' Acrobat. PDF is the file format for representing documents in a manner that is independent of the original application software, hardware, and operating system used to create those documents. A PDF file can describe documents containing any combination of text, graphics, and images in a device-independent and resolution-independent format.

photogrammetry The process of making maps, surveys or scale drawings by referring to photographs, especially aerial photographs.

plaintiff A person who brings (starts) a lawsuit against another person.

pleading 1. The process of making formal, written statements of each side of a civil case. First the plaintiff submits a paper with "facts" and claims, then the defendant submits a paper with "facts" (and sometimes counterclaims), then the plaintiff responds, and so on, until all issues and questions are clearly posed for a trial. 2. Any one of the papers mentioned in no. 1. The first one is a complaint, the response to the complaint is an answer, etc. The pleadings are the sum of all these papers.

pre-litigation report A report that was prepared during the ordinary course of business.

pre-litigation video Video recordings made before a lawsuit was ever anticipated, such as television newscasts, surveillance videos from businesses, and "how-to" videos relating to specific products.

post-litigation report A report prepared, usually by an expert witness, with the specific purpose of helping to prove or disprove facts or allegations made in a case.

preservation of evidence letter A letter sent to an opposing party who is in possession of key evidence, putting the party on notice that litigation is contemplated and instructing the party to preserve the evidence.

privilege The right to prevent disclosure, or the duty to refrain from disclosing information communicated within a specially recognized confidential relationship; for example attorney-client privilege, clergy's privilege, doctor-patient privilege, executive privilege, journalists' privilege, and marital communications privilege.

probative Tending to prove or actually proving something.

procedural law The rules of carrying on a civil lawsuit or a criminal case (how to enforce rights in court) as opposed to substantive law (the law of the rights and duties themselves).

product liability The responsibility of manufacturers (and sometimes sellers) of goods to pay for harm to purchasers (and sometimes other users or even bystanders) caused by a defective product.

proof A body of evidence supporting a contention. Those facts from which a conclusion can be drawn. In this sense, proof can be convincing or unconvincing. 2. The result of convincing evidence. The conclusion drawn that the evidence is enough to show that something is true or that an argument about facts is correct. There are various standards of proof including: beyond a reasonable doubt (how convincing evidence must be in a criminal trial); by clear and convincing evidence; and by a preponderance (greater weight) of the evidence. In this sense, proof is always convincing.

proponent The person who offers something, puts something forward, or proposes something.

propound To offer, propose, or put forward something. For example, to propound discovery is to put discovery forward.

public documents Documents that have been submitted to, filed with, or prepared by a public agency.

R

real evidence Objects seen by the jury; for example, wounds, fingerprints, weapons used in a crime, etc.

receive evidence To admit into evidence.

record 1. A formal, written account of a case, containing the complete formal history of all actions taken, papers filed, rulings made, opinions written, etc. The records also can include all the actual evidence (testimony, physical objects, etc.) as well as the evidence that was refused admission by the judge. Courts of record include all courts for which permanent records of proceedings are kept. 2. Public records are documents filed with, or put out by, a government agency and open to the public for inspection. For example, a title of record to land is an ownership interest that has been properly filed in the public land records. 3. A corporation's records include its charter, bylaws, and minutes of meetings.

redress Satisfaction or payment for harm done.

relevant Tending to prove or disprove a fact that is important to a claim, charge, or defense in a court case. Information must be relevant to be admitted as evidence in a case. All relevant evidence is admissible in a case unless excluded by a specific rule, such as the hearsay rule. Relevant evidence may also be excluded if its value as evidence is outweighed by the possibility of unfair prejudice, the time wasted in presenting it, the possibility of confusing the issues, etc.

remand To send back a case from one court to another, usually to a lower court or administrative agency. In criminal law, to send an accused back into custody, or to turn a prisoner over for continued detention.

request for admissions A discovery request by one side in a lawsuit giving a list of facts to the other and requesting that they be admitted or denied. Those admitted need not be proved at the trial.

request for production A discovery request served by one party on another party seeking the inspection of specified documents or items or permission to enter on and inspect land and property in the responding party's possession or control.

right 1. Morally, ethically, or legally just. 2. One person's legal ability to control certain actions of another person or of all other persons. Most rights have a corresponding duty.

S

safe harbor A statement in a statute or regulation that a good faith attempt to comply is sufficient, even if the attempt has failed.

sanction A court-ordered payment by the side in a lawsuit that abused the discovery process, made to the side that was hurt by the abuse.

settlement An agreement between and among parties that resolves and concludes some or all of the disputed matters.

Shepardize To use the Shepard's citation system to trace the history of a case after it is decided to see if it is followed, overruled, distinguished, etc.

spoliation Destruction of evidence.

statute A law passed by a legislature.

stipulation An agreement between lawyers on opposite sides of a lawsuit. It is often in writing and usually concerns either court procedure (for example, an agreement to extend the time in which a pleading is due) or agreed-upon facts that require no proof.

submit 1. To put into another's hands for a decision. 2. To attempt to introduce evidence. 3. To offer something for approval.

subpoena A court's order to a person that he or she appear in court to testify in a case.

subpoena duces tecum A subpoena by which a person is commanded to bring certain documents to court or to an administrative agency.

sub-rosa investigation A confidential, secret, private or covert investigation.

substantiate To establish the existence of something or prove its truth; verify.

substantive law The basic law of rights and duties (contract law, criminal law, accident law, etc.) as opposed to procedural law (law of pleading, law of evidence, law of jurisdiction, etc.).

summary judgment A final judgment for one side in a lawsuit, or in one part of a lawsuit, without trial, when the judge finds, based on pleadings, depositions, declarations, etc., that there is no genuine factual issue in the lawsuit, or in one part of the lawsuit.

T

tangible evidence Evidence that can be touched; real. Also known as physical evidence.

testify To give evidence under oath.

testimony Evidence given by a witness under oath.

transcript A copy, especially the official copy, of the record of a court proceeding.

trial de novo A trial in a higher court in which all issues of law and fact previously heard in a lower court are reconsidered as if the earlier trial had not occurred.

trier of fact The jury, or the judge if there is no jury.

V

verify To swear in writing to the truth or accuracy of a document.

video text synchronization Technology that allows digitized videotaped depositions to be linked with corresponding transcripts or deposition exhibits and shown on a monitor to the jury.

W

WAN Wide Area Network. A communications network or system, including electronic devices such as telephone lines, satellite dishes, and/or radio waves, that covers a wide geographic system such as a city, county, or state.

witness A person who observes an occurrence, such as an accident, an event, or the signing of a document.

witness statement A written or oral statement made by a witness to an investigator, law enforcement personnel, or other third party, either informally or under oath, that sets forth the witness's knowledge of facts he or she observed.

writings Anything expressed in words, symbols, and numbers, whether written, printed, photocopied, etc.

Index